Cultures in Contrast

The Immigrant; dir. Charlie Chaplin, 1917, U.S.

Cultures in Contrast

Myra Shulman

Ann Arbor

THE UNIVERSITY OF MICHIGAN PRESS

Copyright © by the University of Michigan 1998
All rights reserved
ISBN 0-472-08485-2
Library of Congress Catalog Card No. 97-80103
Published in the United States of America by
The University of Michigan Press
Manufactured in the United States of America
⊗ Printed on acid-free paper

2008   2007   2006   2005   7   6   5   4

To my students, who have taught me so much

I didn't understand much at first—what was said around me, the words, the locations, the terms; what was done, the mannerisms, the poses; what was worn, the clothes, the colors. Everything was new and had to be absorbed. It was scary, yet it made my heart soar with happiness and longing. I hadn't the courage or the honesty to come right out and say to people, "Please explain this to me." I didn't want them to despise me or ignore me or make fun of me. So I had to learn while pretending I already understood everything. That meant putting on my own act within the larger social play taking place among the students on campus, in the little town, and in silent, heartland America.

—Philippe Labro, *The Foreign Student*

Preface

Cultures in Contrast is designed for intermediate to advanced foreign students who are studying English as a second or a foreign language. It offers these students a means for analyzing and evaluating the complex social and moral issues that young adults throughout the world have to deal with today. The text encourages the development of the requisite coping skills and opens the door to a free-spirited discussion of various ways of looking at the world. As students examine their own cultures and compare them with others, culture shock and cultural conflict may be lessened, and enjoyment of cultural differences may be strengthened.

International students in the United States face the challenges of understanding and integrating new customs and values into their own lives while maintaining their own cultural traditions and identities. Although we all have core values that reflect the culture to which we belong, when living in a foreign culture, we may begin to question these values. As Madeline E. Ehrman says in *Understanding Second Language Learning Difficulties*:

> There may be aspects of the new culture that conflict with important values the students hold. In particular, for ESL students in the U.S., acceptance of American culture may (to them) imply rejection of their culture of origin. It is a sad fact that it often takes a high level of sophistication and maturity to see differences among people as opportunities, not threats.[1]

Cultures in Contrast provides a forum to examine and clarify these differences. Such an examination may make it easier for international students living in the United States to feel comfortable and function successfully in the current moral and social climate while remaining loyal to their cultural values and traditions.

Today, more than ever, students on college campuses are expected to have a sensitivity to and respect for diversity as well as a heightened awareness of individual rights and responsibilities. This text attempts to prepare students for this academic environment. In each chapter, students move from a general exploration of their beliefs to an analysis of a case study, a discussion of readings, and finally a specific choice of a coping strategy for a hypothetical dilemma. The case studies and readings, while providing various perspectives on life in the United States, are also meant to strengthen students' cultural self-awareness. The anthropologist Edward T. Hall writes: "One of the most effective ways to learn about oneself is by taking seriously the culture of others. It forces you to pay attention to those details of life which differentiate them from you."[2]

The chapters begin with a question about the major issue each chapter presents, followed by an exploration activity in which students are asked to assess their personal and cultural beliefs. Next they read a case study, discuss the questions, and write a case study

---

1. Madeline E. Ehrman, *Understanding Second Language Learning Difficulties* (Thousand Oaks, CA: Sage Publications, 1996), 172.
2. Edward T. Hall, *The Silent Language* (Garden City, NY: Anchor Press, 1973), 32.

report, usually as a group activity. The case is a realistic scenario that requires the students to sort out the ethical possibilities within the context of their own experiences, traditions, and cultures. The discussion questions serve as a guideline to writing the report and establish the nonjudgmental environment necessary for a lively comparison and contrast of ethics, values, and beliefs. (Examples of case study reports are provided in Appendix B and in the *Instructor's Manual.*)

Interactive tasks, including two role play scenarios, expand upon the case study, and a vocabulary task reinforces both vocabulary acquisition and major concepts from the case. Following these activities are related readings from a journal, newspaper, or book and comprehension questions on the readings. In the chapter's closing activity, students choose the strategy they prefer for coping with a difficult situation. Finally, specific films, articles, and book chapters are listed for those who wish to expand their knowledge of the topic. Through the process of reading, discussion, analysis, writing, and role playing, students will enrich their understanding of today's global society while at the same time they are sharpening their academic English skills.

The overall goals of *Cultures in Contrast* are to increase linguistic competence and to improve intercultural communication skills. The specific objectives are the following:

1. to develop students' reading, writing, listening, and speaking skills through discussion and analysis of current issues;
2. to facilitate students' social and academic adjustment to a new culture;
3. to present students with a multiplicity of viewpoints on social ethics;
4. to encourage students to clarify their own values and ethics;
5. to help students acquire coping strategies for dealing with ethical dilemmas; and
6. to discourage misunderstandings due to cultural differences, stereotyping, and prejudice.

Finally, since this is a book about culture, it would be helpful to define this term. Most anthropologists do not agree on an exact definition, but according to Margaret Mead:

> *Culture* means human culture, the whole complex of traditional behavior which has been developed by the human race and is successively learned by each generation. *A culture* is less precise. It can mean the forms of traditional behavior which are characteristic of a certain society, or of a group of societies, or of a certain race, or of a certain area, or of a certain period of time.[3]

In fact, cultures are dynamic. They undergo growth, development, and change, which makes an analysis of cultural behavior and values challenging. Also, there is a great diversity of values, beliefs, and traditions within any one culture. Every generalization has many exceptions, and especially within the multicultural U.S. society, a broad continuum of attitudes and opinions exists. For these reasons, the case studies and readings do not present a falsely uniform picture of American values, attitudes, or ethics but recreate the ambiguity that characterizes much of human behavior.

---

3. Margaret Mead, *Cooperation and Competition among Primitive Peoples* (New York and London: McGraw-Hill Book Company, 1937), 17–18.

Acknowledgments

First, I thank all my students throughout the years, whose lives and experiences are reflected in this book, and in particular, my students from Georgetown University in the summers of 1996 and 1997. Also deserving special thanks are my editors, Kelly Sippell and Christina Milton of the University of Michigan Press, with whom it is always a pleasure to work. My deep appreciation goes to Joyce Hutchings, Penny Wheeler, and Nancy Marwin, master ESL teachers whose sensitive and insightful comments have much to do with the final form of the text.

My most sincere thanks to David Francis, who first suggested using film stills as illustrations for the text, and to Terry Geesken and Mary Corliss of the Museum of Modern Art, who assisted me in the challenging task of choosing the film stills from the museum's collection. Finally, I am grateful to my family, whose expertise in a number of areas, ranging from computers to films to legal matters, was invaluable to me: Deana Shulman, David Shulman, K. W. Gooch, Margot and Ken Sarch, Vera and Marc Ovadia, Elsa and David Smithgall, and Eve Mezvinsky.

Grateful acknowledgment is given for use of the following copyrighted material:

The Associated Press for "Pakistani Court Clears Couple Who Wed for Love," *Washington Post,* March 11, 1997. Reprinted with permission.

Carol Baum for "First Person: Teacher and Student," *Humanist* 55 (July 1995). Reprinted with permission.

The Chronicle of Higher Education for "Note Book," *Chronicle of Higher Education* 43 (November 22, 1996) and for "One Strike, You're Out at Saint Mary's Dorms," *Chronicle of Higher Education* 43 (October 4, 1996). Copyright 1996. *Chronicle of Higher Education.* Reprinted with permission.

K. Anne Eston for "Learning the Language of Humility and Heart," *Christian Science Monitor,* October 7, 1996. Reprinted with permission.

Tom Gerety for "Students, Soldiers, Justice," *Christian Science Monitor,* January 2, 1997. Reprinted with permission.

Debbie Goldberg for "Getting Beyond a Culture of Cheating" and "On Your Honor: Fostering a Community of Trust," *Washington Post,* November 5, 1995. Reprinted with permission.

Heldref Publications for "Telling Students about Copyright" by Paulette Bochnig Sharkey, *Clearing House* 65 (March–April 1992): 213–14. Reprinted with permission of the Helen Dwight Reid Educational Foundation. Published by Heldref Publications, 1319 Eighteenth St., N.W., Washington, DC 20036-1802. Copyright © 1997.

The New York Times for "When Life's Partner Comes Pre-Chosen" by Shoba Narayan, *New York Times,* May 4, 1995. Copyright © 1995 by The New York Times Co. Reprinted by permission.

Nicholas Brealey Publishing for "The Use of Time" from *When Cultures Collide: Managing Successfully across Cultures* by Richard Lewis; 1996; Published by Nicholas Brealey Publishing, 36 John Street, London WC1N2AT,UK £18.00.

Phi Delta Kappan for "On Alienation and the ESL Student" by Laura Carey, *Phi Delta Kappan* 71 (September 1989). Reprinted with permission.

Population Reference Bureau for "Most U.S. Unwed Mothers Are Not Teenagers" by Daphne Spain and Suzanne M. Bianchi, *Population Today* 24 (November 1996). Reprinted with permission.

J. Peter Schineller for "Culture Shock on Returning to America." *America* 164 (June 29, 1991). Reprinted with the permission of J. Peter Schineller and American Press, Inc., 106 West 56th Street, New York, NY 10019. Originally published in *America*'s June 29, 1991 issue.

Jay Sekulow for "Stop the Discrimination," *USA Today,* April 27, 1995. Reprinted with permission.

Time Life Syndication for "No One Has to Send a Gift" by David Mixner, *Time* 149 (December 16, 1996), copyright © 1996; for "Romancing the Student" by Nancy Gibbs, *Time* 145 (April 3, 1995), copyright © 1995; for "Search for a Gay Gene" by Larry Thompson, *Time* 145 (June 12, 1995), copyright © 1995; and for "The Story in Our Genes" by Sribala Subramanian, *Time* 145 (January 16, 1995), copyright © 1995. Reprinted with permission.

Universal Press Syndicate for "The Snare of Illegal Drugs" by Abigail Trafford. *Washington Post Health,* December 12, 1995. Copyright © 1995 Universal Press Syndicate. Reprinted with permission. All rights reserved.

University of California Press for "Eating in America" in *Land without Ghosts,* edited by R. David Arkush and Leo O. Lee (Berkeley: University of California Press, 1989). Copyright © 1989 The Regents of the University of California. Reprinted with permission.

U.S.A. Today for "Myths Propel the Push for Prayer in School," *USA Today,* April 27, 1995, copyright 1995, USA TODAY. Reprinted with permission.

U.S. News & World Report for "Living with a Stranger," *U.S. News & World Report* 119 (September 25, 1995). Copyright, Sept. 25, 1995, *U.S. News & World Report,* and for "Bare Facts on Childbearing," *U.S. News & World Report* 120 (April 1, 1996). Copyright, April 1, 1996, *U.S. News & World Report.* Reprinted with permission.

The Washington Post for "Single Mother, and Proud" by Stephanie Crockett, *Washington Post,* July 14, 1996, and for "These Dorm Rooms a Study in Sobriety" by Fern Shen, *Washington Post,* September 3, 1996. © 1996, The Washington Post. Reprinted with permission.

Photos were provided by the Film Stills Archive of the Museum of Modern Art, New York.

Every effort has been made to trace the ownership of all copyrighted material in this book and to obtain permission for its use.

Contents

To the Student

Cultures in Contrast focuses on improving competence in the area of cross-cultural communication, which is communication between members of different ethnic and cultural groups. In order to successfully communicate across cultures, we must be willing to recognize and accept beliefs and values that do not match our own. We may have problems in cross-cultural communication if we lack understanding of and compassion for the value systems of others. Furthermore, we often tend to prefer our own worldview, which can lead to prejudice and stereotyped thinking. Stereotypes are barriers to listening to people in their own voices and to forming meaningful relationships.

Becoming skilled in cross-cultural communication involves educating ourselves and increasing our empathy for others. It means developing an open-minded attitude toward cultural differences, an attitude of inclusion rather than exclusion. Such tolerance does not imply a weakening in our own beliefs and values; however, it does demand that we honor and respect the cultural beliefs and traditions of others. As Richard D. Lewis writes in *When Cultures Collide:* "We may enrich our own existence by absorbing certain features of other cultures—change them by our own efforts we will not."[1]

Cross-cultural communication requires not only knowledge of another language but also familiarity with nonverbal behavior (gestures, facial expressions) and cultural practices, values, and customs. Extending beyond an understanding of the words, it is the ability to understand hidden meanings, motivations, and intentions. Mastery of these intercultural skills is essential because they will play a major role in determining your academic success. Of course, the learning process is not easy, and your cultural practices and perspectives may need to be expanded to allow for cultural differences.

As *Cultures in Contrast* sharpens your cross-cultural communication skills, it prepares you for the experience of living and studying in the United States. The following case studies, readings, and accompanying activities are intended to ease your social and academic adjustment to North American life. In addition, they will assist you in formulating and articulating your point of view on the complex social, cultural, and ethical dilemmas that students have to deal with today. You will encounter a multiplicity of viewpoints on sensitive topics ranging from academic motivation to sexual harassment and be exposed to various coping skills and strategies for such situations.

After completing an exploration task, you will read a case study and identify the major points of concern and conflict. Then, working in a group, you and your team members will write a report that offers a solution to the problem, bearing in mind that many valid solutions to each scenario exist. A vocabulary task clarifies your understanding of the topic, as do the readings, which present a variety of authors and styles. The related activities include role plays, writing assignments, surveys, and debates. A strategy session in which you confront a hypothetical dilemma closes each chapter, followed by recommended movies and articles.

1. Richard D. Lewis, *When Cultures Collide: Managing Successfully across Cultures* (London: Nicholas Brealey Publishing, 1996), 315.

Reading and writing about these issues and discussing them openly may increase your understanding of and tolerance for ways of life that contrast with your own. Having such a multicultural perspective will be an advantage in the twenty-first century, when communicating across cultures will be the norm rather than the exception. With the advent of global communication, the world has grown smaller, and distant countries and cultures have become more closely connected. Nevertheless, the differences and misunderstandings among people remain large, and prejudice, stereotyping, and discrimination still exist. The more we can discover about the values, beliefs, and traditions of others and empathize with them, the more likely it is that we will be able to live together in an atmosphere of mutual respect, goodwill, and harmony.

A Note on Terminology

The following are current definitions of terms that will be part of your discussions while you are using this text. The source of the definition is given in parentheses where appropriate.

cross-cultural: dealing with or offering comparison between two or more different cultures or cultural areas (*Merriam Webster* 1996).

cultural relativism: a belief that there are no absolute values that apply equally to all cultures, so all values are relative to time, place, and circumstance.

culture: the behaviors and beliefs characteristic of a particular social, ethnic, or age group (*Random House* 1996).
the customary beliefs, social forms, material traits of a racial, religious, or social group (*Merriam Webster* 1996).

culture shock: a sense of confusion and uncertainty that may affect people exposed to an alien culture or environment without adequate preparation (*Merriam Webster* 1996).
a state of bewilderment and distress experienced by an individual who is exposed to a new, strange, or foreign culture (*Random House* 1996).

custom: long-established practice considered as an unwritten law; the whole body of usages, practices, or conventions that regulate social life (*Merriam Webster* 1996).

diversity: the condition of being composed of unlike elements (*Merriam Webster* 1996).

empathy: the capacity for understanding, being aware of, being sensitive to, and vicariously experiencing the feelings, thoughts, and experience of another person (*Merriam Webster* 1996).

ethics: (1) a set of moral principles or values; (2) the principles of conduct governing an individual or a group (*Merriam Webster* 1996).

ethnic group: a group that shares a common, distinctive culture, religion, or language (*Random House* 1996).
a large group of people classified according to common racial, national, tribal, religious, linguistic, or cultural origin or background (*Merriam Webster* 1996).
"An *ethnic group* is broadly defined as a group with which individuals are identified, or with which they identify themselves, on the basis of cultural characteristics. Every person has one or more ethnic origins, although not all individuals identify themselves strongly or consistently with an ethnic group" (Schwartz 1995, 43–44).

ethnocentrism: the attitude that one's own group is superior (*Merriam Webster* 1996).

moral: conforming to a standard of right behavior (*Merriam Webster* 1996).

multiculturalism: relating to, reflecting, or adapted to diverse cultures (*Merriam Webster* 1996).

race: (1) a family, tribe, people, or nation belonging to the same stock; (2) a class or kind of people unified by community of interests, habits, or characteristics (*Merriam Webster* 1996).
(1) a group of persons related by common descent or ancestry; (2) *anthropology:* a classification of physical characteristics such as skin color, facial form, eye shape,

and now frequently based on such genetic markers as blood groups; (3) any people related by common history, language, cultural traits (*Random House* 1996).

"The word *race* refers to a category of people identified on the basis of similar visible physical characteristics—sometimes characteristics perceived by the writer but having no scientific basis. Because even scientists disagree about the criteria for defining specific races, the term should be avoided or used cautiously" (Schwartz 1995, 43).

relativism: a view that ethical truths depend on the individuals and groups holding them (*Merriam Webster* 1996).

religion: (1) the service and worship of God or the supernatural; (2) commitment or devotion to religious faith or observance; (3) a personal set or institutionalized system of religious attitudes, beliefs, and practices; (4) a cause, principle, or system of beliefs held to with ardor and faith (*Merriam Webster* 1996).

"Not all belief systems are religions" (Schwartz 1995, 45).

society: a community, nation, or broad grouping of people having common traditions, institutions, and collective activities and interests (*Merriam Webster* 1996).

value judgment: a judgment assigning a value (as good or bad) to something (*Merriam Webster* 1996).

values: principles or qualities intrinsically valuable or desirable (*Merriam Webster* 1996).

References

Merriam Webster's Collegiate Dictionary. 10th ed. Springfield, MA: Merriam Webster, 1996.

Random House Webster's College Dictionary. New York: Random House, 1996.

Schwartz, Marilyn. *Guidelines for Bias-Free Writing.* Bloomington: Indiana University Press, 1995.

Chapter 1
Social Adjustment: Culture Shock

El Norte (The North); dir. Gregory Nava, 1983, U.S.

What would you do if you came to study in the United States but after several months you discovered that you could not adjust to living in the culture?

Exploration

This activity will prepare you to read the case study by presenting you with the basic issues that the case study will address. Read the following statements. Then respond to each one by writing *yes* or *no* in the blanks to express your agreement or disagreement. Although your first response to some statements may be "I don't know," try to make a decision about as many statements as possible. After completing the activity, discuss your answers with the members of the class.

1. I experienced culture shock and feelings of alienation after I arrived in the United States. _____

2. Life in the United States is not that much different from life in my country. _____

3. North Americans are much more liberal in their attitudes toward moral issues than I am. _____

4. The food in the United States is not very appealing to me. _____

5. I have had trouble getting used to the climate here. _____

6. It is hard to make friends with North American students in the United States. _____

7. Almost all of my close friends here are from my native country. _____

8. Although most North American students are friendly, their friendliness seems superficial and insincere. _____

9. I feel worried about whether I will be able to master the English language. _____

10. I have not had many problems coping with life in the United States. _____

11. I accept and respect most North American customs and traditions. _____

12. Universities and colleges should provide their international students with support in order to help them adjust socially and academically. _____

Glossary

adapting	modifying oneself according to changing circumstances
adjust	to adapt or conform to new conditions; to become familiar with a new culture, its language and behaviors
alienation	isolation and withdrawal from the values of the society
appealing	attractive, interesting
assimilated	absorbed into a culture or society
barriers	obstacles that prevent progress or achievement
bland	without spice or strong taste
bold	assured, confident, daring
climate	prevailing weather conditions (temperature, wind velocity, precipitation)
coping	dealing with and attempting to overcome difficulties
counselor	person who gives advice or counseling
culture	ideas, customs, skills, arts of a given people in a given period; customary beliefs, social forms, material traits, and behaviors of a racial, religious, or social group

culture shock	state of emotional and physical distress resulting from living in a culture that is different from your own; sense of confusion and uncertainty sometimes with feelings of anxiety that may affect people exposed to an alien culture without adequate preparation
customs	social conventions carried on by tradition and enforced by social disapproval of any violation
depression	state of severe sadness and lack of energy
empathize	to understand, be aware of, be sensitive to the feelings, thoughts, and experience of another person
insincere	not honest or genuine; hypocritical
liberal	broad-minded; not strict in observance of traditional forms
master	to become skilled or proficient in the use of
moral	relating to principles of right or wrong in behavior
optimistic	anticipating the best outcome
preconceived	formed prior to actual knowledge or experience
self-reliant	believing in one's ability to handle problems and make decisions
stereotype	standardized, oversimplified mental picture of a person or group
superficial	lacking in depth; presenting only an appearance
thrilled	extremely excited and happy
traditions	long-established customs or practices that have the effect of unwritten laws
values	ideas, beliefs, practices that are important to an individual or a group; principles of ethical behavior

Case Study: Coming to North America

This problem-solving activity offers the opportunity for group work in analyzing a case study and writing a case study report. Each case presents a dilemma that may be resolved in a number of ways; no one solution is correct. The cases are built around realistic situations that raise a number of complex questions.

After you read the case study, discuss the major problem the case presents and answer the discussion questions with the members of the class. Then write a case study report following the format that is provided.

> Anandita Rantung (called Dita for short) was in the middle of her first semester as a college student. Because of Dita's superior academic achievement in her secondary school in Indonesia, she had been awarded a full scholarship by the Indonesian government to attend college in the United States. When Dita arrived from Jakarta just two months ago to study at a small liberal arts college in the Boston area, she couldn't have been happier. She was excited finally to be in the land of her dreams, the country where she was planning to accomplish her goal of getting a B.A. degree in communications.

America, America; dir. Elia Kazan, 1963, U.S.

Dita knew that it would not be easy to attend college in the United States; her English was still not perfect, and she would have to take several semesters of English courses to prepare her for her academic program. Also, she had lived in Jakarta all her life and had never been away from her family before, and she had many close friends that she would miss very much. Nevertheless, she was thrilled that she had been given this opportunity and was certain that she could overcome any barriers she might face. Dita was an optimistic and enthusiastic person with a strong sense of moral values. She welcomed challenges and maintained her sense of humor, no matter what happened.

Everything had started off well for Dita. She liked Sandra, her roommate from Chicago, and her academic counselor helped her to choose one academic course (Studio Art) that she could take along with her three English courses. She did have a bit of trouble with the food in the college cafeteria. It never tasted right to her. The food was too bland, and it was greasy compared to what she had eaten in Indonesia. No matter what she tried, none of it was delicious. She considered eating at the fast food restaurants in town, but Dita couldn't stand the hamburgers or chicken sandwiches either. Several weeks went by before Dita noticed that her clothes seemed loose, and she realized that she must have lost weight. But she wasn't really concerned. After all, being thin was what many young women wanted.

In terms of her academic work, Dita was not certain how she was doing. Her English classes were small, and the teachers were kind and patient. Yet Dita kept getting low grades on her quizzes, tests, and essays. The studio art class was also causing her trouble. Dita had always enjoyed drawing, so naturally she was pleased that she was taking the art course. Her only problem, though, was that the professor spoke so quickly that Dita could rarely understand what he was telling her. Dita hoped that her work was satisfactory, and she tried to listen carefully to the professor. Still, it was quite upsetting to her when during class in the third week of the semester, the professor told Dita that there had been a misunderstanding and her drawing was not what the professor had assigned.

In the fourth week of her semester, Dita began feeling extremely tired. She could hardly stay awake past ten o'clock at night, and in the morning, if she didn't hear her alarm, she would sleep until eleven or twelve. Since all her classes were in the afternoon, it didn't matter that much. Once her roommate asked her why she was sleepy all the time, but Dita said that it probably was because she had to study so hard. "My English classes take a lot of work, and maybe that's why I'm tired," she told Sandra.

Actually, Dita would have enjoyed going out more often and not just studying all the time, but nobody asked her to go places or do things. And she hadn't met any other Indonesian students yet. As for getting to know some American students, it wasn't that easy. One night when Sandra and two of her friends were talking in the room, Dita came over to listen and try to take part in the conversation. But when they began describing their sexual activities with their boyfriends, Dita got embarrassed and left the room. She just wasn't used to such frank talk about sex. Her friends had not talked like that in her country, and she didn't feel comfortable listening. Besides, she wasn't all that interested in discussing sexual relationships, especially since she hadn't had any.

Although her roommate continued to act quite friendly to Dita, after that, she rarely invited Dita to join her group of friends. Once in awhile Dita thought about asking Sandra if she could come along when they all went out to clubs or parties on the weekends, but she hesitated to be so bold.

"Maybe she'll realize that I am alone tonight and will say something," Dita frequently thought.

But Sandra was caught up in her own world, and she didn't pay much attention to her, except for one time when she invited Dita to dinner. During that dinner, Dita had tried to explain how lonely she was, but Sandra seemed unsympathetic.

"There are plenty of activities you could become involved in or clubs to join. And you just need to become more self-reliant," Sandra told Dita.

Dita smiled shyly. "I guess I still miss my friends and family," she confessed.

"Don't worry. You'll feel better soon," was Sandra's casual comment.

That evening was the last time Dita and Sandra went out together. In fact, Dita rarely left her room unless she had a class. She mostly lay on her bed writing letters to her friends at home. One day two weeks later, after Dita had spent the morning in a state of deep depression and loneliness, she decided that she would go to the advising center and get some suggestions about how to adjust better to her new life. However, when she called to make an appointment with the foreign student adviser, she was told to call back the next week because the adviser was on vacation and no one else could see her.

At that point, Dita began to cry. It occurred to her that maybe it wouldn't be all that bad for her to withdraw from school and return to Indonesia even though it would mean losing her scholarship. Her family and friends might consider her a failure for giving up the chance to get a degree from a college in the United States, but Dita didn't really care what other people would say. They weren't the ones who had to live all alone in a foreign country. She knew she had tried her best, and she was ready to call it quits. Her English wasn't improving anyway, she hated the food, and the weather was getting colder every day. Worst of all, she had no close friends, Indonesian or American, nor any other sources of support, so what was the use of trying to live in the States? It seemed to Dita that coming to North America had been a really bad decision.

Discussion

Answer the following questions about the case study before writing the case study report.

1. Can you understand what Dita is going through and empathize with her?
2. What kind of person is Dita? How would you describe her?
3. How well has she been coping with her college life?
4. What specific problems is Dita having in adapting to American college life?
5. What kind of person is Sandra, Dita's roommate? How would you describe her?
6. What types of support does Dita's college offer to international students?
7. How important are friends in helping a student adjust to a new life?
8. What steps could Dita take to become more comfortable in the United States?

Case Study Report

Working with the whole class, write a case study report analyzing the problems Dita Rantung is having. Use brainstorming[1] to come up with the four sections of the report, which should be written in the format given in the outline that follows.

After you have completed the report, turn to Appendix B, "Case Study Report" (p. 219), and read the model case study report for chapter 1.

   I. Statement of the Problem
      A. Definition
      B. Analysis
  II. Suggestion of Possible Solutions
      A. Solution 1
      B. Solution 2
      C. Solution 3
 III. Evaluation of Possible Solutions
      A. Solution 1
         1. Advantages
         2. Disadvantages

---

1. Brainstorming is the unrestrained offering of suggestions by members of a group to seek solutions to problems. No idea is considered too absurd to mention. The purpose is to generate as many ideas as possible.

  B. Solution 2
   1. Advantages
   2. Disadvantages
  C. Solution 3
   1. Advantages
   2. Disadvantages
IV. Selection of a Solution
  A. Choice
  B. Justification

Vocabulary

This activity will reinforce your understanding of the important concepts and vocabulary words found in this chapter. Fill in the blanks with the most appropriate words to complete the following paragraphs. Use each word only once.

barrier	coping	liberal	appealing	bland
superficial	adapt	traditions	assimilated	differ

When international students attend schools in the United States, they often experience varying degrees of emotional and physical distress in the first few months of living in the new country. These feelings of distress and alienation, known as culture shock, tend to disappear with time although some students suffer more than others. Research shows that this "uprooting disorder" will be less severe if students are highly motivated, psychologically mature, experienced in living in other countries, and competent in the language.[2] Of course, if students don't have a good command of English, the language _____ will make it even harder for them to learn the appropriate social skills they need in their new environment.

  First of all, in trying to _____ to the customs and _____ of this country, students may find the general pace of life a problem. This is particularly true for students who are attending schools in large cities because life in large cities in the United States is lived at a fast pace. People seem to rush around and don't take time to relax, except on weekends. Families rarely eat lunch together, and some don't even eat dinner at the same time because they are just too busy trying to keep up with all their activities. According to one Chinese visitor, "The average American does not understand the calm conversing, nap-

---

2. Adrian Furnham and Stephen Bochner, *Culture Shock: Psychological Reactions to Unfamiliar Environments* (London, New York: Routledge, 1989), 126.

ping, strolling, sitting quietly, and various other kinds of leisurely relaxation that Chinese enjoy. They think they are alive only when they are 'doing' and 'moving.'"[3]

Another problem is caused by the fact that most new students lack the social support systems they had in their home countries. A network of friends can enable an international student to overcome many difficulties, and it is especially helpful to form friendships with native English speakers.[4] However, although North American students can seem friendly, their friendliness is rather _____ and insincere. "Let's get together," they say, without setting a definite date. "Hi. How're you doing?" they ask, without expecting or waiting for an answer. To international students, Americans appear to be self-absorbed and uninterested in making friends.[5]

Also, ethical beliefs and value systems _____ from culture to culture, and students may feel anxious about living in a society whose values do not match theirs. For instance, some international students may consider the attitudes of Americans much too _____ in regard to moral issues, such as young men and women having intimate relationships or living together before marriage. Moreover, the use of drugs and alcohol may be unacceptable to them.

Finally, the _____ North American food is usually not at all _____ to students whose native food is spicy, healthful, and full of variety. Hot dogs, hamburgers, potato chips, and french fries can become boring on a daily basis, and they aren't as healthful as fresh fruits and vegetables or rice and beans. Because they dislike the food, many students do not eat properly during their first few months in the United States. Therefore, it is fairly common for them to lose weight or get sick during this period of adjustment.

Despite these various problems, most international students are flexible enough to acquire the_____ skills required in their new surroundings as they become more aware of others' values and practices.[6] Gradually, they grow accustomed to the lifestyle

3. Jiejun, "A Family Christmas," in *Land without Ghosts,* edited by R. David Arkush and Leo O. Lee (Berkeley: University of California Press, 1993), 231.
4. Furnham and Bochner, 129, 139, 250–51.
5. Elisabeth Gareis, *Intercultural Friendship: A Qualitative Study* (Lanham, MD: University Press of America, 1995), 65.
6. Furnham and Bochner, 250.

in the United States, build a network of friendships, and learn to enjoy the benefits of living abroad. Actually, culture shock can be a positive experience of growth and learning and is a normal response to change.[7] In fact, students who have become _____ into North American culture may even have reverse culture shock when they return to their home countries.

What is your opinion on this topic?

Write a paragraph or two expressing your point of view on the issues discussed above.

7. Furnham and Bochner, 49–50.

Dim Sum: A Little Bit of Heart; dir. Wayne Wang, 1984, U.S.

Activities

1. Fill out the questionnaires on culture shock and culture fatigue in Appendix A (p. 215). After you have completed the questionnaires, discuss your answers with the class.

2. Researchers have found that the greater the distance (both objectively and subjectively) between the visitor's country and the host country, the greater the amount of stress or difficulty experienced by the visitor.[8] Was this true in your case? Write an essay describing the amount of stress or difficulty you faced when you first became a student in the United States and explain how you adjusted to your new life.

3. Write a letter from Dita to her parents in Indonesia. In this letter Dita tells them about the problems she is having in getting used to college life in the United States.

4. Make a list of the support services that an educational institution should offer to its international students to help them adjust academically and socially. Then find out what support services are offered by your school. Share both your lists with your classmates by writing them on the chalkboard.

---

8. Furnham and Bochner, 121, 122, 139.

5. In a debate, two teams present opposing arguments on a controversial topic with the goal of convincing the audience of their point of view. After the class is divided into two teams, have a debate on the following topic: International students should not come to the United States to study until they have mastered English.

   These general guidelines will help you prepare for and carry out your debate.

   • Each team should have approximately the same number of members.
   • Each team should elect a leader who will give the three-minute opening presentation and the three-minute closing summation.
   • All members of the team should be prepared to speak at least once and to give a rebuttal (answering argument) to the opposing team's statements.
   • No one person should dominate the debate; all team members must contribute equally to the debate.
   • The person who is speaking should not be interrupted.

6. Choose one of the following role plays for presentation in class.

   (A) Act out the scene between Dita and Sandra when they go out to dinner together and Dita tries to tell Sandra how unhappy she is, but Sandra is unsympathetic.

   (B) Act out a scene in the future in which Dita meets with her adviser and receives some moral support and practical advice.

   The guidelines given here will help you to plan, practice, and present your role play.

   • Work in teams of two or three. The third person serves as a coach to help the two actors prepare and rehearse the role play (unless a third person is needed for the role play).
   • Discuss the role play scenario with your partner(s), choose your role, and reread the case study.
   • Develop several objectives for your role play and put them in writing. For example, your objectives for the first role play (A) for chapter 1 could be the following:
     1. to show that two people can look at the same situation from opposite points of view;
     2. to show that it is difficult to reveal one's true emotions and ask for help;
     3. to show that North Americans emphasize self-reliance and individualism.
   • Think about your character and plan what your character will say.
     1. Make notes about the broad ideas and emotions you will act out.
     2. Decide how to achieve your objectives for the role play.
   • Rehearse your role play with your partner.
     1. Do not try to write out the dialogue.
     2. Let your dialogue develop naturally and spontaneously.
   • Present your role play to the class (about five minutes in length).
     1. Speak in a loud and clear voice and don't be afraid to exaggerate your actions.
     2. Listen carefully to what your partner is saying before you respond.
     3. Pay attention to nonverbal communication signals of eye contact, facial expressions, gestures, and body language.

- Discuss the issues seen in the role play with the class afterward.
    1. What reactions did your classmates have?
    2. Were your objectives achieved?

Oral Presentation

Prepare and give an oral presentation on one of the topics listed. Use the suggested methods of development to organize your presentation and do library research to gather information. You may also find the additional readings at the end of the chapter helpful in preparing your talk. Guidelines for presentations and a model outline are in Appendix C (p. 222). An outline for the first topic is provided below.

- Three Reasons International Students Attend College in the United States (enumeration, analysis)
- Three Major Cultural Differences between the United States and My Country (enumeration, contrast)

Three Reasons International Students Attend College in the United States

   I. Introduction
      A. Background: Challenging experience to study in the U.S. (must leave family and friends, must master the English language, must adjust to a new culture)
      B. Main Idea: Many international students prefer to attend college in the United States for three reasons: the up-to-date curriculum; improved job opportunities; and the exposure to a global perspective.
  II. Reason 1
      A. Up-to-Date Curriculum
      B. Analysis: Newest courses, theories, textbooks, and technology
 III. Reason 2
      A. Improved Job Opportunities
      B. Analysis: Increasing value of college degree from the United States
 IV. Reason 3
      A. Exposure to Global Perspective
      B. Analysis: Vital approach for the twenty-first century
  V. Conclusion
      A. Summary: The advantages of attending college in the United States
      B. Restatement of Main Idea: Many international students prefer to attend college in the United States.

Chapter Readings

On Alienation and the ESL Student

As an American alone in Barcelona, Ms. Carey came to better understand her English-as-a-second-language students back home in California.

Laura Carey

Among the clutter of ads on the bulletin board in the neighborhood bookshop, I found a notice about a political organization I would have liked to have joined. Every month, people with whom I shared basic principles met to discuss their frustrations, griefs, and small triumphs and to bask in the luxury of common thought.

Next to that notice in the bookshop hung another, inviting women of all ages to informal biweekly potluck suppers. I wanted to go. I hadn't seen any of my women friends or my mother or my sister for six months. I was an American alone in Barcelona. But every time I bought a new supply of books, I stared at those notices longingly and then headed home to my tiny *piso* to read. I knew that I should go to the meetings and the potluck suppers; I knew that I should make the most of my year in Spain. Attending such gatherings would mean that I was at least trying to stave off my homesickness and the occasional bouts of loneliness by joining some of the groups whose addresses, meeting dates, and times I knew by heart.

But I just couldn't—or wouldn't. I felt uneasy about joining such groups. It was the language barrier—and probably the culture barrier, too, though I rarely admitted it even to myself. If these barriers loomed so large for me—an adult with a loving family and a modest bank account waiting back home—how formidable must they seem to the students in my English-as-a-second-language (ESL) classes in California? I've always known that their lives have been traumatic: escaping from war-torn Laos in the middle of the night or fleeing from screaming poverty in Mexico, only to meet with frustration and alienation in the promised land. I felt sympathy for these students, but I couldn't feel their feelings.

I still can't know what it is like to be a child wrenched from home and tossed into dangerous foreign waters. But I have been given a glimpse of life as an alien, and my heart hurts when I think of my students. They wouldn't want my sympathy, though. They are human beings, and, at 16 or 17 years of age, they are more adult and worldly than I; they would insist on their dignity.

I knew no Spanish when I arrived in Barcelona. As I had stated in my request for a leave of absence, I came to *learn* Spanish and to teach English as a foreign language, so that I could better serve my ESL students. I studied Spanish every day before work. I used it in the bread shop, in the butcher shop, in the taxi. I practiced on the *portero* in my building, and sometimes I asked my adult students to clarify some vague grammatical rule that I had just learned.

But I couldn't for the life of me picture myself in a social situation: the gawky American who says everything in the present tense, the woman with the vacant or puzzled look on her face, who can come, go, have, or be but can't walk, run, or laugh for lack of the appro-

Laura Carey, "On Alienation and the ESL Student," *Phi Delta Kappan* 71 (September 1989): 74–75.

priate verbs. What if they asked me a question? What if someone told a funny joke, and I didn't laugh? What if it were a racist joke, and I did laugh? And worst of all, what if I reached out to people, did my best to be warm and make a friend or two, and they turned away from me, embarrassed or impatient? What then?

It was much easier to be friendly with the other Americans that I met. Most of them were English teachers too, and we shared our daily experiences in the classroom. We discussed our students' progress, and we practiced rolling our r's together. We mourned the exchange rate for U.S. currency, we wondered about politics back home, and we reminisced about tortilla chips, bad coffee, and peanut butter.

Never again will I wonder why my ESL students segregate themselves by nationality. I used to be baffled over the way they grouped themselves in the classroom: Mexicans on the right, Laotians on the left, Hmong in the middle. "But you're all in the same boat!" I would cry. "You should stick together." They would only smile, amused; I didn't know what I was talking about.

I learned quite a bit about language acquisition during the time I spent in Spain, far from the land of convenience stores and fenced backyards. I was exposed to all sorts of materials for teaching English, and I discovered that the books and cassettes that personalize the material and tell a story are more effective than straight grammar, that drills are not as evil as I once thought, that role playing eventually eases anxiety, and that the daily lives of the students should be incorporated into every lesson plan. I filled notebooks with tips from other teachers, and I compared and contrasted bits and pieces of information from English, Irish, Scottish, and American teachers. But nothing has been more valuable to my life as a teacher than my own fear.

My fear—unfounded, silly, not terribly adult—made me long for the days when the vagaries of the copy machine posed my greatest frustrations. In California I could explain my flu symptoms to my doctor in complex linguistic structures: "Well, my stomach started to hurt the other day after dinner, although even at the dinner table I wasn't as hungry as usual, and the pain is low, almost abdominal." But in Spain I had a brief bout of something intestinal and, pointing at my stomach, I said to the doctor something like: "Me bad." In California I could call virtually anyone on the telephone, ask for instructions or directions, chat about personal or professional subjects, discuss prices, complain. In Spain a telephone call was a major event requiring several minutes with an English/Spanish dictionary and grammar book, a page of carefully drawn notes, and a pushup or two. I phrased my questions so that a simple yes or no would suffice as an answer, and a string of fast Spanish in reply would throw me into despair. But mine was the Caspar Milquetoast of despairs compared to what my ESL students must have endured.

I arrived in Spain by plane, after a movie and chicken cacciatore. Khammay crossed the Mekong River, her stomach empty, her little brother wiggling and crying under one arm. At the airport in Barcelona I caught a taxi; the smiling driver jabbered away while I repeated, "No entiendo." I don't understand. Khammay walked barefoot to a Thai refugee camp, where she was greeted by uniformed soldiers with rifles who leered at her and shouted at her mother, "Stay away from our food. Do not cause trouble."

I stayed in a pension room with a single gas burner for cooking and two hangers in the closet. Mai's family of seven shared a room with a dirt floor with two other families for their entire first year in Thailand. On some days they had no food at all.

While in Spain I took to reading in solitude for entertainment. Occasionally, I found a film in English with Spanish subtitles, and on those rare evenings I felt rich pleasure. Somsack found a cigarette in the refugee camp. He found it in the pocket of someone else's jacket. Somsack learned the value of stealing and the luxurious escape of nicotine.

Although I have brown eyes and brown hair, I didn't wear the black loafers and leather coat so typical of the modern young Barcelona woman that year. My hair was cut in an American style, and sometimes I felt a little conspicuous. People did look at me. They knew I wasn't native. But Juan, with his strikingly high cheekbones, baggy pants, slicked-back hair, and rusty girl's bicycle, which he pedals faithfully to school and then to work in the orchards every day, is so different from the others in the sophomore class that he has ceased to be conspicuous. He is *mas guapo*. In Mexico he would be the object of enormous yearning, but in California he is invisible. And that, I think, is worse.

My responsibility as an educator involves more than what is written in my contract. Every teacher knows this, and some even enter the field because of it. We are role models—expected to exhibit good health and happiness, to show our students what a solid education did for us. "If you want to live the good life, follow my example," we say, although not in so many words. But in Spain I saw myself becoming a hypocrite. My wealth and my security, even thousands of miles from home, were insulating me. When the next potluck supper was held, I brought an apple pie.

Eating in America

Cai Nengying

American restaurants are all the same. They prepare food in only three ways: boiled in water, grilled, and deep-fried; apart from these there is no other variety. Then, on the table a lot of "condiments" are served so that customers can make things as sweet, salty, sour, or peppery as they like. All over the whole country food stands on the street sell the same hot dogs, hamburgers, sandwiches, french fries, and so on; wherever you go the taste is the same. Especially for someone who has just arrived in America, the sight of a hot dog dripping with red tomato sauce and yellow mustard is enough to take your appetite away. But when you are hungry, there is nothing to do but close your eyes and swallow it. Hamburgers are even worse: semiraw beef with a slice of raw onion and a slice of raw tomato, and then some hamburger sauce—one dares not try it. Sandwiches sound good, but are in fact bland and tasteless. So eating is the most troublesome aspect [of living in America].

 Being invited to dinner is a big treat for Americans, but I find it a painful assignment. First, I cannot get used to eating sweet and salty things together. Second, terrible-tasting food must be praised to the skies. Third, it is not filling, and you have to make yourself another meal after going home.

Cai Nengying, "Eating in America," in *Land without Ghosts*, edited by R. David Arkush and Leo O. Lee (Berkeley: University of California Press, 1993), 219–21.

One time a colleague said to my husband, Fan Guangling, "My father is a good cook and invites you two to have a taste of his culinary skill this weekend." It would have been embarrassing to refuse, so we had to accept. The meal turned out to be canned chicken with vegetables and rice, which tasted funny. Following this dish was a dessert of cored apples stuffed with plum jam and coated in sugar. Eating it made me feel like vomiting, but I had to say, "Delicious! Delicious!" It was unspeakably painful.

Often when we were invited to dinner by Americans I felt that they were not inviting us to eat but to look at the tableware. They do not use rice bowls. At the beginning of the meal the table is set with three plates for each person, three glasses, knife, fork, big spoon, and little spoon. The big spoon is seldom used, however, for they do not drink soup but lots of cold water, so the glasses see much service. The first course is usually raw salad or fruit salad, followed by bread and butter. After that some strange-looking and odd-tasting little dishes are served while people eat and talk. Then comes the main course, usually a piece of chicken or steak or a slice of ham, with a few fried potatoes, and some peas, or whatever, boiled to a pulp. When this is finished dessert is served, fruit pie or ice cream and cake, which is murder to eat for it is tasteless. Moreover, it is not a lot of food in the end, but just a lot of dishes and silverware on the table. Last comes coffee or tea. American tea is a bag of tea leaves in a cup of hot water, at which point the dinner is considered over. Then you are invited into the living room to talk for two or three hours. The foreigners talk and laugh, and we Chinese do not understand what is being said. It is really unbearably painful. That is why I find eating American meals most troublesome.

Cai Nengying, who was from Taiwan, was the wife of a graduate student. This excerpt is from her article "A Housewife Staying in America Talks about Household Matters."

Culture Shock on Returning to America

It took me more than six months to readjust to American culture, and even after that, I was never fully at home. What was this other side? What did I see that I didn't like?

J. Peter Schineller

Everyone was concerned that I would suffer culture shock when I went to Nigeria in 1981. Could I adjust to that foreign culture? Was it safe? Would I ever adapt? The adjustment for me, however, was surprisingly easy. No one at that time spoke about the culture shock when you return home. And yet, for me it was far more difficult, far more painful and time-consuming, to readjust to American culture than it was to go from the United States to Africa. When I say this to friends, they are amazed, and in many ways so am I. Yet for me it is a clear, indisputable fact. Moreover, most foreign missionaries would agree with this view, that the reentry to the United States is more painful than the entry from America to Africa or Latin America.

How do I explain it? What was so difficult in returning home? Why such a slow re-adjustment? I have tried to reflect on this, and now at a distance of a few years, when I am settled back in Africa, I will try to express what I saw and felt.

J. Peter Schineller, "Culture Shock on Returning to America," *America* 164 (June 29, 1991): 676–78.

First of all, I must say that there are many wonderful aspects of American society. It is always good to get back to U.S. soil, and I look forward to my next home visit. Telephones work, television has an amazing variety of programs, transportation systems can be relied upon, stores and shopping centers usually have whatever you want in stock, business and legal systems can, for the most part, be trusted. Things usually work, or if they are broken, can be readily repaired. The melting pot is a reality in the major cities, where peoples of various races and creeds live and work together.

And yet, it took me more than six months to readjust to American culture, and even after that, I was never fully at home. What was this other side? What did I see that I didn't like? What did I miss?

Perhaps the best way to depict the shock or difficulty of reentry is to set forth a series of vignettes, with some comments. . . .

Children. In Cambridge, Mass., I used to walk back and forth from school along Brattle Street, 20 minutes each way. It is an historic and beautiful street, with large spacious homes on both sides and overarching trees. But something was lacking—people, and especially children! Sure, this was expensive Cambridge, but it is, I feel, becoming more typical. Except in inner cities, one does not see many children. In Nigeria, one cannot avoid them, and one does not want to. Children show forth life, hope, joy, play, a sense of the future. In my more cynical moments, I think that the lack of children in the United States results from self-centeredness, the desire to have it one's own way without any strings or obligations. There is something unreal, something that worries me, about so many beautiful houses, mansions, with so few children playing around them.

So much did I miss the smiling faces of children in Nigeria that for the first five months back in the United States, I had to get out my photo album once a week, and spend a few minutes looking at their faces, being with the children once again, at least in my imagination.

Shopping Center and Supermarket. One is overwhelmed upon entering a modern supermarket. There are long aisles of breakfast cereals alone. The quantity and variety are shocking. Then half an aisle for pet foods, including diet food for dogs and cats. I can understand why one missionary from a poor country, upon entering a supermarket, broke down and wept. Instead of low-cal foods, in Africa many simply need food. Of course it is marvelous, a tribute to U.S. enterprise to see such well-stocked stores, and yet there is another world, most of the world that will never have the opportunity to share that consumer abundance.

Conversation. So much American conversation, it seemed to me, was about the latest and often fast-fading fads. Concern with health, foods safe or unsafe, with the latest theory on exercise, with the latest on cholesterol, seemed to take up a disproportionate amount of time. One must talk not about cooking but about cuisine. Again, these can be wonderful. I enjoy a good, healthy meal, but there is more to life than that. And is everyone expected not only to have seen the latest film at the nearby cinema, but also to be able to talk at length about it?

Family. One finds a high and growing percentage of single-parent families. Divorce and second marriages are often talked about with no sense of failure, with little sensitivity to their effects on the children. Stories of child neglect or child abuse dot the newspapers. The elderly have special homes with good health care, yet so often they are distant from the children and grandchildren they cared for and loved. This is in notable contrast with Nigeria, where the elderly are so often in the center, where family life revolves around them, with their wisdom and experience.

Television. No longer for the living room or recreation room, the television is now found in the kitchen and bedroom. The children have their own. Sure, there are many good programs, but then there is the rest. While the quantity of programming has increased, what about the quality? So much television is very provincial and narrow, American-centered. The vision extends beyond the bounds of the United States only to bring us the latest news on the latest crisis. Instead of being with one another, we go to our room or den and turn on the television.

Morality in Media. One does not have to go to 42nd Street or Times Square to see pornography. The local newspaper stand has more than enough. Or videos on the top shelves of rental stores, or special telephone numbers promising thrills. It hurts to see how all this has increased, and with seemingly little question, discussion or opposition. The truly human is being denigrated.

Artificiality. By this word, I mean a distancing from the natural, from nature, or from personal interactions. We live in a world of machines, from our cars to our computers. The marvels of television bring the world of nature into our homes, and yet something—namely, more direct contact—is missing. Our experience is increasingly indirect, filtered, packaged, dished out to us piecemeal. Deep realities of human existence, such as sickness, old age and death, are specialized, sanitized, separated off to the hospital or the old folks home. We don't have to visit there. We don't come face to face with these harsh aspects of life, and yet we expect to have a full, rich emotional experience.

Time. Americans are always short of time, caught up in the race, the fast lane. Microwave ovens, fast foods, 15-second commercials, digital watches that cut the seconds up into hundredths of a second. Time is for doing things, getting things done, rather than (as in Africa) for being with people. . . .

How does one keep a balance? How does one continue to cherish and appreciate the virtues of American culture, and yet not lose a critical perspective? . . . The theologian Paul Tillich praised America, but then reminded us that all people and nations, especially the strong, should constantly be self-critical and aware of the deep ambiguities within them. "He who is not aware of the ambiguity of his perfection as a person and in his work is not yet mature; and a nation which is not aware of this ambiguity of its greatness also lacks maturity. Are we mature as a nation, are we aware of the ambiguity even in the best of us?" Good questions, and questions which the outsider/insider perspective of the returning missionary can help us address.

J. Peter Schineller, S.J., is regional superior of the Nigeria-Ghana Mission, Nigeria, Africa.

Comprehension

After completing the chapter readings, answer the following questions. You may look back at the readings in order to find the answers.

"On Alienation and the ESL Student"
1. Why did Laura Carey go to Barcelona, Spain?
2. Why didn't Laura join the political organization or go to the potluck suppers?
3. What was Laura worried about in social situations?
4. What proved to be most valuable to her life as a teacher?
5. Why was her experience much less difficult than the experiences of her ESL students?
6. What made Laura decide to attend the next potluck supper?
7. What are the similarities and what are the differences between Laura Carey and Dita Rantung, the young woman in the case study?
8. What is the central point (main idea) of the reading selection "On Alienation and the ESL Student"?

"Eating in America"
1. How does the author feel about hot dogs, hamburgers, and sandwiches?
2. Why is being invited to dinner in an American home a painful assignment for the author?
3. What does the author think about the amount of food at an American meal?
4. Why doesn't the author enjoy being invited into the living room to talk for two or three hours?
5. What is your opinion about American food? Which American foods do you like the best?

"Culture Shock on Returning to America"
1. How did the author feel about his readjustment to American culture compared to his adjustment to Africa?
2. What does the author like about the United States?
3. Why did the author miss the smiling faces of Nigerian children when he returned to the United States? What does the author believe this lack of children results from?
4. What is the author's attitude toward the shopping centers and supermarkets in the United States?
5. How does the author describe conversations in the United States?
6. Explain the differences the author sees between Nigerian and American families.
7. What does the author think of American television?
8. Describe the author's view of morality in the U.S. media.
9. What has caused the artificiality of life in the United States?
10. How do Americans use time in contrast with Africans?
11. Why did the theologian Paul Tillich remind us that all people and nations, especially the strong, should be self-critical and aware of the deep ambiguities within them?
12. What is the central point (main idea) of "Culture Shock on Returning to America"?
13. What is your reaction to the author's opinions? Do you agree or disagree with his descriptions of life in the United States? Explain your answer.

Walkabout; dir. Nicolas Roeg, 1971, Australia

Strategy Session

In this final activity, you will be confronted with a hypothetical dilemma. You should evaluate the pros and cons of the suggested coping strategies and then choose the strategy you find most appropriate. There are no right or wrong choices, but you must write a well-thought-out justification for your decision.

> Imagine that you are an international student who has been studying at a college in the United States for the past four years. You have just graduated with a bachelor's degree in business. You enjoy living in the States because you have made many friends and feel comfortable living in the culture. Although your parents expect you to return to your native country in a few weeks, you would prefer to stay in the United States for several more years, either to get a job or to get a master's degree.

Which strategy would you use in this situation and why? Provide a written justification for your decision. If none of the listed strategies would be your choice, you may develop your own strategy.

1. Write a letter to your parents explaining your feelings and plans and asking for their permission to remain in the States for another year or two.

2. Telephone your parents and explain to them that you have decided to stay in the States for another year or two in order to get a job or a master's degree.

3. Buy a round-trip airplane ticket to your country (returning to the United States in three weeks) so you can talk to your parents face-to-face about what you plan to do.

4. Return to your native country and start looking for a job there, with the hope that you can return to the States in a year or two.

5. Find a job immediately, even if it isn't exactly what you want, so you can tell your parents that you are staying in the States because you already have a job.

6. Other: _____

Suggested Films

The films listed here are related to the topic in this chapter. After you view one of these suggested films, you should fill out the Film Analysis Form in Appendix D (p. 224). (See p. 225 for an example of a completed form.)

America, America (1963)
The Brother from Another Planet (1984)
College (1927 silent film)
Coming to America (1988)
"Crocodile" Dundee (1986 Australia)
Dim Sum: A Little Bit of Heart (1984)
El Norte (The North) (1983)
Foreign Student (1994)
The Gods Must Be Crazy (1981 Botswana)
The Joy Luck Club (1993)
Jungle 2 Jungle (1997)
Knowing Her Place (Women Make Movies: 1990)
Mi Familia (My Family) (1995)
The Milagro Beanfield War (1988)
Moscow on the Hudson (1984)
Someone Else's America (1996)
Walkabout (1971 Australia)

Additional Readings

These readings will expand your knowledge of the topic in this chapter. They include articles from newspapers and magazines and a book. After you complete your reading, fill out the Reading Report Form in Appendix E (p. 226). (See p. 227 for an example of a completed report.)

Dembner, Alice. "Help Exists for Foreign Students." *Boston Globe,* May 31, 1995, 24.

Dodge, Susan. "Culture Shock and Alienation Remain Problems for Many Foreign Students on U.S. Campuses." *Chronicle of Higher Education* 36 (March 7, 1990): A33.

"Freshman Survival Tips." *USA Today: The Magazine of the American Scene* 125, November 1996, 7.

Gose, Ben. "A New Approach to Ease the Way for Freshmen."*Chronicle of Higher Education* 42 (September 8, 1995): A57–58.

Hanson, Jennifer, and Wanda Fox. "Communicating across Cultures." *Training & Development* 49 (January 1995): 56–58.

LeWine, Sarah. "Is It Romantic?" *Boston Globe,* February 8, 1996, CAL 8.

Melton, R. H. "George Mason's Ethnic Diversity Runs into a Cafeteria Wall." *Washington Post,* November 7, 1995, B1, B5.

Newman, Richard. *The Complete Guide to College Success: What Every Student Needs to Know.* New York: New York University Press, 1995.

Ning, Qian. "Almost Made in America." *Newsweek* 130 (October 27, 1997): 38.

Rubin, Amy Margaro. "Under One Roof." *Chronicle of Higher Education* 42 (February 2, 1996): A35–36.

Smolowe, Jill. "The Pursuit of Excellence." *Time* 139 (April 13, 1992): 59–60.

"Students from Afar." *U.S. News & World Report* 119 (November 20, 1995): 38.

Chapter 2
Academic Motivation: Miscommunication

N'Diangane (Njangaan); dir. Mahama Traore, 1975, Senegal

How would you react if your teacher told you that you had a failing grade in the course after the midterm exam?

Exploration

After reading the following statements, respond to each one by writing *yes* or *no*.

1. A teacher's expectations strongly affect the academic performance of a student. _____

2. It is a teacher's responsibility to motivate students by creating a positive learning environment in the classroom. _____

3. It is a student's responsibility to let the teacher know about his or her academic problems or concerns. _____

4. Grades should reflect a student's effort more than a student's ability. _____

5. Students who do not attend class regularly should receive lower grades. _____

6. It is not appropriate for students to question what their teacher says. _____

7. The relationship between a student and his or her teacher should be informal. _____

8. I will do better work when my teacher is very demanding. _____

9. I enjoy participating actively in a class by asking and answering questions. _____

10. In my culture, students are expected to sit quietly in class and listen to their teacher lecture. _____

11. In my country, students and teachers have a more formal relationship than they do in the United States. _____

12. Teachers in my country are treated with great respect and honor by students. _____

Glossary

affect	to have an effect on; to influence
appropriate	right for the purpose; suitable, proper
complain	to make an accusation; to express displeasure
defensively	serving to defend or protect
demanding	making difficult demands on one's resources, patience, energy
differ	to be unlike; to disagree
effort	a hard attempt to achieve a particular goal
expectations	what one is looking for as likely to occur, proper, or necessary
formal	stiff in manner; not warm or relaxed; according to prescribed rules
influence	to have the power to affect others
interpretation	one's own understanding of the meaning of something
midterm	examination given in the middle of a semester
miscommunication	failure of communication; misunderstanding
morale	the mental and emotional condition of an individual
motivation	incentive, drive, or stimulus to accomplish something
nature	inborn character or disposition
participating	taking a part or sharing with others in an activity
performance	accomplishment; execution of tasks and assignments
question	to dispute or challenge; to doubt
reflect	to show or make apparent
regular	consistent or habitual in action
turn things around	to change for the better
volunteer	to offer or give of one's own free will without being asked

Girls' Dormitory; dir. Irving Cummings, 1936, U.S.

Case Study: A Question of Interpretation

After you read the case study, discuss the major problem the case presents and answer the discussion questions with the members of the class. Then write a case study report, following the format that is provided.

Mei Chang is from mainland China. She is a sophomore who is studying for a B.A. in computer science at a large state university on the West Coast of the United States. Mei is having trouble in several of her college courses because her English is not at a high enough level for her to speak with confidence, and sometimes she doesn't understand what other people are saying. She tends to be quiet by nature anyway, and in class she almost never asks any questions or volunteers her opinions. She just listens respectfully, as she was trained to do in China. She is also afraid that the other students will laugh at her poor pronunciation. Most of her grades are in the C to C+ range although in computer programming courses she gets B's.

Mei is taking an advanced English course for non-native students. It is a requirement for graduation from the university. In this class (College Reading and Writing) Mei has been doing rather badly, especially because she doesn't take part in the class discussions on the works of literature the students are reading. Her teacher, Ms. Kramer, often calls on Mei, but Mei rarely has an answer to give. In fact, since Ms. Kramer has noticed Mei's lack of participation, she has begun to call on her even more often. This has caused Mei to feel uncomfortable and somewhat annoyed.

"Why does she have to keep on calling on me?" she wondered. "I wish she would just leave me alone."

Besides the problem with participating in the discussions, Mei has also been having trouble with the writing assignments. Because her grades have been low, she knows she should rewrite the essays. But she can't understand the meaning of Ms. Kramer's comments on her papers: "Organization is illogical and unclear. Topic sentences are not correct. Be more specific. Try to come straight to the point." Although Ms. Kramer encourages students to come to her if they have questions, Mei hasn't tried to see Ms. Kramer during her office hours to ask her for help in rewriting the essays.

After the midterm exam, Ms. Kramer announced that she would meet with the students to give them a written and an oral evaluation of their performance at midpoint in the semester. Mei did not look forward to meeting with Ms. Kramer. She was nervous about having to talk with her and even considered skipping class, but at the last minute she decided to go. When it was her turn to go into the conference room, her heart began to beat quickly.

"Well, hello, Mei," said Ms. Kramer. "Please sit down. I'm sorry to report that your midterm exam was a C-, and your midterm average is also C-. It would have been higher if you had participated more in class and rewritten your papers that had the lowest grades. And I wonder if you are doing all the reading assignments."

Mei stared at Ms. Kramer. She couldn't say a word. But she knew that C- was a failing grade in this course. Her eyes began to fill up with tears, and she looked away so Ms. Kramer wouldn't notice.

"Unless you work very hard to raise your average by rewriting your papers and speaking up in class, you may have to take this course again. What can I do to help? How can I encourage you to participate in the class?" said Ms. Kramer in a kind voice.

Mei shook her head slowly and tried not to cry. "I don't know," she answered. Then she stood up.

"I'm sure you can turn things around if you put more effort into your English," Ms. Kramer continued, as Mei left the conference room.

Mei's attendance in College Reading and Writing became quite irregular in the second half of the semester. She really didn't care about English anymore, and she was so busy with her four other courses that she rarely had the time to do the reading or complete the writing assignments. Two weeks before the final exam, Ms. Kramer asked Mei to stay after class for a few minutes to talk with her. With embarrassment, Mei noticed that many of her classmates were still in the room when Ms. Kramer began her remarks.

"Mei, I'm worried about your work, and I just wanted to remind you that your final grade partly depends on class participation and attendance. You've missed a lot of classes, you don't contribute much in the class, and you also owe me two essays." Ms. Kramer's voice sounded louder than usual to Mei.

"I can't do them, and anyway, why does it matter? You told me I was going to fail when we had the midterm conference," replied Mei.

"I said no such thing! You must have misunderstood me. I simply asked you to work harder in this course," Ms. Kramer answered in surprise.

"That's not what you told me," Mei responded angrily, "and after you said I was going to fail, I lost my motivation."

Ms. Kramer looked worried as she tried to remember exactly what she had said at their conference, but Mei continued to argue.

"Why should I write these essays and why should I come to class or even bother to take the final if you have already decided not to pass me?" she asked, getting even angrier.

"Of course you should take the final, and I'm so sorry about this misunderstanding," was all Ms. Kramer could say as Mei walked out of the classroom.

The following morning Ms. Kramer received a call from the chairperson of her department, Dr. Harris. "A student named Mei Chang just came to see me. She complained that you told her at midterm that she would never pass College Reading and Writing, which upset her and destroyed her morale," said Dr. Harris.

"What? I certainly didn't say that. She completely misunderstood me. I told her that she had a failing grade at midterm and had to study hard in order to pass. And I reminded her that poor attendance would affect her final grade. I was only trying to motivate her," answered Ms. Kramer somewhat defensively.

"Well, this seems to be a question of interpretation, and the student believes she should have another chance to pass the course. You had better be in my office at 3 o'clock so we can try to settle this with her," Dr. Harris replied.

Discussion

1. How can teachers motivate students to study and also keep their morale high?
2. What could Mei have done to improve her performance in College Reading and Writing?
3. What could Ms. Kramer have done to motivate Mei and improve her attitude in College Reading and Writing?
4. Were Ms. Kramer's remarks to Mei at the midterm conference appropriate? How would you have interpreted them? Would you have felt motivated to do better or discouraged?
5. Should Ms. Kramer have talked to Mei about her academic work in front of her classmates? How could she have handled this differently?
6. How did Mei's interpretation of Ms. Kramer's remarks to her differ from Ms. Kramer's interpretation?
7. Should Mei have gone to Ms. Kramer's department chairperson to complain about Ms. Kramer?
8. Does Mei still deserve a chance to pass the course? Why or why not?
9. What could have caused the miscommunication between Ms. Kramer and Mei?
10. Can their misunderstanding be resolved? If so, how?

Case Study Report

Working with a partner or in a small group, write a case study report analyzing the problem that has arisen between Ms. Kramer and her student Mei Chang. Follow this format, which is in Appendix B (p. 219), when writing your report.

I. Statement of the Problem
    A. Definition
    B. Analysis
II. Suggestion of Possible Solutions
    A. Solution 1
    B. Solution 2
    C. Solution 3
III. Evaluation of Possible Solutions
    A. Solution 1
        1. Advantages
        2. Disadvantages
    B. Solution 2
        1. Advantages
        2. Disadvantages
    C. Solution 3
        1. Advantages
        2. Disadvantages
IV. Selection of a Solution
    A. Choice
    B. Justification

Vocabulary

Fill in the blanks with the most appropriate words. Use each word only once.

effort	reflect	affected	participating	regular
morale	performs	motivate	expectations	demanding

Students who attend schools outside of their native countries may be surprised by the educational methods and materials they will encounter. This results from the fact that different cultures have different _____ of how students and teachers should behave in a classroom, what their roles should be, and how learning is best accomplished.[1] Of course, students enrolled in schools in the United States will find a variety of teaching styles

---

1. Danling Fu, *My Trouble Is My English: Asian Students and the American Dream* (Portsmouth, NH: Boynton/Cook–Heinemann, 1995), 197–99.

and academic standards, and they will be more comfortable with some than with others. Nevertheless, several general factors determine how well a student _____ in a course.

First, studying on a daily basis, in order to keep up with both reading and writing assignments, is essential. Developing good study habits is a smart idea because there definitely is a relationship between the amount of time devoted to a course and the final grade. Although grades sometimes _____ how much ability a student has rather than how hard the student has worked, a student who makes a serious and intense _____ to learn may be just as successful as the student with natural ability who doesn't work as hard.

Second, _____ actively in class generally raises a student's grade since being outspoken and behaving assertively are seen as positive traits in the United States. Such behavior is not easy for someone who is used to a formal classroom with a teacher who lectures while students listen quietly and respectfully, rather than speaking up.[2] However, if a student rarely asks or answers questions, the teacher may doubt his or her ability to understand the content of the lesson or may think that the student isn't interested in the class.

Third, _____ attendance can also improve a student's grade. Professors often try, through their lectures, to provide additional information that students can't learn solely from reading their textbooks. While attending class is not always a major requirement at universities in other parts of the world, in the United States it is important. In fact, at most universities, missing more than fifteen percent of the semester's classes can result in failing the course.

Finally, a positive and supportive learning environment encourages academic achievement. Just as a teacher's style and technique can be influenced by the students, the academic performance of a student can be _____ by the attitude of his or her teacher. Thus, a _____ teacher who expects a student to do well may _____ the student to work harder. On the other hand, if a teacher has

2. David F. McCargar, "Teacher and Student Role Expectations: Cross-Cultural Differences and Implications," *Modern Language Journal* 77 (Summer 1993): 192–93.

unrealistic goals for his or her student, the student may fail to achieve those goals and suffer a loss of _____. Moreover, when professors do not clearly explain their course objectives, standards, or grading system, this causes problems for their students, who will be confused about how best to meet the course requirements. In such a situation, students should not hesitate to ask their teachers for clarification and help.

What is your opinion on this topic?

Write a paragraph or two expressing your point of view on the issues discussed above.

Activities

1. In *Writing across Cultures*, Kenneth Wagner and Tony Magistrale suggest that students living in a foreign culture should write in an "analytical notebook" at least four or five times a week, using the language of the new culture. According to Wagner and Magistrale: "Writing about your everyday cultural experiences will help you discover and understand your new culture."[3]

   Begin to write in a notebook or journal on a regular basis. The journal will allow you to express your personal thoughts and feelings about your life in a new culture as well as to practice thinking and writing in English.

2. Liu Zongren, a Chinese journalist, studied for two years in the United States. In his book *Two Years in the Melting Pot,* he describes his experiences as a student:

   > In China, teacher-student relationships have a long tradition of being as important as that between a father and a son. At Medill [Northwestern University School of Journalism] I had found the relationship between students and teachers rigid; they had little to do with one another outside the classroom. At Circle [the University of Illinois in Chicago] I felt the students behaved too freely in the classroom. They drank coffee and ate food in class,

---

3. Kenneth Wagner and Tony Magistrale, *Writing across Cultures: An Introduction to Study Abroad and the Writing Process* (New York: Peter Lang, 1995), 146.

Qingchun Ji (Sacrificed Youth); dir. Zhang Nuanxin, 1986, China

and put their feet on the desks in front of them. Nevertheless, I did like the way classes were conducted and how students were encouraged to take part in class discussions. At first I thought the professors might not be well prepared and therefore didn't have much to say. But later I learned that through debate and discussion the students are encouraged to develop independent thinking.[4]

Write an essay in which you compare and contrast studying in your country with studying in the United States. Discuss the three points Liu Zongren raises: the relationship between teacher and student, the classroom behavior of students, and the way classes are taught.

3. Make a list of the characteristics of an ideal (superior) teacher, for example, *patience*. Then make a list of the characteristics of a poor teacher, for example, *impatience*. Share your lists with your classmates by writing the words on the chalkboard.

4. Liu Zongren, "Two Years in the Melting Pot," in *From the Outer World,* edited by Oscar Handlin and Lilian Handlin (Cambridge: Harvard University Press, 1997), 422.

4. In three paragraphs, describe the best teacher or the worst teacher you have ever had.
5. After the class is divided into two teams, have a debate on the following topic: Students should challenge their teachers during class if they disagree with their grades or with the teachers' comments and answers to their questions.
6. Choose one of the following role plays for presentation in class. Plan and practice your dialogue before presenting it.
   (A) Act out the scene that took place two weeks before the final exam, when Ms. Kramer asked Mei to stay after class.
   (B) Act out the same scene but with a positive ending. Show how Mei and Ms. Kramer could have handled this situation more effectively and communicated more clearly, resulting in a better outcome for both individuals.

Oral Presentation

Prepare and give an oral presentation on one of the topics listed. Use the suggested methods of development to organize your presentation and do library research to gather information. Appendix C (p. 222) provides an example of an outline for the first topic.

- Communication Styles in the United States and My Country (comparison-contrast)
- Teaching Methods in the United States and My Country (comparison-contrast)

Chapter Readings

First Person:
Teacher and Student

Carol Baum

I stood in front of my desk and waited, hands on hips, for the students to straggle in. My "hellos" were enthusiastic, but I was nervous. I had rehearsed my lines on the long drive to work, still with opening-day jitters after years of teaching. My students were anxious, too, as I outlined the workload for Advanced English As a Second Language. When I had finished, one student raised her hand. "What about *Sula?*" she asked.

I put *Sula* on the reading list the day Toni Morrison won the Nobel Prize. The book was about the lifelong relationship of two African-American women from a small Ohio town—Sula defying convention, Nel embracing it. Yes, Morrison was tough going and my students weren't native speakers, but I wanted them to be challenged, to see America's best. A new teacher at the community college, I was filled with schemes. I wanted to make a difference in their lives.

The Friday of the second week, we formed a circle and I asked the students what they thought of the book. The response was immediate and angry: "It's too hard! Why are we reading this?"

Carol Baum, "First Person: Teacher and Student," *Humanist* 55 (July 1995): 46–47.

Horse Feathers; dir. Norman Z. McLeod; the Marx Brothers, 1932, U.S.

"Just think, you're reading the winner of the Nobel Prize for Literature, not the literary equivalent of McDonald's," I reminded them. I looked at their faces. They liked McDonald's.

I called upon Vladimir, a Russian, to describe the book's setting. He answered confidently. I cheered him on—if he understood, others must.

"How do you like it?" I asked the moment he finished.

"I hate it," he answered without missing a beat.

I took a breath and called on someone else to read aloud.

At the beginning of the next week, the students handed in their first essays. The topic: a meaningful event in their lives. Vladimir wrote an emotional account of the devastating earthquake in Armenia, in which he apologized to the "dear reader" for his faltering English. Clara, from Honduras, described how terrified she'd been of caterpillars and how mercilessly her brothers had teased her. "But now when I look back, I can laugh. . . . It is very comfortable to be able to see through my memories all those faces that I love." I was struck by how something as unremarkable as caterpillars could impart such meaning.

For the moment, my own life had lost its comfortable definition. For 23 years I'd planned my escape from Los Angeles with fantasies of a small New England town, changing seasons, the charm of brick sidewalks and village greens. I'd finally done it nine months before. But I'd failed to consider what I was leaving behind. I missed many things . . . and the list grew steadily. When I walked into the center of my postcard-perfect town, I looked around in utter disbelief. Where was I? The only familiar ground was in class. And class wasn't going well.

On Friday I polled the students to see how many had read the second chapter. Fewer than half. As they yawned and groaned, I tried to understand. They had a lot more to contend with than taking up the challenge of a difficult book. Alina, in her late forties and a graduate of a Russian university, wanted to find a job, not sit in a classroom. Hareq, homesick for her family in Ethiopia, was working a full-time job when not in class. Svetlana was about to return to Russia for three weeks because her mother was dying. How could she even bear to be here?

I attempted a new tack. I reconstructed the story of Shadrack, who'd gone off to the First World War (as Morrison puts it) "a young man of hardly twenty . . . his mouth recalling the taste of lipstick," and returned to his hometown emotionally destroyed by combat. Once I had finished, I asked, "Kalsavoeun, what about your experiences in Cambodia?"

My Cambodian student stretched out his legs and stared at me from under his baseball cap. He used his time in class to sketch heads on elongated necks. Now he spoke softly.

"When we were running from war, we didn't eat for four days. We only had a very little water to survive. Our clothes were lost. After three months, we found a camp. My mother made bread and soup to sell. About half a year later, a bullet passed over my head. And the war started all over again."

Solomon broke in with stories of famine and war in Ethiopia; the Russians, with accounts of their flight from anti-Semitism. A lively discussion ensued, and it made me smile. My students were no longer bored.

It was the worst winter in 50 years. Ice everywhere and the days were dark and gloomy. Bad luck flourished. Solomon was clobbered on the head outside his apartment and required 12 stitches. Clara's stepbrother died in a motorcycle accident. Svetlana had seen her mother for the last time.

But the students were doing the reading. If I forgot to put the study questions on the board, a chorus of voices reminded me. We explored the theme of friendship in *Sula,* and everyone had something to say. Sula and Nel met at age 12. Reuniting after 10 years of separation was like "getting the use of an eye back." Their friendship endured betrayal, death. My students spoke sadly of friends they'd never see again, and I shared their loss. The letters and phone calls from Los Angeles couldn't replace the intimate contacts that had made up my daily rhythm.

In the book, Nel's husband "longed" for work which went to "thin-armed white boys from another state."

"Have you encountered racism in the United States?" I asked.

"Definitely not," responded Vladimir emphatically. "There is no racism here."

"Where have you been?" a Japanese and several Dominicans chimed in together. They glared at him while citing examples from their lives.

"Well . . . " Vladimir seemed to think this over. He excused himself and dashed from the classroom so as not to be late picking up his daughters.

Then came the day we formed a circle for the last time. I ended where I'd begun: "What did you think?"

Vladimir raised his hand. "I was very impressed by certain scenes like when the mother set her son on fire. . . . In short, I'll never forget this book." I clutched my copy of *Sula* fondly. "But," he added, "I would've preferred *The Bridges of Madison County!*" Most of the others nodded in agreement.

We had a party. I had wanted a festive atmosphere; instead, everyone glanced longingly at the clock. In the final moments, Clara pulled "Pin the Tail on the Donkey" from her school bag. Suddenly the room reverberated with laughter as one after another, we stumbled blindfolded toward the donkey.

I watched the students go. They walked proudly. Here they were, hungrily taking on the trappings of everything American while I couldn't even adjust to a new state. I would miss them. Would they think of me or of Advanced English—today, tomorrow, five years from now? I wrote their names carefully on the back of the class photo and placed it in my briefcase next to the tattered paperback copy of *Sula*. Then I followed them out the door and drove home.

Learning the Language of Humility and Heart

K. Anne Eston

As a third-year Spanish student, I joined 21 other students and two professor-guides on my college's first study-abroad program to Argentina. I knew how to ask for the bathroom and call home, so I wasn't panicked about dinner. Yet my second night in Buenos Aires, to my horror, I ordered the squid stew instead of stuffed shrimp.

The next evening was a triumph: I managed to order the most succulent filet mignon I had ever eaten, along with salad *without* salt and soda *with* ice, in defiance of local customs. Then I pored over the dessert menu as my waiter stared down at me in anticipation.

"Chocolate caliente, por favor." Hot chocolate, I said. No adjectives or verb conjugations.

"Chocolate caliente," he repeated, a mixed expression of confusion and irritation on his face.

"Si, chocolate caliente," I repeated confidently, but politely.

"Muy bien." He nodded curtly and walked away. Clearly, to him, I was a pompous American with no taste and no etiquette.

Moments later, he returned with exactly what I had asked for: a demitasse of bitter, steaming chocolate syrup. Touché.

I learned to order my hot chocolate *con leche* (with milk), but there were larger lessons in communication in store. I was still relying on my status of intermediate fluency to carry me through my coursework at the Instituto Americano where we attended classes daily. As long as I could order the steak and learn the tango, I was not concerned.

But our instructor in Argentinean culture viewed my status and progress differently. While her classes included music, dance, and art, the study of literature was a large part of

K. Anne Eston, "Learning the Language of Humility and Heart," *Christian Science Monitor*, October 7, 1996, 17.

learning the culture. And "Don Segundo Sombra," the dramatic tale of an early *gaucho* (cowboy), became a weight on my mind.

One of the first assignments she gave us was to take an excerpt from that work and give an oral presentation retelling it, emphasizing cultural themes. My study partner and I prepared that evening. We skimmed the story in about 15 minutes, before trading *boleros* for boy-watching. We had more important missions, like cruising the avenue. We were, after all, of the intermediate level, not requiring extensive practice for a simple improvisation about a cowboy who slung his bolero around the pampas all day.

We failed miserably. At center stage, and under the instructor's eagle eyes, one of us would mumble some chopped-up Spanish and pass the verbal baton to the other, who would inevitably drop it somewhere in the middle of the wrong verb tense or a gender disagreement. Hanging our heads, we slunk back to our seats, vowing to make up for our linguistic fiasco.

And try we did, though success continued to elude me. For every assignment thereafter, I made painstaking efforts to choose just the right vocabulary words. I pored over the Spanish dictionary until I was certain I understood every nuance of every passage I read.

But to no avail. The C's kept coming, along with what I felt was cruel criticism from my teacher. She exuded control and superiority when listening to or reading our attempts at fluent Spanish. Yet when she spoke English, she became a child, full of humility, modesty, and wonderment.

On only one occasion did I connect with my teacher on a bridge other than words. Our professors had invited her to join our group at a local *estancia* (ranch), for a day of horseback riding, folk dancing, and an *asado,* a feast of grilled meats with all the trimmings. With her family there, watching us absorb the best of what her country had to offer in music, art, and food, my teacher glowed.

She laughed and ate with us. And with the afternoon sun lighting up her shiny black hair and glassy, dark eyes, she sang the most beautiful gaucho love song we had ever heard.

Back in the classroom, I continued to disappoint her, and she continued to burden me. I plodded through the rest of the coursework, with no expectation of success. I filled my experience with ballet at Teatro Colon. I scoured the shops for the perfect leather jacket and pondered a date with the bellboy (an Erik Estrada look-alike) at the hotel.

Our *compadres* at the Instituto gave our group a reception on the last day of class. Our semester-long assignment had been to keep a journal in Spanish about our impressions and experiences of the culture. As I snacked on a shortbread sandwich cookie with *dulce de leche* (caramel) in the middle, my instructor came toward me with my journal in hand.

The expression on her face was one I had not seen since the day at the ranch.

Reaching out to touch my arm, she said to me in Spanish, "This is the first thing you have given me that I have understood." And I understood her, too, every word.

I had written in my journal about the families we stayed with on weekends, where no spoken language was needed to express the love they showed in taking us in. I had told of the growth in friendship between my American classmates and me, some of whom would never have befriended me back home on campus. I wrote of the humility we'd needed to demonstrate to the families that had rebuilt their homes in preparation for our arrival because they believed we all lived like J.R. Ewing of "Dallas" fame. It was not perfect Spanish, but it was from my heart.

And everything I have written since then, if it has been devoid of judgment and criticism, has been well-received, if not completely understood.

I think my teacher would be proud.

Comprehension

"First Person: Teacher and Student"
1. What did Carol Baum want to do for her students in her Advanced English as a Second Language class?
2. Why wasn't the English class going well at first?
3. What happened to get the students interested in the class?
4. Why does the teacher admire her students?
5. What is the main idea of this reading?

"Learning the Language of Humility and Heart"
1. Why was Anne Eston in Argentina?
2. What was her attitude toward her studies in Argentina?
3. How did Anne's teacher feel about the study of Spanish literature?
4. How well did Anne and her partner do on their presentation?
5. Describe Anne's feelings about her teacher.
6. On what occasion did Anne and her teacher seem to connect? Why?
7. How did Anne do in the classroom after that experience?
8. Why did Anne's teacher appreciate Anne's journal writing?
9. Describe the similarities and the differences between Anne's teacher and Carol Baum, the author of "First Person: Teacher and Student" (p. 32).
10. Describe the similarities and the differences between Anne and Mei Chang, the young woman in the case study.
11. What is the main idea of this article?

Strategy Session

Imagine that you and your teacher are having trouble communicating, and you are worried that your teacher does not understand your problems or your learning style. It is the midpoint in the semester, and you are wondering what to do.

Which strategy would you use in this situation and why? Provide a written justification for your decision. If none of the listed strategies would be your choice, you may develop your own strategy.

1. Wait to see if the situation will improve by itself as time goes by.

2. Make an appointment to meet with the chairperson of the department, your teacher's supervisor, in order to inform the chairperson of your concerns about the teacher.

3. Make an appointment to meet with your teacher to try to clarify your concerns and straighten out any misunderstandings.

4. Write a note to your teacher asking her several questions about her teaching methods and grading system and stating your complaints.

5. Persuade some of your classmates who have similar concerns about the teacher to join with you in bringing up these issues during the next class.

6. Other: _____

Suggested Films

Bill & Ted's Excellent Adventure (1989)
Blackboard Jungle (1955)
The Blue Angel (1930 Germany)
The Browning Version (1994 U.S.-Britain)
Children of a Lesser God (1986)
Dangerous Minds (1995)
Dead Poets Society (1989)
Goodbye, Mr. Chips (1939 and 1969 U.S.-Britain)
High School High (1997)
Higher Learning (1995)
Mr. Holland's Opus (1995)
Sarafina! (1992 U.S.-Britain-France)
Stand and Deliver (1987)
The Substitute (1996)
To Sir, with Love (1967 Britain)

Additional Readings

Borkat, Roberta F. "A Liberating Curriculum." *Newsweek* 121 (April 12, 1993): 11.
Curwin, Richard L. "Teaching At-Riskers How to Hope." *Education Digest* 60 (October 1994): 11–15.
Goodman, Allan E. "What Foreign Students Contribute." *Chronicle of Higher Education* 42 (February 16, 1996): A52.

McCarthy, Colman. "School Days: Beyond Carrots and Sticks." *Washington Post Education Review,* July 28, 1996, 13, 26.

McMillan, James H., and Daisy F. Reed. "At Risk Students and Resiliency: Factors Contributing to Academic Success." *Clearing House* 67 (January 1994): 137–40.

Nzelibe, Jide. "America's Wild Kingdom: A Nigerian Immigrant Is Shocked by His U.S. High School." *Policy Review* (Fall 1993): 40–43.

Chapter 3
Group Learning: Unethical Behavior

The Paper Chase; dir. James Bridges, 1973, U.S.

What would you do if your teacher caught you cheating during an exam?

Exploration

After reading the following statements, respond to each one by writing *yes* or *no*.

1. I am accustomed to working in groups in school. _____

2. Working in groups is an effective learning technique. _____

3. The better skilled members of a group should help the weaker ones by doing their work for them. _____

4. If my friend asked for help in doing his or her homework assignment, I would do it. _____

5. If my writing skills were weak, I would ask someone to do my written assignments for me. _____

6. Doing academic work for a friend is a way to show friendship and support. _____

7. Many students behave unethically in school, so it doesn't matter if I do also. _____

8. I have not cheated in school in any way. _____

9. I have helped another student to cheat. _____

10. If I discovered that a student was cheating during an exam, I would report that student to the teacher. _____

11. Unethical behavior is more prevalent in schools in the United States than in schools in my country. _____

12. What is considered ethical behavior in one culture may be considered unethical in another culture. _____

Glossary

academic	relating to performance in academic courses
cheating	violating rules dishonestly by deception
complain	to make an accusation; to express displeasure
consider	to regard as
contribute	to give or provide jointly with others
diagnostic	of value for deciding the level of competence
encourage	to give courage, hope, confidence, or support
ethical	conforming to moral standards
ethics	a set of moral principles or values governing an individual's conduct
explicitly	leaving no question as to meaning or intent; unambiguous
format	general arrangement or plan of a document
generosity	willingness to give or share; unselfishness
grateful	thankful, appreciative; feeling gratitude
insecure	not confident; filled with anxieties
integrity	firm adherence to a code of moral values
loyalty	faithfulness to a person, government, cause, or duty
obligation	moral responsibility; a duty imposed legally or socially
plagiarism	passing off the words or ideas of another person as one's own
prevalent	widespread; generally accepted or practiced
problematic	difficult to solve or decide

reasonable   sensible, just, rational
resolve   to find the solution or answer to a problem; to solve
sternly   severely, strictly, firmly
stressed   emphasized
struggled   made great efforts or attempts
superior   excellent in quality; above average
unreasonable   not rational; excessive, immoderate

She's Working Her Way through College; dir. Bruce Humberstone; Ronald Reagan, 1952, U.S.

Case Study: A Little Help from My Friends

After you read the case study, discuss the major problem the case presents and answer the discussion questions with the members of the class. Then write a case study report, following the format that is provided.

Mehmet Kaya Ozul is in the MBA program at Ace University in Ohio. He has recently arrived from Istanbul, Turkey. Mehmet is very pleased to be attending Ace University. His father owns an import-export business that is expanding, and he wants Mehmet to work in the company after Mehmet completes his master of business administration (MBA) degree. Although Mehmet is highly intelligent and hardworking, reading and writing in English are still difficult for him. Shortly after Mehmet arrived at the university, he had to take a diagnostic test of his English language skills. After receiving a low score on the grammar and writing sections of the test, he was advised to enroll in grammar and writing courses at the university's English Language Institute. Mehmet signed up for the courses, but because of his heavy course load in the MBA program, he has rarely attended the English classes.

In the first-year MBA program, all the students were divided into groups of five and told that these groups would be working on the required projects together. Mehmet had not done any group work in his classes before, but this seemed like a good idea to him since he felt insecure about his own ability to complete the various assignments success-fully. The first assignment for each group was to do a human relations analysis for the course in Organizational Behavior. The professor emphasized that each member of the group was to complete one of the five sections of the written analysis.

Mehmet's group consisted of three American students (John, Mary, Susan), Sung Ho Kim from Korea, and himself. At the first meeting, the students elected John the group leader. John assigned each member one section of the analysis and asked the group to meet again in one week with the completed sections of the paper. Although Mehmet struggled through the readings and sat in front of his computer for hours, he was unable to get started writing his section. The ideas were so complicated, and the vocabulary was quite difficult for him.

Finally, on the day of the group's meeting, Mehmet wrote two pages and brought them to the library, where the students were to meet. The five members of the group began to read one another's sections of the paper, but the students who read Mehmet's two pages were laughing and shaking their heads.

"What are you trying to say here?" asked John.

"I guess I should have told you that writing is hard for me," Mehmet replied with a sigh.

"Well, we'll just have to do your section ourselves. We get one grade for all of us, so we better not let you lower our group grade. Anyway, what's wrong with getting a little help from your friends?" said Mary, a practical person.

Kim, the graduate student from Korea, had also had trouble writing his section of the analysis, and his few sentences didn't seem logical or understandable to the American students, so they decided to write his section as well as Mehmet's. Kim was grateful for their support. Although Kim had been attending daily English classes at the English Lan-guage Institute, he knew his writing skills were still weak, and he had never liked writing, even in his native language. It seemed reasonable to him to let his American friends help out, especially since they were together in this group.

At the next meeting of the group, the five students looked over the twenty-five-page paper and prepared to hand it in.

"What if Professor Mallory finds out that Mehmet and Kim didn't really do any work? Isn't that slightly unethical?" asked Susan with a serious look on her face.

"That's what I was wondering," said Mehmet. "But this is a group project, so I guess it's OK for you to help us. In my country, we often help each other in school, even when taking tests, because we have to support our friends. It shows our loyalty and generosity. In fact, if I ask my friend to help me do my assignment and he refuses, I will not consider him my friend any longer."

"Well, since we want to get the highest grade possible, it seems as if we have no other choice than to do your writing for you," said John. "Anyway, how would Professor Mallory know what we did? Don't worry about it."

Mary nodded in enthusiastic agreement. "What Professor Mallory doesn't know can't hurt him."

Professor Mallory read the paper by Mehmet's group and found it unusually clear and well written; the analysis was first rate, and the format was professional. Of course, he gave the group an A for that assignment, and he even praised the group in the class. For the next three assignments, Mehmet and Kim did nothing except staple the pages of their group project together. And each project received an A. Then Professor Mallory gave his midterm examination, which was an in-class essay answering two questions about organizational strategy and analysis. Mehmet, even though he had studied hard for the exam, received a C-, and so did Kim.

Shortly afterward, Kim and Mehmet were told to meet with Professor Mallory to discuss their midterm exam results. At the meeting with the students, Professor Mallory asked about how Mehmet and Kim could have done such superior work on their group projects but such poor work on their in-class essays.

Mehmet admitted that the other students had helped him with his writing. "But it was mainly a little help with the grammar and vocabulary," he said.

"Just a little help," repeated Kim. "Anyway, weren't these supposed to be group projects?"

"Yes, but I explicitly asked each individual to be responsible for a section of the analysis, so this really is unacceptable. Unequal participation is unethical," Professor Mallory said sternly.

Then he explained again that each student had to do his or her own work and that certainly, in a group project, it was essential for all members of the group to divide the work and contribute to the final project equally.

After Mehmet and Kim had left his office, Professor Mallory called the director of the English Language Institute to check on how Mehmet was doing in his language courses.

"He hasn't attended since the second week of class. How is he doing in the MBA program?" asked the director.

"Well, since he has been getting group grades, he has done fine, but on his own he can hardly write a correct paragraph. This situation is definitely problematic. I can see that Mehmet, Kim, and probably some of the other students aren't doing their own work," said Professor Mallory. "I doubt that they understand what collaborative work really means, so I'm going to discuss it in our next class, and maybe you and I should get together to try to resolve these issues."

The next time the class met, Professor Mallory gave all the students a lecture on group dynamics and team management. He explained that students were responsible for doing their own work and that the group projects should not be done by only a few members of the group. He stressed that any group project that was not completed by all members of the group would receive a failing grade and mentioned that there would be an increase in the number of essays and reports written in class. He ended with an explanation of academic integrity, emphasizing that academic violations could result in dismissal from the university.

After Mehmet's group received a grade of C on the next project, John, Susan, and Mary went to Professor Mallory to tell him it was unfair to have both Mehmet and Kim in their group. Mehmet wrote to his father and mother to complain about the unreasonable rules at the university, and Kim decided to drop out of the MBA program and return to Korea.

When Professor Mallory called the director of the English Language Institute to arrange a meeting, he mentioned that the foreign students were not learning English fast enough. In response, the director of the English Language Institute asked why the MBA program would admit graduate students whose English skills were not at the level required for graduate work. Professor Mallory had no satisfactory answer to that question.

Discussion

1. What is your understanding of the meaning of *group work?*
2. Is it unethical for students with strong skills to help students with weak skills do their assignments?
3. What instructions did Professor Mallory give about the group work projects?
4. What were the attitudes of John, Mary, and Susan toward doing Mehmet's and Kim's parts of the group project? Was their behavior ethical?
5. How did Mehmet and Kim feel about having someone else do their parts of the project? Was their behavior ethical?
6. What could Professor Mallory have done to prevent this problem from occurring?
7. How can Mehmet and Kim succeed in the MBA program at Ace University?
8. What should the MBA professors at Ace University do to make group learning more effective?

Case Study Report

Working with a partner or in a small group, write a case study report analyzing the problem that the Ace University professors and MBA students are facing.

   I. Statement of the Problem
  II. Suggestion of Possible Solutions
 III. Evaluation of Possible Solutions
 IV. Selection of a Solution

Vocabulary

Fill in the blanks with the most appropriate words. Use each word only once.

insecure   problematic   ethics   obligation   plagiarism
explicitly   resolved   academic   superior   stress

Unethical behavior by students is quite common on college campuses in the United States. Although most professors _____ the importance of honesty, the question of how to prevent ethical violations still has not been _____. Not only the weak and _____ students but also the _____ students sometimes engage in dishonest activities. Moreover, research shows increases in test cheating among women and in unpermitted collaboration among all students on written work.[1] Even students with strong personal _____ may be tempted to take the answers into an exam, copy from another student during a test, or let someone complete their assignments for them if they are under a lot of pressure.

Another type of academic dishonesty occurs when writers fail to acknowledge the sources of their information. For example, students who are writing papers have a(n) _____ to use quotation marks around words taken from another writer's book or article and to insert a footnote or an in-text citation for the quotation. In addition, they should list all their sources in a bibliography or reference list at the end of the paper. Nevertheless, students often use someone else's words without documentation or citation of the source, an illegal behavior that is called _____.

In order to deal with these _____ situations, nearly every university or institution of higher learning has some form of a(n) _____ integrity code, which _____ outlines the different types of unethical behavior and the punishments a student could receive for such behavior. There is a wide range of punishments, including a letter of warning or a failing grade in the course for minor offenses and suspension or expulsion from the university for more serious or repeat offenses.

1. Donald L. McCabe and Linda Klebe Trevino, "What We Know about Cheating in College," *Change* 28 (January 1996): 31–32.

Some universities, such as the University of Virginia and Princeton, have honor codes that were established when the universities were founded. All students who enter these universities must agree to abide by the honor code's requirements. These usually include the promise not to cheat on examinations and the responsibility to report any student suspected of violating the code. The basic premise behind such codes is that "professors trust students enough not to monitor them as they take exams."[2] Schools with honor codes report fewer problems with cheating. At Princeton, only two to four students each year are found guilty of unethical behavior.[3] The success of honor codes results from the fact that they create an environment among students in which academic integrity is a core value and, therefore, cheating is not socially acceptable.[4]

What is your opinion on this topic?

Write a paragraph or two expressing your point of view on the issues discussed above.

Activities

1. Write a letter from Mehmet and Kim to Professor Mallory, explaining why they let the students in their group do their sections of the analysis and asking for his understanding of their language problems.
2. Does the university or school you are attending have a code of academic integrity? (It is probably part of the student handbook.) If so, get a copy of it and read it carefully. Then discuss it with members of your class.
3. Make a list of activities and behavior that would be considered unethical in schools in your country. Share your list with your classmates by writing the words on the chalkboard.

2. "A Code of Honor Troubles Princeton," *New York Times,* March 4, 1996, B5.
3. "A Code of Honor Troubles Princeton," *New York Times,* March 4, 1996, B6.
4. McCabe and Trevino, 33.

Horse Feathers; dir. Norman Z. McLeod; the Marx Brothers, 1932, U.S.

4. A survey involves asking people questions in order to gather data for analysis of a subject. Conduct a survey on the subject of unethical behavior. Ask at least ten people the questions listed here. Then make a chart containing the information you have gathered, and report your results to the class.[5]

Tests
1. Have you ever copied from another student?
2. Have you ever helped another student cheat?
3. Have you ever used cheating notes?
4. Have you ever obtained unauthorized advance knowledge of test questions?

Written Work
5. Have you ever copied material without footnoting?
6. Have you ever plagiarized?

5. These questions are taken from Donald L. McCabe and Linda Klebe Trevino, "What We Know about Cheating in College," *Change* 28 (January 1996): 31.

7. Have you ever turned in work done by another person?
8. Have you ever collaborated on assignments requiring individual work?

5. After the class is divided into two teams, have a debate on the following topic: Working in groups is a better method of learning than working individually.
6. Choose one of the following role plays for presentation in class. Plan and practice your dialogue before presenting it. (Five people are needed for these role plays.)
   (A)   Act out the scene in which John, Mary, and Susan read what Mehmet and Kim wrote for the group project and decide to do the writing for them.
   (B)   Act out the same scene but show how the students could have handled the situation in an ethical manner.

Oral Presentation

Prepare and give an oral presentation on one of the topics listed. Use the suggested methods of development to organize your presentation and do library research to gather information.

- The Advantages and Disadvantages of Group Learning (enumeration and analysis)
- Causes of Cheating by College Students (enumeration and cause)

Chapter Readings

On Your Honor: Fostering a Community of Trust

Debbie Goldberg

With the leaves starting to turn color across its tree-lined campus, Haverford College in autumn looks like the quintessential American college, a secluded, intellectual oasis just miles from the Philadelphia city limits. Despite their proximity to the city, students at Haverford don't live like big-city neighbors. Rooms are often left unlocked, found money is returned via bulletin board notices, and scores of backpacks—containing wallets, books and whatnot—are simply tossed in piles outside the dining hall while students eat.

One recent Monday, Chris Osgood was eating a quick lunch because he had a take-home economics test due by 5 p.m. The Vermont freshman had been carrying the test around in his backpack for three days, waiting for the right time to take it, and hadn't even been tempted to sneak a peek. After lunch, he would go to the library, take the test, check the time on his watch and stop working, whether he was finished or not, after one-and-a-half hours.

What fosters this atmosphere of trust at Haverford is its honor code, in effect since 1897, which sets social and academic standards for students to live by. At Haverford, students who accept the college's offer of admission don't even have to send in a deposit to secure their spot in the freshman class.

Debbie Goldberg, "On Your Honor: Fostering a Community of Trust," *Washington Post Education Review,* November 5, 1995, 12–13.

Haverford may be the most typical of honor code colleges—a small, competitive liberal arts college—but recently there has been renewed interest in establishing some form of honor system at very different types of institutions. Like the University of Maryland, for instance—a large, bustling public institution on the fringes of Washington, D.C., which in 1990 adopted a Code of Academic Integrity that the school's 38,000 students pledge to live by when they enroll.

"It's a new day for honor codes," asserts Gary Pavela, Maryland's director of judicial programs. "Administrators are beginning to realize the only way to address the high rate of academic dishonesty is by reaching the student peer group and culture."

Next fall George Washington University will fully implement its new academic integrity code. The hope there—according to Scott Mory, the senior and student senate member who has been working for two years on a joint student-faculty committee to create the code—is that it will not only police dishonesty, as the school's former policies did, but promote academic honesty.

Honor codes typically cover a broad range of academic infractions, such as copying test answers, plagiarizing, creating false data, stealing tests and making up a medical excuse. Some schools' codes, such as Haverford's, cover social behavior as well, talking about mutual respect and concern for others. The University of Virginia's honor system, a revered tradition since 1872, says students shall not lie, cheat or steal. Virginia students are bound by the honor code even off campus; students who knowingly write bad checks to local merchants are brought before the honor committee for investigation.

In addition, many honor codes refer to such ideals as maintaining trust in the community. At Virginia, students found guilty of an honor violation must leave the university. As Raya Papp, this year's honor committee chair, notes: "We don't feel they can be part of . . . the trusting community we all believe exists here."

But no one is naive enough to think that simply having an honor code eliminates cheating, plagiarism and petty larceny on campus. "Honor codes are not a panacea," says Sally Cole, executive director of the Center for Academic Integrity, based at Stanford University, a consortium of more than 70 higher education institutions concerned with such issues. But, she adds, "they're definitely a means of encouraging academic honesty."

At the University of Virginia's orientation, for instance, freshmen participate in an honor education ceremony, signing their pledges on parchment paper. Applicants to Haverford must submit an essay on what the honor code means and how they would uphold it. Every time an honor case is heard, every student gets a copy of a detailed abstract (no names mentioned), which students say fosters spirited debates among friends and in residence halls.

But honor codes are not without their critics. Christopher Leggett, for one, thinks student-run honor councils have too much freedom to trample on students' rights without any administrative oversight. In February 1993, Leggett, then a sophomore at the University of Virginia, was accused of cheating on a computer science exam. He says his rights were violated during the honor proceedings, in part because he wasn't allowed to present certain evidence at his trial. Leggett also was shocked at how adversarial the proceedings were, and feels the student prosecutor was trying to win at all costs. Leggett was judged guilty by an all-student hearing panel and told in the middle of the night that he had to leave school, recalls his mother, Carol Leggett, who works at The Washington Post.

Leggett hired a lawyer from the prestigious Williams & Connolly law firm to fight his case, and in July 1994 he was quickly exonerated at a second trial. The case caused an uproar on campus. Papp, the current honor committee chair, says there is disagreement among students and alumni on whether Leggett was indeed wronged by the system or got away with cheating because he brought in a high-priced lawyer.

Robert T. Canevari, the university's dean of students, says it is not unusual for students to have attorneys representing them in honor code cases. "What is unusual here is the fact that Mr. Leggett and his attorneys were able to uncover serious flaws in the system," he says.

Leggett, who graduated from Bucknell University last spring and is now in an M.B.A. program at Wake Forest University, is bitter about his experience. "I feel those people in the honor system took what were supposed to be the best years of my life and made them a nightmare." The ordeal cost the family about $75,000, even though the university ultimately paid the Leggetts' lawyer about $45,000. But "it was worth every penny," says Carol Leggett, who worries about students who can't hire a lawyer.

Another controversial aspect of some honor codes requires students to turn in fellow students who don't uphold the standards. These "non-toleration" or "policeman's" clauses are considered ratting by students and aren't too effective. They also tend not to be enforced.

There are exceptions. In 1994, after a well-publicized cheating scandal, 24 midshipmen were expelled from the U.S. Naval Academy, several on grounds that they had withheld information and covered for their classmates, says Col. David A. Vetter, character development officer at the academy, whose job was created in the aftermath of that scandal. "Truth versus loyalty [to classmates] is a tough issue," he says.

Penalties for violating honor codes generally depend on the severity of the violation, and may range from redoing an assignment or taking an academic integrity seminar to getting a failing grade or being suspended or expelled from school. As the Leggett case demonstrated, the University of Virginia is unusual in that it only has one sanction: separation from the university. Because the punishment is so severe, the panel of up to 12 students who hear a case must consider three criteria—act, intent and seriousness—when deciding a case. In other words, if the panel agrees a student did violate the honor code but decides that the act was minor or inadvertent, they might find the student not guilty anyway.

Pavela rejected the single-sanction approach when drafting Maryland's honor code because "it leads to a toleration for a low level of cheating," he says. "We think if there is cheating, there should be a penalty, and it shouldn't be expulsion."

What Maryland came up with is an "XF" grade penalty: the "X" indicates on a student's transcript that the course was failed because of academic dishonesty—and it's right there for potential graduate schools and employers to see. In addition, students with an "XF" grade can't participate in extracurricular activities, including intercollegiate athletics. While the "XF" is a severe sanction, first-time offenders can petition to have the "X" removed after one year if they successfully complete an academic integrity seminar, a six-week, non-credit course dealing with personal ethics and values.

In addition to imposing sanctions, honor codes can mean academic privileges for students, especially at institutions such as the University of Virginia and Haverford, where take-home tests and unproctored exams are the norm. For instance, Haverford students have a two-week finals period during which they can take any of their exams any day they choose at three set times each day. Students can take tests when they're ready, and don't have to worry about having several scheduled for the same day, as happens at other schools, says Stacey Jacobs, a junior and student council president. And Haverford professors don't worry that students taking the test first will blab information to other students.

Advocates also believe that the merits of honor codes extend well beyond graduation day. "As students graduate and enter the work force, they appreciate the honor system to a much greater extent," says the University of Virginia's Papp. And at Haverford, at least one alumnus every year voluntarily reports an honor code violation committed as a student, says Dean Randy Milden. "Maybe they cheated in class, and five or ten years out, it's hanging over their heads," she explains. In such a case, the graduate may be asked to, say, write to his or her classmates about the violation. "The focus of sanctions isn't punitive," Milden says. "It's repairing the breach of trust with the community and recommitting to its values."

Getting Beyond a Culture of Cheating

Debbie Goldberg

Honor Code or not, student cheating—a habit many students picked up in high school—is prevalent on American campuses. "We get them only three months after they leave high school, and I think a majority of kids from both public and private high schools are leaving a culture where there's a fair amount of cheating," says Gary Pavela, director of judicial programs at the University of Maryland.

But when freshmen arrive, colleges have an "opportunity to break that cycle." Pavela says, "Some will actually reinforce the attitude that cheating is okay, because they don't deal with it, or faculty look the other way. Other schools make a real effort from the beginning [to] break habits from high school."

Donald McCabe, associate professor of management at Rutgers University in Newark, N.J., and a founder of the Stanford-based Center for Academic Integrity, says there is less cheating at honor code schools.

"It's not the code per se, but the environment the code creates on campus," he says. "Code schools talk about cheating a lot more, it's a more significant value discussed at orientation and meetings, students may sign a pledge that they will do their work honorably, and they look around and don't see a lot of cheating going on."

Debbie Goldberg, "Getting Beyond a Culture of Cheating," *Washington Post Education Review,* November 5, 1995, 12.

McCabe's data suggest that about 20 percent of college students will cheat no matter what, and another 20 percent will not cheat under any circumstances.

"The battle is fought over the 60 percent in the middle, and that's where [honor] codes make a big difference," McCabe explains. The single most significant factor is the behavior of other students, what McCabe calls the "cheating culture."

At code schools, he says, the impressionable students in the middle "look around and don't see a lot of cheating going on, and they're slowly convinced to do their work in an honorable fashion as well."

McCabe's data show that the level of cheating at honor code colleges is lower than at other institutions, and there are fewer repeat offenders. For instance, in his 1990–91 survey of 31 mostly private, competitive institutions, 57 percent of students at honor code schools admitted to cheating at least once, compared with 78 percent at colleges without honor codes. And 20 percent of students at non-code campuses said they had cheated three times or more, compared with only 5 percent of students at honor-code campuses.

The students most likely to cheat come from both ends of the educational spectrum: those doing so poorly that they have little to lose by cheating, and those who are competing fiercely for coveted spots in selective graduate schools.

"At competitive schools where a disproportionate number of students go to law school or medical school, if students see others cheating they don't want to disadvantage themselves," McCabe explains.

He says that cheating seems to occur less frequently at smaller, residential campuses, where students are less anonymous and it's easier to achieve some sense of community responsibility among them.

Comprehension

"On Your Honor: Fostering a Community of Trust"
  1. How does the Honor Code encourage the atmosphere of trust at Haverford College?
  2. What does George Washington University hope to accomplish by establishing a new academic integrity code?
  3. What do honor codes cover?
  4. Explain the case of Christopher Leggett at the University of Virginia.
  5. What are the "non-toleration" and "policeman's" clauses, and why are they not too effective?
  6. What is the only penalty for violations of the honor code at the University of Virginia?
  7. What penalty does the University of Maryland impose for academic violations?
  8. What privileges do honor codes give to students?

"Getting Beyond a Culture of Cheating"
  1. What is the single most significant factor in determining whether a student will cheat?

2. How do honor code schools compare to other schools in regard to percentage of students who cheat?

Strategy Session

Imagine that you are a teacher who is assigning your students to work in groups of four in order to complete their first major group project, which involves research, analysis, and writing.

   Which strategy would you use in this situation and why? Provide a written justification for your decision. If none of the listed strategies would be your choice, you may develop your own strategy.

1. Discuss the theory and procedure of group work with the students in class.

2. Give the students a written handout on the theory and procedure of group work.

3. Let the students discover, through trial and error, how to do the project instead of first giving them a lot of information about how to work in groups.

4. Ask the students to read several books on the topic of group work in college classes.

5. Make one student in each group the leader and assign him or her the responsibility of ensuring that the group functions effectively.

6. Other: _____

Suggested Films

Bill & Ted's Excellent Adventure (1989)
The Breakfast Club (1985)
Cooperative and Student Team Learning (NEA Professional Library: 1989)
Fast Times at Ridgemont High (1982)
if. . . . (1968 British)
The Interactive Classroom (NEA Professional Library: 1989)
The Paper Chase (1973)

Additional Readings

Caplan, Lincoln. "'Gouging' the Honor System." *Newsweek* 123 (June 6, 1994): 33.
"Cheating in School: How Common Is It?" *Current Events* 94 (February 20, 1995): 5.
"A Code of Honor Troubles Princeton." *New York Times*, March 4, 1996, B5.
Croucher, John. "The Complete Guide to Exam Cheating." *New Scientist* 142 (June 11, 1994): 48–49.

Innerst, Carol. "Honor Thy Alma Mater." *Insight on the News* 11 (December 18, 1995): 34.

Kibler, William L., and Pamela Vannoy Kibler. "When Students Resort to Cheating." *Chronicle of Higher Education* 39 (July 14, 1993): A131–132.

Levine, Daniel R., and Gary Pavela. "Cheating in Our Schools: A National Scandal." *Reader's Digest* 147 (October 1995): 65–70.

McCabe, Donald L., and Linda Klebe Trevino. "What We Know about Cheating in College." *Change* 28 (January 1996): 28–33.

Ogilby, Suzanne M. "The Ethics of Academic Behavior: Will It Affect Professional Behavior?" *Journal of Education for Business* 71 (November 1995): 92–96.

Spaid, Elizabeth Levitan. "Honor Codes: Newest Pledge on Campuses." *Christian Science Monitor,* December 6, 1995, 3.

Tetzeli, Rick. "Business Students Cheat Most." *Fortune* 124 (July 1, 1991): 14.

"UMass Be Not Proud." *Boston Globe,* August 15, 1996, A22.

Chapter 4
Campus Living: Roommate Relations

Carnal Knowledge; dir. Mike Nichols, 1971, U.S.

How would you react if you walked in and found your roommate having sex with someone in your dormitory room?

Exploration

After reading the following statements, respond to each one by writing *yes* or *no*.

1. The United States is a permissive society. _____

2. Young people in the United States do not behave as morally as young people in my

   country. _____

3. Each person must develop and live by his or her personal moral code. _____

4. College students in the United States have too much freedom. _____

5. Premarital sex (engaging in sexual relations before getting married) is immoral.

   _____

6. Students should not be allowed to have sexual relations in a college dormitory or residence hall. _____

7. Universities should impose strict rules on the students who live in their dormitories or residence halls. _____

8. Drugs and alcohol should not be allowed in college dormitories or residence halls.

   _____

9. The universities in my country have stricter rules than the universities in the United States. _____

10. College students are adults and have the right to manage their own lives. _____

11. Roommates should respect each other's rights. _____

12. I would rather live alone than live with a roommate. _____

Glossary

amazed	surprised, astonished
compromise	settlement of differences in which each side makes concessions
dormitories	residence halls providing rooms for students
down	depressed, dejected; being in a state of reduced or low activity
eventually	in the end; finally
handle	to deal with; to manage
homesick	unhappy or depressed at being away from home and family; longing for home
immoral	not in conformity with accepted principles of right and wrong behavior; not in conformity with the accepted standards of proper sexual behavior
impose	to establish or apply by authority
morality	rules of right human conduct
outgoing	sociable, friendly
permissive	tolerant of behavior or practices disapproved of by others; lenient
premarital	before marriage
privacy	freedom from unauthorized intrusion
shocked	affected with great surprise, distress, or disgust
sin	transgression of the law of God; an offense against religious or moral law

strange	new, unfamiliar; not before known, heard, or seen
strict	inflexibly maintained; stringent in requirement
thoughtful	anticipating the needs and wants of others; considerate, kind
values	ideas, beliefs, practices that are important to an individual or a group; principles of ethical behavior

College; dir. James W. Horne; Buster Keaton, 1927, U.S.

Case Study: Three's a Crowd

After you read the case study, discuss the major problem the case presents and answer the discussion questions with the members of the class. Then write a case study report.

> Maria Franchino comes from Venezuela. She has just arrived in Texas, where she will be attending a large university. Maria is excited about beginning her life in the United States and also a bit frightened. This is the first time she has ever been far away from her family and friends. But as the youngest of six children, Maria is used to lots of activity and is an outgoing young woman who loves to make friends and have new adventures.

After Maria met her roommate, Jennifer Robertson, she felt lucky. Jenny seemed to be a warm and lovely person who immediately made Maria feel at home. She took Maria all around the campus and even to the bookstore during the first week. Of course, after getting to know Jenny better, Maria realized that their personalities were quite different. For one thing, Jenny loved hard rock music, but Maria hated it, and Jenny didn't mind a messy room, but Maria couldn't stand disorder. Nevertheless, Maria wanted to be friends with Jenny, so she was determined to make the best of the situation.

On Saturday night, Jenny invited Maria to go to dinner with her and her boyfriend, Jack, who was a junior at the university. Although Maria had lots of fun eating with them at a Chinese restaurant near the campus, Jack wasn't really Maria's type. He told many jokes she couldn't understand at all and drank a lot of beer. Still, Maria was happy to be included, and she tried to keep up with the conversation using her less-than-perfect English. Jenny said good-bye to Maria after dinner and told Maria not to wait up for her, as she would be late. When Maria fell asleep around midnight, Jenny hadn't come home yet.

The next weekend, on Friday night, Maria went to the movies with her friend Elena, who had come to the university the year before and was also from Venezuela. Elena was telling Maria all the inside information on what courses to take and which professors were considered the best.

Maria began to talk about her roommate, Jenny, and Elena told her that she had had a bad experience with her roommate in her first year and had eventually moved out of the dorm and into her own apartment. "But don't worry. I'm sure you will not have the problems I had," said Elena. "You sound as if you have met a good friend. Just don't be surprised if sometimes Jenny does things that will seem strange to you."

Maria didn't ask Elena what she meant by strange. She figured she would find out sooner or later.

That night when Maria came back to her dorm room, no one was there. She was exhausted, so she got undressed and into her bed and had almost fallen asleep when she heard the door opening and some footsteps entering the room. It sounded like two people were whispering, and then Maria realized Jenny and Jack were both standing in the room. They talked quietly as they moved toward Jenny's bed and sat down on it. At first Maria pretended to be asleep, but suddenly she saw that Jenny and Jack were lying down on Jenny's bed, and she knew she had to say something.

"Hi!" she called out softly. "It's me—Maria."

"Oh, we thought you were sleeping," said Jenny, giggling.

"Well, I'm not!" Maria replied in a louder voice.

"Three's a crowd. Maybe I'd better leave. I'll see you later," said Jack, and he got up quickly and walked out of the room.

Jenny went running after Jack, so Maria just lay in bed and tried to get to sleep. It took a long time, and she had bad dreams all night. She dreamed she was walking along a path, looking for her house in Caracas, but she couldn't find it, and it was getting dark and she was frightened because she was all alone.

The next day, Saturday, Maria called Elena to tell her what had happened the night before. Maria was shocked and upset. In Venezuela, men and women didn't sleep together in the college dorms. In fact, Maria wasn't even allowed to go on dates unless her older brothers or sisters went along, and sex before marriage was considered a sin.

"I warned you that Jenny might do something that would surprise you," said Elena. "I had that same situation last year, only it was worse because my roommate was unfriendly to me and didn't care what I thought about her. She and her boyfriend slept in our room almost every weekend, so I finally moved out. At first I was amazed by their behavior, but my friends explained that many American college students act like this."

"But isn't there a rule against having an overnight guest without the roommate's consent?" Maria asked. "I think I saw that in my student handbook in the section on residence halls."

Elena laughed. "Sure, there's a rule like that, but nobody pays attention to it."

Maria shook her head. "Well, I want my privacy, so I might have to sleep at your apartment tonight, if that's OK."

"Of course that's OK," Elena answered. "Just call me later if you decide to come."

At about ten o'clock Maria phoned Elena. "Can I stay with you? I have a feeling Jenny and Jack will come to the room again," she said.

"Sure, and maybe you should even move in with me. I have two bedrooms, you know, so there's plenty of room, " Elena replied warmly.

On Sunday, when Maria went back to her room, it was a total mess. Jenny's clothes and books were all over the room, along with several empty beer cans and soft drink cans. This was disturbing to Maria, who was already feeling kind of down and homesick. Images of her house in Caracas and her family sitting around the dining table eating a delicious lunch of empanadas, chicken, and rice kept floating through her mind. Finally she decided to call home because she wanted to hear her mother's voice.

"Hello, Maria! I'm so glad you called! How are things?" asked her mother.

"Just fine, I guess, but I really miss all of you," replied Maria, doing her best to sound cheerful.

"Well, remember we love you and try not to get too homesick. How's school? Do you like your classes? And how's your roommate? I hope you're getting along. Are you having any problems adjusting to your new life?"

"No, not really. Things aren't that different here. Anyway, I can handle it," Maria said bravely. After talking a few more minutes, she hung up the phone. Then she got out her suitcases and began to pack her clothes.

Discussion

1. Is it a good idea for universities to allow men and women to live in the same dorms, or should dorms be single sex?
2. Should universities allow men and women to visit each other in their dorm rooms at night?
3. What kind of person is Maria? What kind of person is Jenny?
4. Why was Maria surprised by Jenny's behavior?
5. Should Jenny have asked Maria's permission to bring Jack to their room?
6. Why didn't Maria try to talk to Jenny about how she felt?

7. Whose right to privacy was being violated—Jenny's or Maria's?
8. Would it be helpful for Maria to go to her adviser and to talk about the problem with Jenny?
9. Should either Maria or Jenny move out of the dorm room?
10. How could Maria resolve her problem with Jenny? What sort of compromise could they reach?

Case Study Report

Working with a partner or in a small group, write a case study report analyzing the problem Maria is facing concerning her roommate.

I. Statement of the Problem
II. Suggestion of Possible Solutions
III. Evaluation of Possible Solutions
IV. Selection of a Solution

Vocabulary

Fill in the blanks with the most appropriate words. Use each word only once.

| sin | permissive | amazed | dormitories | shock |
| impose | premarital | handle | strict | values |

The United States is considered to be a(n) _____ society by many international visitors. When people see how some American college students behave, they are _____ at what appears to be their lack of basic morals and traditional _____. Of course, there are exceptions, but in general, college students in the United States live a much freer life, compared to college students of the past, because of the changes that have taken place in the moral and social norms of U.S. society.

For instance, today, unlike a generation ago, it is unusual for college students to think of _____ sex as a(n) _____, so young men and women often form intimate relationships. This has come to be accepted as a natural way of life, especially after students date for a long time and are serious about each other. Indeed, some teenagers become sexually active in middle school.[1]

Also, although most universities still _____ rules on the students living in their _____ , these rules are far less stringent than those in the past. Thirty

1. Patrick Welsh, "Hollow Young Lovers," *Washington Post*, April 28, 1996, C1.

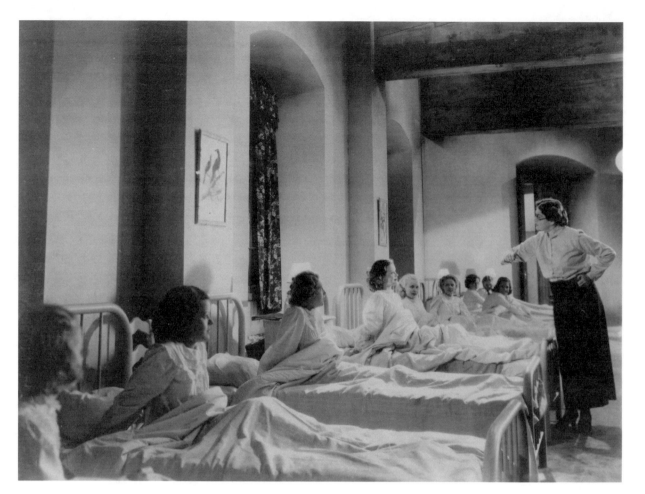

Girls' Dormitory; dir. Irving Cummings, 1936, U.S.

years ago, college dorms were single sex, with men living in one building and women in another. The dorm residents had curfews (10:30 P.M. on weekdays and midnight on weekends) and rules about when students could have visitors in their rooms. Today, men and women share the same dorms, frequently living on the same floors; curfews have been abolished; and visitors have few restrictions, other than not staying longer than three days. Such conditions may _____ those parents who believe their college-age children need rigorous guidelines to follow to ensure a proper lifestyle.

However, there are those who think that this loosening of restrictions has had positive results. Because many young adults in the United States were given so much freedom at an early age, they may have learned how to _____ situations involving drinking, drugs, and sexual relationships. According to certain psychologists, having these first-hand experiences sometimes proves to be a better form of education than simply reading books or being given lectures by their parents or teachers.

On the other hand, there are people who are concerned about the weakening of moral values and would like to see universities return to the days of _____ rules and regulations. One person who disapproves of the liberal atmosphere at most academic institutions is the journalist Michael Novak. He does not trust universities "because the faculties as a whole seem to be so far out of tune with the rest of the American public, politically and culturally. . . . It seems that every other view is protected at the university today except the convictions and values of the parents—and of the public as a whole."[2]

What is your opinion on this topic?

Write a paragraph or two expressing your point of view on the issues discussed above.

Activities

1. Write a letter from Maria to Jenny, explaining that she needs privacy, so she has decided to move out of their dorm room as soon as possible.
2. Develop a set of regulations for university students living in dormitories on a campus in the United States. Then get a copy of the regulations that your educational institution has for students living in its dormitories or residence halls. (The student handbook should have the regulations for student conduct in residence halls.)
3. Write a questionnaire that will be sent to new college students in order to put compatible roommates together. The questionnaire should have at least five questions that will reveal the student's personality, likes and dislikes, and habits.
4. Make a list of arguments against premarital sex and a list of arguments supporting premarital sex. Share your list with your classmates. Then write a three-paragraph essay describing your attitude toward premarital sex.
5. After the class is divided into two teams, have a debate on the following topic: Sexual activities in a college dormitory or residence hall should be prohibited.

2. Michael Novak, "Thought Police," *Forbes* 146 (October 1, 1990): 212.

6. Choose one of the following role plays for presentation in class. Plan and practice your dialogue before presenting it.
   (A) Act out the scene in which Maria tells Elena about Jenny coming to the dorm room with Jack.
   (B) Act out a scene in the future in which Maria tries to talk to Jenny about her need for privacy, her feelings when Jenny brought Jack to the dorm room, and her plan to move out of the dorm.

Oral Presentation

Prepare and give an oral presentation on one of the topics listed. Use the suggested methods of development to organize your presentation and do library research to gather information.

- How to Live in Peace with Your Roommate (process, examples)
- Changing Moral Standards in My Country: Past, Present, Future (chronology, examples)

Chapter Readings

Living with a Stranger

Thrown together, roommates can become the best of friends—or enemies.

Viva Hardigg with Caitlin Nobile

Identical twins Katie and Sarah Monahan arrived at Pennsylvania's Gettysburg College last year determined to strike out on independent paths. Although the 18-year-old sisters had requested rooms in different dorms, the housing office placed them across the hall from each other. While Katie got along with her roommate, Sarah was miserable. She and her roommate silently warred over matters ranging from when the lights should be turned off to how the furniture should be arranged. Finally, they divided the room in two and communicated primarily through terse notes.

During this travail, Sarah kept running across the hall to seek solace from Katie. Before long, the two wanted to live together again. Sarah's roommate eventually agreed to move out. Soon the beds in the room were hauled back from their separate corners and covered with matching quilts. "From the first night we lived together again, we felt so comfortable," says Sarah. "We felt like we were back home."

Sarah's ability to solve her dilemma by rooming with her identical twin is unusual, but the conflict she faced is not. Despite extensive efforts by many schools to make felicitous roommate matches, unsatisfactory outcomes are common. When personalities don't gel, it's even worse than going out on a seemingly endless blind date, since the bad match can last for a semester or longer. Moreover, roommates can affect each other's psychological well-being. A recent study published in the *Journal of Personality and Social Psychology*

Viva Hardigg, "Living with a Stranger," *U.S. News & World Report* 119 (September 25, 1995): 90–92.

reports that depression among college roommates is often contagious. "The roommate situation is the first challenge students face," says Dennis Murphy, associate dean at Gettysburg. "If they can get through that successfully, they've achieved one of the hardest parts of their education."

Learning to tolerate a stranger's idiosyncrasies may teach undergraduates flexibility and the art of compromise. But the learning process is often painful. Julie Noël, a 21-year-old senior at Ithaca College in Upstate New York, recalls that she and her freshman year roommate were uncommunicative and uncomfortable throughout the year. "I kept my stereo up once for a whole day just to test her because she was so timid," says Noël. "It took her until dinnertime to finally turn it off." Near year's end, the two ended up in a screaming fight. "Looking back, I wish I had talked to her more about how I was feeling," says Noël.

Most roommate conflicts spring from such small, irritating differences rather than from grand ideological disputes. "It's the specifics that tear roommates apart," says Christine Hollow, assistant director of residential programs at the University of Dayton in Ohio.

In extreme cases, roommate conflict can lead to serious violence, as it did at Harvard last spring: One student killed her roommate before committing suicide. Many schools, like Gettysburg and Pennsylvania State University, have initiated conflict mediation programs to defuse tensions between students before frustrations explode into physical violence. Other colleges have resorted to "roommate contracts" or "bills of rights" to open channels of discussion between feuding and often noncommunicating roommates. The University of Dayton, for instance, requires all freshmen to fill out and sign a contract after attending a seminar on roommate relations. Students detail behavioral guidelines for their room, including acceptable hours for study and sleep, a policy for use of each other's possessions and how messages will be handled. Although the contracts are not binding, copies are given to the floor's residential adviser in case conflicts later arise. "The contract gives us permission to talk about issues which students forget or are afraid to talk about," says Hollow.

Some schools try to head off feuding before it begins by using computerized matching, a process that nevertheless remains more a guessing game than a science. Students are put together on the basis of their responses to housing form questions about smoking tolerance, preferred hours of study and sleep, and self-described tendencies toward tidiness or disorder. Parents sometimes undermine the process by intercepting the forms and filling in erroneous and wishful data about their children's habits, especially on the smoking question. Suzie Orr, director of residence life and housing at Indiana's St. Mary's College, says that the matching process is also complicated by a philosophical debate among housing administrators: "Do you put together people who are similar—or different, so they can learn about each other?" A cartoon sent to a Gettysburg freshman by her mother sums up the way many students feel the process works: Surrounded by a mass of papers, a housing worker picks up two selection forms and exclaims, "Likes ballet, likes football; they're perfect together!"

Alan Sussman, a sophomore at the University of Maryland at College Park, says that his school's housing office must have favored this approach when it matched him with a roommate. "I think they must have known each of our personalities and picked the opposite," he recalls, citing the shouting matches in his tiny, baby-blue cinder block room last year. While Sussman was neat and a compulsive studier, his roommate was messy and liked to party into the early hours. "People in the hall were putting up wagers about who was going to knock out who first," he says. Sussman considered moving at the end of the semester but decided to stay and "fight it out." Against all odds, the two ended up being friends. Says Sussman: "We taught each other a lot—but I would never do it again."

Residential advisers, who are usually upperclassmen, can play a vital role in mediating squabbles like that faced by Sussman. Says Gary Barone, 22, who was an RA at the University of Maryland for three years while studying elementary education: "A lot of times students acted like the first graders I was teaching." In his years as an RA, Barone defused more than a few conflicts. "A lot of freshmen," he explains, "worry that they will have some evil biker guy as a roommate."

To minimize the likelihood of such mismatches, the University of Nevada at Las Vegas has developed an elaborate questionnaire to gauge roommate compatibility. Instead of asking obvious questions, UNLV's form solicits reactions to a series of scenarios. For example:

"Struggling to wake up, you open your eyes to a gray, overcast morning. You survey your room from the bed and see books and papers piled on dressers among hairbrushes, mirrors, apple cores, clothes draped over chairs and on the floor, and newspapers piled up under the window. What a sight! Response: (a) This sounds like my room all the time—messy, but lived in. (b) I would probably clean my room, but who knows when. (c) My room would seldom be that messy. (d) This doesn't apply to me; I would always keep my room neat and clean."

After the university began to use this approach five years ago, requests for roommate switches dropped by 50 percent, and they have remained quite low.

Out of the blues. For all the downsides of living together, there are many stories of college roommates becoming lifelong friends, business partners or creative collaborators. Singers Jean Norris and Renée Neufville of the soul duo Zhane started writing songs while rooming together in 1990 at Temple University in Philadelphia. After breaking up with their boyfriends within 24 hours of each other, they managed to compose their way out of the blues.

But for each success story, there is more than one tale of woe. An Internet bulletin board—alt.flame.roommate—serves as a kind of ad hoc support group for those who need to vent. Recently, a student nearing the end of his patience offered a top 10 list of roommate gripes. His No. 1 complaint was simple and to the point: "[My roommate] is socially inept and most everybody hates him upon meeting him." Having vented his spleen, the frustrated student concluded by saying: "I feel better. Thank you."

One Strike, You're Out at Saint Mary's Dorms

Orchard Lake, Mich.— Students at Saint Mary's College caught drinking, taking drugs, or having overnight guests in dormitory rooms used to get three warnings before they were

"One Strike, You're Out at Saint Mary's Dorms," *Chronicle of Higher Education* 43 (October 4, 1996): A6.

kicked out of campus residence halls. But starting this semester, even first-time offenders at the Roman Catholic college will lose their housing privileges and their $200 security deposit.

Joanne Bellaire, the college's new dean, initiated the stricter policy. She said it was intended to help the college avoid serious problems that arise from the use of drugs and alcohol.

But some students, who see the penalties as a way to curb sex in the dorm rooms, are upset about the change.

"We know that premarital sex is against the Catholic Church," said Maria M. Stancati, a junior. "But the Catholic religion teaches forgiveness more than it bans premarital sex."

Actually, Saint Mary's hasn't changed that particular policy. The college has long held that students caught having sex in dorm rooms could face expulsion, said Thaddeus C. Radzilowski, the president. He added that no students in recent memory have been kicked off the campus for breaking dorm rules.

Comprehension

"Living with a Stranger"
 1. Why are conflicts between college roommates serious?
 2. What can students learn from living with others?
 3. What causes most conflicts between roommates?
 4. What methods do colleges use to lessen tensions between roommates?
 5. Explain the advantages and disadvantages of computerized matching of roommates.
 6. How has the University of Nevada solved the problem of roommate incompatibility?
 7. What is the main idea of the article?
 8. How compatible are Maria and Jenny, the two students in the case study?

"One Strike, You're Out at Saint Mary's Dorms"
 1. What will happen to students who are caught drinking, taking drugs, or having overnight guests in the dorms at Saint Mary's College?
 2. How does this differ from the previous punishment for such actions?
 3. Why did the dean initiate the stricter policy?
 4. Why are some students upset about the change?
 5. What particular part of the policy is not a change?

Strategy Session

Imagine that you are a new student who has just arrived at your college. You have been assigned a roommate who comes from a country different from yours and does not speak your language very well.

Which strategy would you use in this situation and why? Provide a written justification for your decision. If none of the listed strategies would be your choice, you may develop your own strategy.

1. Write out a detailed list of rules that you want your roommate to agree to follow and give it to your roommate.

2. Have a long talk with your roommate to make sure you are in agreement about basic issues and rules for living together.

3. Invite your roommate out to dinner so you can get acquainted in a friendly setting.

4. Avoid spending time with your roommate until you have had a chance to get your schedule in order and become familiar with the school.

5. Spend your free time with your old friends from high school and let your roommate make his or her own friends.

6. Other: _____

Suggested Films

1969 (1988)
Carnal Knowledge (1971)
Clueless (1995)
National Lampoon's Animal House (1978)
The Odd Couple (1968)
Real Genius (1985)
The Roommate (PBS: 1984)
Roommates (1995)
Threesome (1994)
With Honors (1994)

Additional Readings

Barry, Rebecca. "Welcome to Roommate Hell." *Seventeen* 53 (September 1994): 123–29.
Collison, Michele N.-K. "Colleges Are Tightening Restrictions on Students Living in Dormitories." *Chronicle of Higher Education* 36 (November 1, 1989): A1, A39.
Gose, Ben. "A New Approach to Ease the Way for Freshmen." *Chronicle of Higher Education* 42 (September 8, 1995): A57–58.
Newman, Richard. "Roommate Dynamics." In *The Complete Guide to College Success: What Every Student Needs to Know.* New York: New York University Press, 1995.
Novak, Michael. "Thought Police." *Forbes* 146 (October 1, 1990): 212.
Perse, Tobias. "Try a Little Tenderness." *Rolling Stone*, October 20, 1994, 132.
Welsh, Patrick. "Hollow Young Lovers." *Washington Post,* April 28, 1996, C1–2.
Williams, Melissa. "Roommate Management 101." *Seventeen* 55 (September 1996): 125–26.
Zevin, Dan. "Roommatism." *Rolling Stone* (October 20, 1994): 131–32.

Chapter 5
Time Management: Punctuality

Safety Last; dir. Fred Newmeyer, Sam Taylor; Harold Lloyd, 1923, U.S.

What would you do if you were continually late to your classes, appointments, and social activities?

Exploration

After reading the following statements, respond to each one by writing *yes* or *no.*

   1. Being on time to class is essential for students attending school in the United States.

      ‾‾‾‾‾‾

2. A student who comes late to class should not be allowed to enter the classroom. _____

3. People who are habitually late are not polite. _____

4. It is more important to do your homework than to come to class on time. _____

5. In my country, it is acceptable for college students to come to class late. _____

6. Teachers should always be on time to their classes. _____

7. It is not necessary to be exactly on time to social events in the United States. _____

8. In my country, a dinner invitation for 7 P.M. means a guest should arrive around 7:30 or 8 P.M. _____

9. The expressions *in time* and *on time* have the same meaning. _____

10. I usually do one thing at a time and follow a strict schedule. _____

11. I usually do several things at once and keep my schedule flexible. _____

12. Attitudes toward time vary from one culture to another. _____

Glossary

annoyance	temporary disturbance of mind caused by something that displeases or irritates
apologize	to acknowledge and express regret for a fault or wrong
attitudes	opinions; mental position with regard to a fact or state
competitive	involving or based on competition
confusing	puzzling, bewildering, perplexing
continually	happening over and over again; repeated often
customary	habitual, usual
depressing	discouraging, saddening; lowering the spirits
energetic	having or showing energy; vigorous, active
exactly	precisely
expression	particular word, phrase, or sentence
flexible	characterized by a capability to adapt to new, different, or changing requirements
habitually	usually, customarily; doing a certain thing by habit
impatiently	feeling or showing annoyance because of delay or opposition
insistence	making a firm demand
in time	before it is too late; eventually
lack	to suffer from the absence of
minor	lesser in importance
misunderstanding	failure to understand; mistake of meaning or intention
on time	at the appointed time; punctually

priorities	things or activities that deserve time and attention
punctuality	being on time for an activity, appointment, or engagement
sneak	to move quietly to avoid being seen or heard
sociable	enjoying or requiring the company of others; friendly or agreeable
strict	inflexibly maintained
time management	using and controlling one's time in an efficient and effective manner
vary	to be different or diverse; to differ

The Pawnshop; dir. Charlie Chaplin, 1916, U.S.

Case Study: Not Better Late than Never

After you read the case study, discuss the major problem the case presents and answer the discussion questions with the members of the class. Then write a case study report following the format that is provided.

> Rajesh Rao, a high school graduate from Madras, India, is enrolled in English language classes at a private language school in San Francisco. He is trying to improve his English skills to the point that he can apply to a highly competitive university in the United States.

In the meantime, Rajesh, a sociable and energetic young man, is having a good time getting to know San Francisco and making friends with the other international students in his school.

Although Rajesh is a pretty hardworking student, lately he has been having so much fun going out to clubs and parties at night that he has had trouble getting up in the morning. His English classes begin at 9:00 A.M. and end at 1:00 P.M. every day during the week, but Rajesh has not arrived on time since the first few days. He just can't seem to wake up early enough in the morning to catch the 8:00 A.M. bus from his neighborhood in Mission to his school in the North Beach area.

Actually, in India Rajesh had usually arrived late to his classes, but so did some of the other students, and even the teacher was late once in awhile. It didn't matter very much, and Rajesh had received excellent grades all through high school in spite of his lack of punctuality. He also tended to be late to his social activities, but that was customary in his country. In fact, it was considered almost rude to be on time to a party.

One morning at the end of the first month of classes, when Rajesh as usual entered the classroom at about 9:45 A.M., his teacher, Mr. Kent, looked at him with annoyance and said, "Well, if it isn't Mr. Rao."

Rajesh laughed and started to apologize for being so late, but Mr. Kent interrupted him by saying: "Better late than never is an expression we use for people who aren't punctual, but I don't really agree with that saying."

Rajesh was upset by Mr. Kent's remark and sat down quickly in his seat.

After class, Mr. Kent asked Rajesh if he could come to his office at 3:00 that afternoon to discuss a few things. Rajesh said he would be there, and then he went to meet several friends who were eating lunch at a nearby Italian restaurant. The time passed so quickly that it was 3:15 before Rajesh looked at his watch.

"Oh, no, I'm supposed to be at Mr. Kent's office!" he exclaimed, leaving some money on the table and rushing out of the restaurant.

When Rajesh knocked on Mr. Kent's door at 3:30, he was slightly worried about how Mr. Kent would react, and he apologized for being late. Mr. Kent just smiled politely and told Rajesh that his lack of concern about being late to class was becoming a serious problem.

"Well," answered Rajesh, "I live quite far from school, so I have to take the bus, and you can never rely on the buses. Sometimes they're right on time and sometimes they're late. But I'll do my best to be on time to class from now on."

"I certainly hope so," said his teacher, "because according to the rules of the school, if a student is continually late, we lower the grade. I'd hate to have to do that."

That night, Rajesh attended a big party that continued into the early hours, and the next morning he again arrived late to class. This time he tried to sneak into the room during the break so his teacher would not notice him. Unfortunately, Mr. Kent ran into him at the door and gave him a dark look.

"Late again, I see," he said to Rajesh. "This is going to affect your grade, as I told you yesterday."

"But why should it matter if I'm late as long as I do all the work and get good marks on my tests?" asked Rajesh with annoyance. "I don't understand why being on time is so very important."

Mr. Kent frowned and answered impatiently, "That's the way it is here, and these are the rules, so you'd better get used to it if you plan to study in the States. Maybe you need a course in time management to get your priorities in order. School should come first, you know."

That evening Rajesh thought about how angry Mr. Kent had seemed and how hard it was to get to class on time. This whole misunderstanding about punctuality was really confusing to him and rather depressing. If his good work on the tests and homework didn't make any difference in how his teacher treated him, he might as well quit going to school. Or maybe he should look into other language schools in San Francisco and even in other cities. They couldn't all have this strict policy about such a minor matter.

Discussion

1. What does being late to classes and appointments reveal about a student's attitude?
2. List Rajesh's priorities in order of importance (1 = most important).
3. What is Rajesh's attitude toward coming to class late?
4. What is Mr. Kent's attitude toward students who come to class late?
5. Did Mr. Kent give Rajesh a good explanation for his insistence on punctuality?
6. How honest was Rajesh when he gave his teacher an explanation for his lateness?
7. How can Mr. Kent convince Rajesh of the importance of being on time?
8. Should Rajesh change his behavior? Explain your answer.

Case Study Report

Working with a partner or in a small group, write a case study report analyzing the problem Rajesh is facing in his English class.

  I. Statement of the Problem
 II. Suggestion of Possible Solutions
III. Evaluation of Possible Solutions
IV. Selection of a Solution

Vocabulary

Fill in the blanks with the most appropriate words. Use each word only once.

lack	priorities	annoyed	flexible	habitually	misunderstanding
rude	vary	punctuality	on time	continued	attitude

The anthropologist Edward Hall writes that most complex societies can be classified in regard to their organization of time as either monochronic or polychronic. In a monochronic society, such as the United States, people tend to do one thing at a time and follow tight schedules. In a polychronic society, such as Spain, people tend to do several things at once and have _____ schedules. Hall believes that each system has strengths and weaknesses but that the systems are not compatible: "Like oil and water, they don't mix."[1] Whether or not Hall is correct, it is obvious that ideas about and perceptions of time _____ a great deal from one culture to another, which sometimes causes problems.

_____, or being exactly _____ for professional activities and social engagements, is valued highly in North America and Northern Europe. According to Hall: "If people are not prompt, it is often taken either as an insult or as an indication that they are not quite responsible."[2] Thus, being _____ late is considered _____ and unprofessional in countries such as Switzerland or Germany. Although a guest could arrive fifteen or twenty minutes late to an informal social event, much later than that would not be appropriate behavior. For business events, being punctual is even more essential. Furthermore, for military or diplomatic personnel, arriving late to an event is completely unacceptable, so they often arrive early.

On the other hand, in most South American, African, and Middle Eastern countries, there is a more relaxed _____ toward punctuality. In Brazil, if you are invited to a party that starts at 9 P.M., you will find hardly anyone at the party if you decide to come before 10 P.M. Concerning business activities, it is good to arrive at the scheduled time, but you will probably not be criticized if you are late for an appointment. Brazilians and other Latin Americans place more emphasis on close human relationships than on rigidly followed schedules and aren't greatly _____ by lateness.

When people from a culture with relaxed ideas about time move to a culture with strict ideas about time, serious problems can arise. If they don't understand the importance of keeping to a fixed schedule and not being late, their _____ may lead to conflicts with their colleagues and friends. Discussing these issues openly is one of the best ways to help avoid _____ conflicts. Nevertheless, there are those who _____ the ability or motivation to change their lifestyle and habits, and

1. Edward T. Hall, *The Dance of Life: The Other Dimension of Time* (New York: Anchor/Doubleday, 1989), 45–46.
2. Edward T. Hall, *The Silent Language* (New York: Anchor/Doubleday, 1973), 9.

being on time is a goal they will never achieve, no matter how hard they try to put their

_____ in order.

What is your opinion on this topic?

Write a paragraph or two expressing your point of view on the issues discussed above.

Activities

1. Write a letter from Rajesh to his parents in India, explaining the problems he is having with his teacher in his English class.
2. Evaluate your time management and your ability to be on time by keeping a time log (record) of all your activities for three days and nights. Mark the times you are late to an appointment, a class, or a meeting with a friend. After analyzing your time log, list the *three* biggest time wasters in your life, for example, watching TV or talking on the telephone. Then write an essay about how you can eliminate these time wasters from your life.
3. Describe the general attitude in your country toward being on time for the situations listed here. In these situations, is it *extremely important, somewhat important,* or *not important* to be on time? Discuss your answers with the class.
   - Classes in school (middle school, high school, university)
   - Business appointments (meetings, conferences, briefings)
   - Informal social events (parties, dinners, movies)
   - Formal social events (weddings, dances)
   - Doctor and dentist appointments
   - Religious activities (church, mosque, or temple services)
   - Sports events (football, basketball, baseball, soccer, polo games)
   - Recreational activities (playing tennis or golf, exercising, jogging)
4. Write a schedule of the average workday in your country. Include the times when businesses and government agencies open, close for lunch, open again, and close for the day. Compare your schedule with your classmates' schedules and with the schedule in the United States by writing your schedule on the chalkboard.

5. After the class is divided into two teams, have a debate on the following topic: It is better to be flexible about the use of time than to be punctual and follow schedules strictly.

6. Choose one of the following role plays for presentation in class. Plan and practice your dialogue before presenting it.

   (A) Act out the scene when Rajesh goes to Mr. Kent's office to discuss being late to class.

   (B) Act out a scene in the future in which Rajesh returns to Mr. Kent's office to try to justify his behavior and Mr. Kent convincingly explains why punctuality is essential.

Oral Presentation

Prepare and give an oral presentation on one of the topics listed. Use the suggested methods of development to organize your presentation and do library research to gather information.

- The Perception and Use of Time in My Country (analysis, examples)
- Effective Time Management for Students (problem solution, examples)

Comprehension

Life by the Clock

Abdul Hamid

I noticed that people are busy and work according to set routines, like the ticking hands of a clock circling around its center. Everyone works like a machine, up in the morning, onto the bus or train to get to the office, where the same people meet daily. How different from my country, where there was less routine, where I could relax, meet friends and relatives, share their happiness and sorrow. I felt homesick enough to wish I was back in Pakistan . . . But after a while I felt better, and by attending to my own work, joined everyone else in a routine. . . . For in the United States, the weather has no effect on daily activities. Whether it is raining, freezing, or snowing, life goes on at supersonic speed, as usual.

People tend to be self-centered in the United States; children leave their parents in lonely nursing homes. These helpless creatures watch life pass by their nursing home windows, hoping for a visit, dying there while waiting. Their children, informed about their parents' death either by phone or letter, have no time to attend the funeral. They might only send a bouquet to be placed on the grave. Sons and daughters are considered independent at the age of eighteen and are then expected by the parents to set up on their own.

I had no idea how valuable time was prior to my visit to the United States. Time and punctuality are the essence of American life; people, slaves of the clock, follow it without complaint. A slight negligence or delay may result in substantial financial losses which

Abdul Hamid, "Life by the Clock," in *From the Outer World*, edited by Oscar Handlin and Lilian Handlin (Cambridge: Harvard University Press, 1997), 448–50.

Americans can hardly afford. Punctuality thus becomes second nature to them. Hence they take light lunches and heavy dinners and work hard, relaxing only during vacations. While at work they waste no time in idle chatter or going about business in a leisurely fashion. They try to do their jobs as efficiently and quickly as possible. Once in a bank to cash a check, it took only forty-five seconds to do so at the counter, in spite of the fact that the cashier performed her duties with a smile on her face and also gave me some necessary information. I also observed that though the higher classes in America have all the vices of the rich everywhere, they seem to complain less about the common people. For the latter are obliging, efficient, and modest, and everything seems to run smoothly and punctually in their domains. . . .

Abdul Hamid is a respected Pakistani author who was invited to the United States by the Voice of America. He later wrote a book, *Amerikano* (published in 1989), in which he described his impressions of the United States.

The Use of Time

Richard D. Lewis

The world views held by different cultures vary widely, as do a multiplicity of concepts which constitute and represent a kaleidoscopic outlook on the nature of reality. Some of these concepts—fatalism, work ethic, reincarnation, *sisu,* Confucianism, *Weltschmerz, dusha,* etc.—are readily identifiable within specific groups, societies or nations. Other concepts—central and vital to human experience—are essentially universal, but subject to strikingly different notions of their nature and essence. Such concepts are those of space and time.

Time, particularly, is seen in a different light by eastern and western cultures and even within these groupings assumes quite dissimilar aspects from country to country. In the western hemisphere, the USA and Mexico employ time in such a diametrically opposing manner that it causes intense friction between the two peoples. In western Europe the Swiss attitude to time bears little relation to that of neighbouring Italy. Thais do not evaluate the passing of time in the same way that the Japanese do. In Britain the future stretches out in front of you. In Madagascar it flows into the back of your head from behind.

Linear time

Let us begin with the American concept of time, for theirs is the most expensive, as anyone who has had to do with American doctors, dentists or lawyers will tell you.

For an American, time is truly money. In a profit-oriented society, time is a precious, even scarce, commodity. It flows fast, like a mountain river in spring, and if you want to benefit from its passing, you have to move fast with it. Americans are people of action; they cannot bear to be idle. Past time is over, but the present you can seize, parcel and package and make it work for you in the immediate future.

Richard D. Lewis, "The Use of Time," in *When Cultures Collide: Managing Successfully across Cultures* (London: Nicholas Brealey Publishing, 1996), 52–58.

Time looks like this:

Figure 13

This is what you have to do with it:

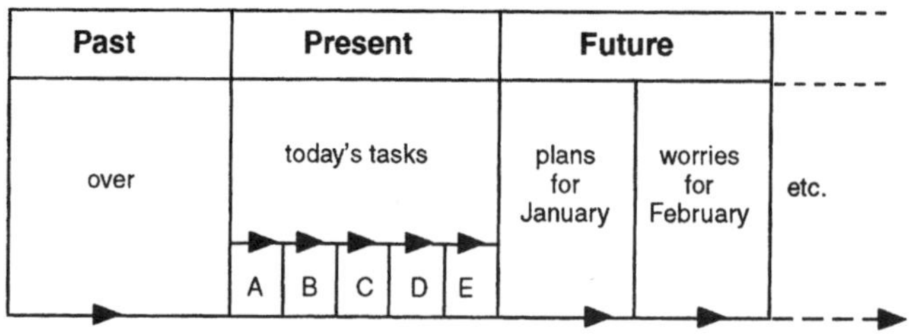

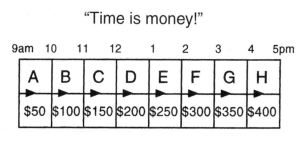

Figure 14

In America you have to make money, otherwise you are nobody. If you have 40 years of earning capacity and you want to make $4 million, that means $100,000 per annum. If you can achieve this in 250 working days that comes to $400 a day or $50 an hour.

Figure 15 suggests that you can make $400 a day if you work 8 hours, performing one task per hour in a planned, time-efficient sequence. In this orientation Americans can say that their time costs $50 an hour. The concept of time **costing** money is one thing. Another idea is that of **wasting** time. If, as in Figure 16, appointments D and E fail to show up, Americans might say that they have wasted 2 hours—or lost $100. Thus:

"Time is money!"

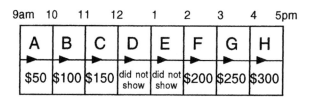

Figure 15

Figure 16

This seems logical enough, until one begins to apply the idea to other cultures. Has the Portuguese fisherman, who failed to hook a fish for two hours, wasted his time? Has the Sicilian priest, failing to make a convert on Thursday, lost ground? Have the German composer, the French poet, the Spanish painter, devoid of ideas last week, skipped opportunities which can be qualified in monetary terms?

The Americans are not the only ones who sanctify timekeeping, for it is a religion in Switzerland and Germany, too. These countries, along with Britain, the Anglo-Saxon world in general, the Netherlands, Austria and Scandinavia, have a linear vision of time and action which the above figures have illustrated. They suspect, like the Americans, that time passing without decisions being made or actions being performed is streaking away unutilized in a linear present and future.

Anglo-Saxon, Germanic and Scandinavian peoples are essentially linear-active, time-dominated and monochronic. They prefer to do one thing at a time, concentrate on it and do it within a scheduled timescale. They think that in this way they get more things done—and efficiently. Furthermore, being imbued with the Protestant work ethic, they equate working time with success. (The harder you work—more hours, that is—the more successful you will be, the more money you will make.) This idea might sound reasonable in American ears, would carry less weight in class-conscious Britain, and would be viewed as entirely unrealistic in southern European countries where authority, privilege and birthright negate the theory at every turn. In a society such as existed in the Soviet Union one could postulate that those who achieved substantial remuneration by working little (or not at all) were the most successful of all.

Multi-actives

Southern Europeans are multi-active, rather than linear-active. The more things they can do or handle at the same time, the happier and the more fulfilled they feel. They organize their time (and lives) in an entirely different way from Americans, Germans and Swiss. Multi-active peoples are not very interested in schedules or punctuality. They pretend to observe them, especially if a linear-active partner insists, but they consider reality to be more important than appointments. In their ordering of things, priority is given to the relative thrill or significance of each meeting. Spaniards, Italians, Arabs ignore the passing of time if it means that conversations would be left unfinished. For them, completing a **human transaction** is the best way they can invest their time. Germans and Swiss love clock-regulated time, for it appears to them as a remarkably efficient, impartial and very precise way of organising life—especially in business. For an Italian, on the other hand, time considerations will usually be subjected to human feelings. "Why are you so angry because I came at 9.30?," he asks his German colleague. "Because it says 9 am in my diary," says the German. "Then why don't you write 9.30 and then we'll both be happy?" is a logical Italian response. The business we have to do and our close relations are so important that it is irrelevant at what time we meet. The **meeting** is what counts. Germans and Swiss cannot swallow this, as it offends their sense of order, of tidiness, of pre-arrangement.

A Spaniard would take the side of the Italian. There is a reason for the Spaniard's lax adherence to punctuality. The German believes in a simple truth—scientific truth. The Spaniard, in contrast, is always conscious of the double truth—that of immediate reality as well as that of the poetic whole.

The German thinks they see eye to eye, as in Figure 17:

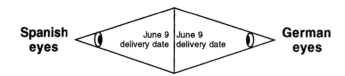

Figure 17

In fact the Spaniard, with the consciousness of double truth, sees it as in Figure 18:

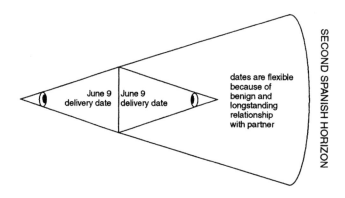

Figure 18

As far as meetings are concerned, it is better not to turn up strictly on time for Spanish appointments. **In Spain, punctuality messes up schedules**, as in Figure 19.

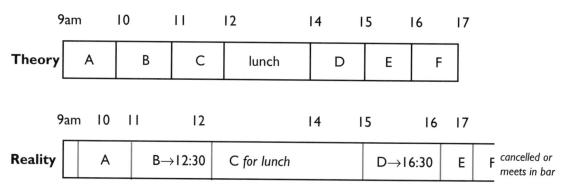

Figure 19

Few northern Europeans or North Americans can reconcile themselves to the multi-active use of time. Germans and Swiss, unless they reach an understanding of the underlying psychology, will be driven to distraction. Germans see compartmentalisation of programmes, schedules, procedures and production as the surest route to efficiency. The Swiss, even more time and regulation dominated, have made **precision** a national symbol. This applies to their watch industry, their optical instruments, their pharmaceutical products, their banking. Planes, buses and trains leave on the dot. Accordingly, everything can be exactly calculated and predicted.

In countries inhabited by linear-active people, time is clock and calendar related, segmented in an abstract manner for our convenience, measurement and disposal. In multi-active cultures like the Arab and Latin spheres, time is event or personality related, a subjective commodity which can be manipulated, moulded, stretched or dispensed with, irrespective of what the clock says. "I have to rush," says the American, "my time is up." The Spaniard or Arab, scornful of this submissive attitude to schedules, would only use this expression if death were imminent.

Cyclic time

Both the linear-active Northerner and the multi-active Latin think that they **manage** time in the best way possible. In some Eastern cultures, however, the **adaptation** of humans to time is seen as a viable alternative. In these cultures time is viewed neither as linear nor event-personality related, but as **cyclic**. Each day the sun rises and sets, the seasons follow one another, the heavenly bodies revolve around us, people grow old and die, but their children reconstitute the process. We know this cycle has gone on for one hundred thousand years and more. Cyclical time is not a scarce commodity. There would seem to be an unlimited supply of it just around the next bend. As they say in the East, when God made time, he made plenty of it.

As many Asians are keenly aware of the cyclical nature of time, business decisions are arrived at in a different way from in the West. Westerners often expect an Asian to make a quick decision or treat a current deal on its present merits, irrespective of what has happened in the past. Asians cannot do this. The past formulates the contextual background to the present decision, about which in any case, as Asians, they must think long term—their hands are tied in many ways. Americans see time passing without decisions being made or actions performed as "wasted." Asians do not see time as racing away unutilised in a linear future, but coming round again in a circle, where the same opportunities, risks, dangers will re-present themselves when people are so many days, weeks or months wiser. How often do we (in the West) say "If I had known then what I know now, I would never have done what I did?" . . .

In a Buddhist culture—Thailand is a good example, although Buddhist influence pervades large areas of Asia—not only time but life itself goes round in a circle. Whatever we plan in our diary, however we organise our particular world, generation follows generation, governments and rulers will succeed each other, crops will be harvested, monsoons, earthquakes and other catastrophes will recur, taxes will be paid, the sun and moon will rise and set, stocks and shares will rise and fall. Even the Americans will not change such events, certainly not by rushing things.

Richard D. Lewis is a managment consultant to international companies. He lives in Great Britain. (This reading uses British spelling.)

Comprehension

"Life by the Clock"
1. What is the difference between Hamid's life in Pakistan and the lifestyle in the United States?
2. To Hamid, how do Americans appear in regard to their use of time?
3. How do children treat their elderly parents in the United States?
4. Why is punctuality so important to Americans?
5. What example does Hamid give to show the way Americans work?
6. Hamid writes: "Time and punctuality are the essence of American life." Do you agree with this statement? Explain your answer by giving examples to support your point of view.

"The Use of Time"
1. Describe the way North Americans view time.
2. Which groups of people are linear-active, time dominated?
3. Explain the meaning of *monochronic*.
4. Which peoples are multi-active, and how do they view time and punctuality?
5. To what do multi-actives give priority and why?
6. What is the major difference between linear-actives like Germans and Swiss and multi-actives like Italians and Spaniards?
7. In Spain and other multi-active cultures, why does punctuality mess up schedules?
8. How do some Eastern cultures view time?
9. How do Asians and North Americans differ in making business decisions?
10. Does Rajesh Rao, the student in the case study, have a linear-active, multi-active, or cyclic view of time? Explain your answer.

Strategy Session

Imagine that you are a professor who, at midpoint in the semester, is having trouble with some of your students. They are not following the rules for the course that were outlined on the course information sheet you handed out in the first week of the semester. Some students come to class late, leave class early, are absent, hand in papers past the due date, and miss exams.

Which strategy would you use in this situation and why? Provide a written justification for your decision. If none of the listed strategies would be your choice, you may develop your own strategy.

1. Hand out another information sheet for all the students, listing your requirements and the penalties for not meeting the requirements, and go over it in class.

2. Have an informal chat with the class, explaining your disappointment with the way some students are behaving.

3. Give the problem students a failing grade at midterm.

4. Take no action and hope that the problem students will settle down after the midterm.

5. Call the problem students in for one-on-one conferences in which you explain your course policies and the penalties for not following these policies.

6. Other: _____

Suggested Films

Back to the Future (1985)
Forever Young (1992)
Four Weddings and a Funeral (1994 Britain)
Groundhog Day (1993)
Peggy Sue Got Married (1986)
Somewhere in Time (1980)

Additional Readings

Cerio, Gregory. "Don't Be Late." *Self* 15 (November 1993): 140–43.

Hall, Edward T. "The Voices of Time" and "Time Talks: American Accents." In *The Silent Language*. Garden City, NY: Anchor/Doubleday, 1973.

Kanekar, Suresh, and Laura Vaz. "Effects of Gender and Status upon Punctuality Norms." *Journal of Social Psychology* 133 (June 1993): 377–84.

Kendall, Peter. "College Degree in 2 Years Isn't the Half of It." *Chicago Tribune*, June 6, 1995, 2C 1.

Levine, Robert, and Ellen Wolff, eds. "Social Time: The Heartbeat of Culture." *Psychology Today* 19 (March 1985): 28–30+.

Newman, Richard. "Time Management." In *The Complete Guide to College Success: What Every Student Needs to Know.* New York: New York University Press, 1995.

Pantiel, Mindy. "Study Tips from Top Students." *Better Homes and Gardens* 71 (December 1993): 36–38.

Perry, John, "How to Procrastinate and Still Get Things Done." *Chronicle of Higher Education* 42 (February 23, 1996): B3.

Smith, Greg. "Surviving Your First Year of College." *Career World* 24 (April 1996): 12–13.

Tierney, John. "Revenge of the Punctual." *Self* 11 (October 1989): 40–42.

Chapter 6
Difficult Decisions: Interpersonal Conflict

The L-Shaped Room; dir. Bryan Forbe, 1963, Britain

What would your advice be to an unmarried friend who discovered she was pregnant?

Exploration

After reading the following statements, respond to each one by writing *yes* or *no*.

1. A woman has the right to make all decisions about her own body. _____

2. Abortion is a sin. _____

3. Abortion should be an option when rape or incest has resulted in a pregnancy or a woman's life is endangered. _____

4. A woman who is considering having an abortion must discuss this with the father of her unborn child. _____

5. Abortions should be against the law. _____

6. Women who have abortions are evil and selfish. _____

7. Getting pregnant when you are not married is a sin. _____

8. I believe in birth control. _____

9. There should be restrictions on the right to have an abortion, such as parental notification. _____

10. Women should not have children unless they want to. _____

11. It is illegal to have an abortion in my country. _____

12. Abortion is a controversial issue in my country. _____

Glossary

abortion	termination of a pregnancy by expulsion of a nonviable fetus
absolutely	completely, wholly
adoption	taking a child into one's own family by legal process and raising as one's own child
birth control	method used to prevent conception of a child
controversial	subject to debate; arousing opposing views
dizzy	having a whirling sensation in the head with a tendency to fall
evil	morally bad or wrong; resulting from conduct regarded as immoral
illegal	not permitted or authorized by law
immature	not mature; not completely grown or developed
incest	sexual intercourse between persons so closely related that they are forbidden by law to marry
kidding	joking; teasing playfully
legal	permitted by law; based upon or authorized by law
mess	state of difficulty, trouble, or confusion
option	choice; the power, right, or liberty of choosing
pale	of a whitish or colorless complexion; pallid
pregnancy	condition of containing the unborn young within the body
pro-choice	for women's right to have a legal abortion
pro-life	against women's right to have a legal abortion
rape	sexual intercourse without consent and chiefly by force or deception
regret	to feel sorry about or remorseful over something that one has done
restrictions	limitations
sin	breaking of a religious law or a moral principle, through a willful act

Ju Dou; dir. Zhang Yi-Mou; Gong Li, 1989, China-Japan

Case Study: A Matter of Life or Death

After you read the case study, discuss the major problem the case presents and answer the discussion questions with the members of the class. Then write a case study report following the format that is provided.

Delashna Amerkere comes from Sri Lanka. She has been attending Millburn College for the past three years. Her roommate, Rachel Bassett, is her best friend, and they have been living together since their freshman year, first in the dormitory and now in an off-campus apartment. Recently, Delashna has noticed that Rachel has been acting strange; she gets up much later than usual and looks rather pale and weak. In fact, just yesterday, Rachel was so sick that she stayed in bed and missed all her morning classes. When Delashna asked what was wrong, Rachel told her that perhaps it was the flu.

Today, Delashna suggested that Rachel go to see the doctor. She offered to go along, and Rachel agreed, so they walked to campus and went to the student health office. After about thirty minutes, Rachel came out of the doctor's office, looking even paler than before.

"What's the matter? Do you have the flu?" asked Delashna. Rachel seemed distressed and wouldn't answer. She just walked out the door and into the street.

"Rachel, tell me what's wrong," said Delashna, running after her friend.

"Well, you don't want to know," answered Rachel.

"Of course I do—tell me right now!" shouted Delashna.

"OK. I'm pregnant, but the good news is that it's early, so I won't have any trouble having an abortion," said Rachel quietly, trying to sound matter of fact.

Delashna suddenly felt weak and dizzy. She couldn't believe what she was hearing. How could it be true that Rachel was pregnant? She and her boyfriend, Max, had never seemed that serious about each other, and Rachel had not mentioned planning to get married. Besides, didn't she use birth control? This doctor must have made a mistake. And the word *abortion*—Rachel couldn't have meant that. If she had said that, it was only because she was upset. Delashna doubted that Rachel would really want an abortion— even if she were pregnant, which she probably wasn't.

"Maybe you should find another doctor and see if there is a mistake," said Delashna hopefully. "Test results are often wrong, especially about stuff like this."

"No chance of that. I am pregnant, and the only thing to do is have an abortion. I don't want to marry Max even though I guess I love him, but he's so immature and irresponsible. And I'm not finished with college. How could I raise a child by myself and go to school at the same time? Thank God I can take care of this right away," said Rachel.

"Oh, please, Rachel, think about what you are saying. Abortion is a sin. You'd be ending the life of a child. If you don't want to marry Max, what about having the baby and giving it up for adoption?" said Delashna.

"I could never do that—go through nine months of pregnancy and give the baby to someone else—that would be terrible!" Rachel responded.

"Well, at least you should wait a few days before making a decision. You could talk to your parents, and maybe you should even talk to Max," said Delashna.

"Are you kidding? I can't tell my parents. No way! They would never understand, and if I tell Max, who knows what he might want to do? That would just complicate things. I'm getting the abortion tomorrow morning. It's the right thing for me. This is my body—not yours or anyone else's," replied Rachel angrily as she walked off alone down the street.

As Delashna walked home slowly, she was praying to find a way to change Rachel's mind. She couldn't let her best friend make such a horrible decision. Delashna believed that except in cases of rape or incest, abortion was absolutely wrong, and she felt that Rachel would probably regret it if she ended her pregnancy. Her mother had told her many times that children were a gift from God, and she had never even mentioned the word *abortion*. No one would ever consider such an action in her family.

Why couldn't Rachel tell her mother about being pregnant? Delashna wondered. She knew she would tell her mother if she were in such a mess. Maybe she should call Rachel's mother herself before it was too late or make Rachel talk to a counselor. Although Delashna felt helpless and terrified, she was determined to try to stop Rachel from going ahead with the abortion. This was a life or death matter, and she was on the side of life.

Discussion

Answer the following questions before writing the case study report.

1. What is Delashna's attitude toward abortion?
2. What is Rachel's attitude toward abortion?
3. Should Rachel talk to her parents about her pregnancy and her intention to have an abortion?
4. Should Rachel talk to her boyfriend, Max, about her pregnancy and her intention to have an abortion?
5. How can Delashna try to change Rachel's mind about having an abortion?
6. Should Delashna tell Rachel's parents about Rachel's pregnancy? Why or why not?
7. How difficult would it be for a single woman like Rachel to raise a child by herself while attending college?
8. What other options besides abortion does Rachel have?
9. How can Rachel make the right decision about her pregnancy?
10. How can the conflict between Rachel and Delashna be resolved?

Case Study Report

Working with a partner or in a small group, write a case study report analyzing the problem Delashna is facing concerning her friend Rachel.

I. Statement of the Problem
II. Suggestion of Possible Solutions
III. Evaluation of Possible Solutions
IV. Selection of a Solution

Vocabulary

Fill in the blanks with the most appropriate words. Use each word only once.

pro-choice	pro-life	abortion	restrictions	rape
legal	incest	pregnancies	controversial	option

On January 22, 1973, the U.S. Supreme Court ruled (seven to two) in *Roe v. Wade* that a state may not prevent a woman from having an abortion during the first three months (trimester) of pregnancy and that it can regulate but not prohibit an abortion during the second trimester.[1] The result of this decision was to make abortions in the early months

---

1. *Roe v. Wade*, 410 U.S. 113 (1973).

_____ in the United States. Since then, pregnant women have had the right to choose whether or not to have a child.

Many women agree with this right to choose, but others do not agree. Today this question is a(n) _____ issue that divides nearly all American people into two groups: those who support abortion rights (_____) and those who are antiabortion (_____). Moreover, some people who are generally against abortions do believe they should be allowed when _____ or _____ results in a pregnancy or when the woman's life is endangered.

The question of whether a woman has the right to make all the decisions concerning her own body is fundamental to the _____ debate. Pro-choice women do not want the federal government or state laws controlling what they do. They believe that they alone must make such personal decisions as whether and when to have children.

Another basic issue surrounding the abortion controversy is the question of when life begins. To those who are antiabortion, life begins at conception, and thus, abortion is the murder of a living being. Supporters of abortion rights see the unborn fetus as not viable until at least five months, and therefore, they believe that abortion should be a(n) _____ until that point in the woman's pregnancy.

Some states are passing laws that restrict a woman's right to an abortion. For example, in certain states, a woman must notify her parents if she is under the age of 18 when she is considering having an abortion. Other _____ on abortion could include the ban of federal funds for abortions and loss of funding for family planning clinics.[2]

About one and a half million abortions are performed in the United States every year.[3] Naturally, this number would be lower if everyone knew how to use effective methods of birth control. These days, schools offer classes in sex education to their students in order to make them aware of the importance of using birth control to avoid unwanted _____ as well as sexually transmitted diseases like AIDS.

2. "The New Threat to Women's Reproductive Health," *Glamour* 93 (March 1995): 110.
3. Frederica Mathewes-Green, "Seeking Abortion's Middle Ground," *Washington Post,* July 28, 1996, C4.

What is your opinion?

Write a paragraph or two expressing your point of view on the issues discussed above.

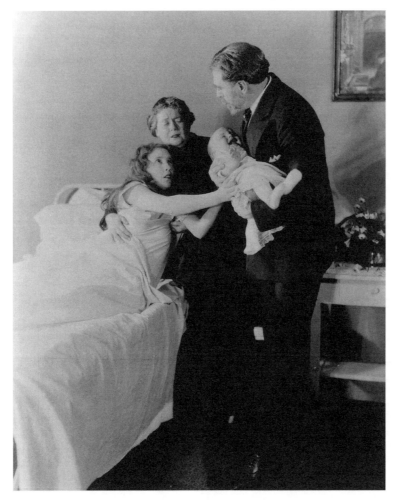

Human Wreckage; 1923, U.S.

Activities

1. Write a letter from Delashna to Rachel in which Delashna tries to convince her friend that she should not terminate her pregnancy.
2. Make a list of the reasons for and the reasons against having an abortion. Compare your list with your classmates' lists by putting them on the chalkboard.

3. Do library research on the topic of abortion laws in the United States. Look up the case *Roe v. Wade* in an encyclopedia and check periodical indexes like the *Reader's Guide to Periodical Literature* and the *New York Times Index,* or do a computer search to find current articles on abortion laws. After reading several articles, write a short summary of the status of legal abortions in the United States.

4. Conduct a survey of at least ten people. Ask them the questions listed here and report your results to the class.

   1. What is your position on the issue of abortion: pro-life, pro-choice, or undecided?
   2. If you are pro-life, do you believe exceptions should be made in cases of rape, incest, or danger to the mother's life?
   3. If you are pro-choice, do you believe there should be restrictions on the right to have an abortion?
   4. If you believe in restrictions on abortion rights, what should they be?

5. After the class is divided into two teams, have a debate on the following topic: Women should not have the legal right to have an abortion except in cases of rape, incest, or danger to the woman's life.

6. Choose one of the following role plays for presentation in class. Plan and practice your dialogue before presenting it.

   (A) Act out the scene on the street between Delashna and Rachel in which Rachel tells Delashna that she is pregnant and wants to have an abortion.

   (B) Act out a future scene in which Delashna and Rachel reach an agreement on what Rachel should do about her pregnancy.

Oral Presentation

Prepare and give an oral presentation on one of the topics listed. Use the suggested methods of development to organize your presentation and do library research to gather information.

- Reasons to Support the Pro-Choice Movement (enumeration, analysis)
- Reasons to Support the Pro-Life Movement (enumeration, analysis)

Chapter Readings

Single Mother, and Proud

Working Two Jobs and Raising a Daughter; What's to be Ashamed Of?

Stephanie Crockett

I vividly recall that hot August day three years ago when I stared disbelievingly at the pink tip of a home pregnancy test that revealed, yes, I was pregnant.

Stephanie Crockett, "Single Mother, and Proud," *Washington Post,* July 14, 1996, C5.

I stretched out on my back on the day bed in my father's living room and rubbed my hands back and forth over my flat, 20-year-old stomach, trying to feel some connection to the life growing inside me.

I was scared to death.

Young, single and pregnant—three of the worst things to be in society today. I had heard the country's movers and shakers who stress the importance of family and values, and who discount those who don't fit their model of the American family. I quickly learned that the world looks at single mothers as a symbol of society's failures, a reminder that the morals and values that America is supposed to stand for have been blurred. Being unmarried and pregnant was *not* something to be proud of.

So I wasn't. I was ashamed. And afraid. For weeks after that day, I would pull the fading pink stick out of my wallet to remind myself that I was still pregnant and, more importantly, that I had to make a decision. Having a child, a year away from a college degree in English, with no real job, no prospects and no husband, was not part of my life's plan.

The father, my fiancé, was thrilled. We began making plans for the future, stepping up things a bit so that we could fit everything into the next nine months. Then there were the arguments, and suddenly, we were no longer engaged, and eventually, not even together. I was left to make the decision on my own. I straddled the choice of motherhood and abortion, weighing each side of the equation and making up my mind more than once. For days I would tell myself that it wouldn't be a big deal to have an abortion. After all, I didn't feel like I was pregnant, and I didn't look like I was pregnant. An abortion couldn't be that bad. Then I would see pregnant women, or babies in strollers, Gerber baby food commercials or little children playing on a playground, and I would get sick to my stomach at the thought of expunging the growing baby I carried.

After weeks of going back and forth, I finally decided that I could take care of a child, that I could be a mother, that I could do it, even if I was alone.

But I worried about what my friends and co-workers would think of me. Would an out-of-wedlock pregnancy prove that I was irresponsible? Would it be a reflection on my job, my ability? On me?

So I didn't tell people until I had to. I waited until the last possible moment, when the largest shirt my 6-foot-2-inch brother had in his closet began to get tight on me, and people started asking questions. I reluctantly told them I was pregnant, and I would watch people's expressions and follow their eyes searching for a ring on my left hand. A few people made absent-minded remarks like, "Oh, I didn't know you were married!" and "But you're not married, are you?"

I wondered what went through the minds of people on the subway when they saw me. I was so ashamed. It seemed as if strangers could somehow tell just from looking at me that I was going to be a single mother. To me their faces had looks of "another fatherless child being brought into the world" and questions of "Is this another child my tax dollars will have to take care of?"

It was at those times when I wanted to justify my pregnancy, tell them how my ex and I had been involved with one another since I was 12, that he was the first person I'd kissed, the first person I'd loved. I wanted to say that we had planned to get married, soon, probably before the baby was born. Anything to make my pregnancy okay, anything to make my baby count. To this day, when I walk down the street with my daughter, her small young hand held in my ringless one, there still are people who glance my way with disgust and pity.

Of course I didn't want to be an unmarried mother. I had the same plans that little girls do when they dream about growing up: getting married to the man of my dreams, having a wonderful job, a wonderful family, a wonderful life. But somewhere, when I was making all my plans, life interfered.

So here I am, at Plan B. Only the people closest to me know how hard it is to balance being a mother, a full-time college student, two jobs and freelance writing. It's difficult to make it day to day with very little sleep or food. Without constant help from my mother and my sister, I probably wouldn't eat or sleep much at all.

But the hardest part was never what I thought it would be. It's not working two jobs to support my daughter. It's not putting that great pair of boots back on the rack and buying a coat for Jordyn instead. It's not wondering what people are thinking behind their blank stares when they learn that I am a single mother at 24, and it's not even being denied the respect that, as a mother, I deserve.

The hardest times are when I get home from work so late that I only can see my daughter while she's sleeping. It's the times that I don't get to kiss her goodbye because I am rushing out the door to start another work day. It's when the only time I get to hear her voice is over the telephone from work and the days that I don't hear her voice at all. It's not being there on Christmas morning to watch her open her gifts because I'm working. It's barely being able to keep my eyes open while we watch "The Lion King" for the 99th time.

Sometimes, when I come home from work, I will spend time watching her while she sleeps. As I think of how proud I am of her, sometimes I curse myself for the time when I wasn't proud of being pregnant, and a wave of guilt washes over me when I think of how close I'd gotten to never knowing her at all. The two of us, however imperfect to the sociologists and the bigwigs, are a family.

I get angry and my eyes fill with tears when I think of the six months I kept her existence a secret, so unlike the joy a married woman feels when she and her husband learn that they are carrying another human being. And then I sigh. Yes, it is hard raising a child alone, but she is well worth it.

Now there is no time to be ashamed. There is only time to change the next diaper, play patty-cake, or recite the alphabet to my daughter. Maybe, if I had a minute, I would be able to pat myself on the back and think "Hey, I am defying the odds, I'm making it," but there are a lot of single mothers who are doing the very same thing. It would be nice to live in a society that recognizes us, that realizes that having a child without a mate isn't the best way to be a parent, but it is certainly not the worst.

Right now, that doesn't matter. I have a child to raise.

Bare Facts on Childbearing

Call it a baby bust. In recent years, fewer women have gotten pregnant. And fewer have had abortions. In 1993, exactly 20 years after the Supreme Court ruled a woman has a right to terminate her pregnancy, the percentage of pregnancies ending in abortion dropped to its lowest level since 1977. The Centers for Disease Control and Prevention, which released its abortion figures last week, attributes the decrease to possible changes in attitudes, contraception use, access to abortion services and, perhaps, a decline in unplanned pregnancies. Among the centers' findings:

- **Prime time.** While the number of women in their childbearing years (15 to 44) has increased 11 percent since 1980, the percentage in their reproductive prime (under 30) has dropped. In 1980, 58 percent of childbearing women were younger than 30; in 1992, just 47 percent were.
- **Deliveries.** From 1992 to 1993, live births dropped by 1.6 percent.
- **Abortions.** In 1993, America had 1.3 million abortions, 99,000 fewer than in 1990, the peak year. In 1993, there were 334 abortions for every 1,000 live births, down from 364 in 1984.
- **Who and when.** Of the women who had abortions in 1993, 79 percent were unwed, 46 percent never had given birth before, 54 percent were under 25 and 52 percent were eight weeks pregnant or less. Sixty-two percent were white and 34 percent were black. Twenty-one years earlier, 77 percent were white and 23 percent were black.

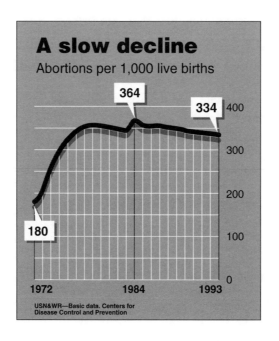

"Bare Facts on Childbearing," *U.S. News & World Report* 120 (April 1, 1996): 16.

Most U.S. Unwed Mothers Are Not Teenagers

Daphne Spain and Suzanne M. Bianchi

The link between motherhood and marriage has become increasingly tenuous in the late 20th century. Over the past three decades, the decline in marital births and the increase in out-of-wedlock births together have resulted in a higher proportion of all births occurring outside marriage. Almost 1 in 3 births took place outside of marriage in 1994, compared with 1 in 5 in 1980 and 1 in 10 in 1970.

The birth rate for all unmarried women has risen steadily since 1940, from 7.1 births per 1,000 women to 46.9 births per 1,000 women in 1994. This trend crosses every age category, and the largest jumps occurred during the 1980s. Women in their early 20s have the highest current nonmarital birth rate, followed by women in their late 20s, and then by teenagers (see table). The rising age at first marriage has contributed to the number of women "at risk" of bearing a child out of wedlock.

Racial differences

Although the birth rates for unmarried white women are lower than those for unmarried black women, they have risen much more rapidly, doubling since 1980. The timing of nonmarital births also varies for blacks and whites: unmarried white mothers tend to be older than unmarried black mothers. Black nonmarital births are most likely to occur to teens and women in their early 20s, while out-of-wedlock birth rates are highest for white women in their 20s.

The dramatic rise in the proportion of black children born outside marriage is not the result of a sharp increase in childbearing among unmarried black women. Between 1970 and 1994, the birth rate to teenage unmarried black women rose only slightly. Rather, births among married black women fell substantially during the 1960s and 1970s, and fewer black women (especially teenagers) are marrying.

The most striking difference between the current fertility patterns of blacks and whites is that a far higher proportion of black children are born to unmarried teenage mothers than are white children. In 1994, 1 in 5 black children was born to an unmarried teenage mother compared with 1 in 13 white children; similar racial differences exist for children born to unmarried women in their early 20s. In 1994, when one-third of all births occurred to unmarried women, 70 percent of all black births occurred out of wedlock, compared with one-quarter of all white births.

Teenage mothers

Although they are separate issues, teenage and out-of-wedlock births are often confused in the public's mind. The reality is that nonmarital births to women in their 20s and 30s exceed those to teenagers. It is true that births to teenagers are more likely to occur outside of marriage now than in the past because contemporary teens are less likely than their prede-

Daphne Spain and Suzanne M. Bianchi, "Most U.S. Unwed Mothers Are Not Teenagers," *Population Today* 24 (November 1996): 3.

cessors to marry in response to pregnancy. But in 1994, only 30 percent of all nonmarital births occurred to teenagers, compared with 50 percent in 1970.

. . . If women continue to bear children, but less often within marriage, the question becomes: are marriages being delayed, or eschewed all together, because women can afford to live independently, or are marriages being postponed, sometimes permanently, because men cannot afford to marry the mothers of their children?

Fertility of U.S. Unmarried Women

Year	Total	Rate per 1,000 unmarried women, ages 15–44					
		15–19	20–24	25–29	30–34	35–39	40–44
All races							
1950	14.1	12.6	21.3	19.9	13.3	7.2	2.0
1960	21.6	15.3	39.7	45.1	27.8	14.1	3.6
1970	26.4	22.4	38.4	37.1	27.0	13.3	3.6
1980	29.4	27.6	40.9	34.0	21.1	9.7	2.6
1990	43.8	42.5	65.1	56.0	37.6	17.3	3.6
1992	45.2	44.6	68.5	56.5	37.9	18.8	4.1
1993	45.3	44.5	69.2	57.1	38.5	19.0	4.4
1994	46.9	46.4	72.2	59.0	40.1	19.8	4.7

Source: NCHS, Advance Report of Final Natality Statistics, various years; and U.S. Bureau of the Census, Historical Statistics of the United States, B28-35, 1975.
Note: Fertility rates are live births per 1,000 unmarried women in a specified age group.

Comprehension

"Single Mother, and Proud"
1. What happened to the author three years before she wrote this article?
2. How does the world look at single mothers?
3. What did the author decide to do about her pregnancy and why?
4. How did the author feel while she was pregnant?
5. What is the hardest part of being a single mother?
6. How does the author feel now?
7. What is the author's central point?
8. What are the differences between Stephanie Crockett, the author, and Rachel, the student in the case study?

"Bare Facts on Childbearing"
1. What may explain the decrease in the percentage of pregnancies ending in abortion?
2. Compare the percentages of childbearing women under age thirty in 1980 and 1992.
3. How many fewer abortions were there in 1993 compared to 1990?
4. What percentage of women having abortions in 1993 were unwed, and what percentage were under 25?

"Most U.S. Unwed Mothers Are Not Teenagers"

1. Compare the numbers of births occurring outside of marriage in 1970, 1980, and 1994.
2. Compare the birth rates for all unmarried women in 1940 and 1994.
3. What age group of women has the highest current nonmarital birth rate?
4. What factor has contributed to the number of women "at risk" of bearing a child out of wedlock?
5. List four differences in nonmarital births between blacks and whites.
6. Why are births to teenagers more likely now than in the past to occur outside of marriage?
7. What question do the authors ask about the trend to delay or avoid marriage?

Strategy Session

Imagine that you are a student adviser in a university in the United States. An unmarried student has come to see you because she has just found out that she is six weeks pregnant.

Which strategy would you use in this situation and why? Provide a written justification for your decision. If none of the listed strategies would be your choice, you may develop your own strategy.

1. Listen carefully to the student and let her do most of the talking. Don't give her advice but just try to discover her feelings and point of view.

2. Give the student information about her options in an objective way, and suggest that she come back to seek you in a week.

3. Give the student information about her options but encourage her to continue the pregnancy.

4. Give the student information about her options but encourage her to get an abortion.

5. Give the student the name, address, and telephone number of a doctor who performs abortions.

6. Other: _____

Suggested Films

Alfie (1966 Britain)
Bed and Sofa (1926 silent film)
Casting the First Stone (First Run Icarus Films: 1991)
Citizen Ruth (1997)
Georgy Girl (1966 Britain)
The L-Shaped Room (1963 Britain)

Life and Choice after Roe v. Wade (PBS Video: 1992)
A Mongolian Tale (1997 China)
Nenette et Boni (1997 France)
Nine Months (1995)
She's Having a Baby (1988)
A Taste of Honey (1961 Britain)
Une Affaire de Femmes (Story of Women) (New Yorker Video: 1990)

Additional Readings

Benshoof, Janet. "Abortion Rights and Wrongs." *Nation* 263 (October 14, 1996): 19.

Carlson, Margaret. "Public Eye: Vigilante Boyfriend." *Time* 146 (October 9, 1995): 70.

Graff, James L. "Calling the Cops on a Pregnant Girlfriend." *Time* 146 (October 9, 1995): 69–70.

Griffin, Katherine. "Sex Education That Works." *Health* 9 (May–June 1995): 62–64.

Mathewes-Green, Frederica. "Seeking Abortion's Middle Ground." *Washington Post,* July 28, 1996, C1, C4.

"The New Threat to Women's Reproductive Health." *Glamour* 93 (March 1995): 110.

Waldman, Steven, and Ginny Carroll. "Roe v. Roe." *Newsweek* 126 (August 21, 1995): 22–24.

Wellbery, Caroline. "Oh, Boy!" *Washington Post Health,* March 11, 1997, 16.

"You're Having What?" *Psychology Today* 27 (March–April 1994): 44–45.

Chapter 7
Gender Issues: Sexual Orientation

Persona; dir. Ingmar Bergman, 1966, Sweden

What would your reaction be if your friend told you that he or she was a homosexual?

Exploration

After reading the following statements, respond to each one by writing *yes* or *no*.

1. Homosexuality is a sin. _____

2. A person's sexual orientation is determined by his or her choice. _____

3. Homosexuality is more a result of genetic factors than environmental factors. _____

4. Being a homosexual or a lesbian is abnormal because it is against the laws of nature.

    _____

5. There is no difference between heterosexual and homosexual people. _____

6. I have friends of various sexual orientations and lifestyles. _____

7. I accept and respect homosexual behavior. _____

8. I would not get involved in a sexual relationship with a person of my sex. _____

9. Homosexuality is expressed openly in my country. _____

10. People who are homosexual should keep their sexual orientation a secret. _____

11. Homosexual behavior should be against the law. _____

12. I believe that same-sex marriages are as valid as marriages between men and women.

    _____

Glossary

abnormal	not normal
conservative	traditional, moderate, cautious, safe
disbelief	absence of belief; refusal to believe
environmental	all the conditions and influences surrounding and affecting the development of an organism
factors	any of the circumstances or conditions that bring about a result
gay	homosexual
gender	male or female sex
genetic	having to do with genes, units by which hereditary characteristics are transmitted and determined
grim	somber, gloomy
hang out	to spend time with someone
heterosexual	characterized by a tendency to direct sexual desire toward the opposite sex
homophobic	irrationally frightened of homosexuality or homosexuals
homosexual	characterized by a tendency to direct sexual desire toward another of the same sex
hung up on	worried about
jealous	hostile toward a rival or one believed to enjoy an advantage
lesbian	female homosexual
lifestyle	typical way of life of an individual, group, society, or culture
narrow-minded	not liberal; prejudiced; limited in outlook
orientation	general direction of thought, inclination, or interest in regard to sexual preference
revelation	an act of revealing or communicating a truth
valid	justifiable; relevant and meaningful; supported by objective truth

Case Study: A Case of Mistaken Identity

After you read the case study, discuss the major problem the case presents and answer the discussion questions with the members of the class. Then write a case study report following the format that is provided.

Alex Mitopolous is studying for a master's degree in international relations at a well-known university in Washington, DC. He is an excellent student who knows English almost as well as he knows his native language, Greek. Alex lives alone in a large apartment in Georgetown, and he studies very hard, so he doesn't enjoy much of a social life. In fact, he is rather shy and has almost no friends except for a few of the other Greek students in the school.

This is Alex's second year in graduate school, and this semester he is enrolled in an honors seminar in Chinese foreign policy. He has really been enjoying this seminar because he has gotten well acquainted with the other students in the class, especially Molly Donnelly, a straight-A student who shares many of Alex's views on foreign policy. Molly and Alex have been working on projects for the seminar and studying together for tests. Since Alex spends a lot of time at Molly's apartment, he has also gotten to know her roommate, Linda, who is an MBA student. Sometimes, the three of them go out for pizza and beer or just hang out. Alex thinks Molly is a terrific person, and he has come to depend on her for advice and encouragement.

One night, Alex and Molly decided to go to the Third Edition, a club in Georgetown. After two hours at the club, Alex was beginning to get bored, so he asked Molly to come over to his place to watch a movie. (He had rented *First Knight* from the video store.) While he and Molly were watching the movie, Alex noticed how totally beautiful Molly was, and suddenly he leaned nearer to her and gently kissed her on the mouth. Molly jumped up from the couch they were sitting on and started to laugh loudly.

"Maybe I shouldn't be laughing," she said, "but this is kind of strange."

Alex was startled and embarrassed by Molly's reaction to his kiss, and he didn't know what to say. Finally, out of nervousness, he started to laugh himself. "Is it so awful that I would want to kiss you and be close to you?" Alex asked. "We've been good friends for quite a long time, and I would like to have a different kind of relationship with you now."

Molly stared at Alex with disbelief. "This sure is a case of mistaken identity," she finally said, shaking her head. "You're mistaken—about my identity, Alex. You really don't know who I am, do you?"

Alex looked puzzled. "What do you mean?"

Molly smiled before she replied. "I guess I just assumed you knew that I'm gay—or should I say a lesbian? Linda and I have been a couple for a year now, and we are perfect for one another. No guy could ever make me as happy as she does!"

Alex was shocked into silence. "I had no idea," he said after a minute had passed. "I—I—don't really know any other women like you—I mean you seem so normal."

Molly looked grim after Alex's remark, and she got up to get her coat and leave.

"I'm as normal as anybody else in this world, Alex. You're looking for love in all the wrong places, and you're too hung up on gender, so you're the one who's weird—and homophobic, too," she added, storming out the door.

After Molly left, Alex stayed up drinking beer and going over everything that had happened. He thought for a long time about whether to call Molly and apologize for his behavior and his remark. But he couldn't get up the courage to make the call. Somehow, Molly no longer seemed like the same person to him. In fact, he was ashamed about how he was feeling, yet Alex had never understood how people could be attracted to members of their own sex. Perhaps he was old fashioned in his idea that men and women belonged together; there was no way he could see being attracted to a man, that was for sure! And the thought of two women together—that was just too much for him to accept. Well, maybe he and Molly and Linda could still be pals, and that would be great, but Alex doubted it would be possible.

Three days later, at the next meeting of the seminar, Alex tried to sit far away from Molly and not to look at her. Once he caught her staring at him, and he turned his eyes away. After class was over, Alex was leaving when Molly stopped him by standing directly in front of him so he couldn't move past her.

"Hey, Alex," she said.

"Hey, Molly, how're you doing?" replied Alex softly.

"I was wondering if we could go out for coffee and, you know, talk things over," said Molly.

"Oh, sorry. I can't. I have to go meet some friends," replied Alex, and then he turned and quickly left the room.

That night Alex really had a hard time trying to fall asleep because he was experiencing many different emotions. He felt jealous of Linda, guilty about his behavior, and, most of all, he felt sad about losing Molly as a friend. Yet he was still upset by her revelation, and nothing could change her back into the woman he had liked so much. Alex wanted to discuss this with someone, but he had no idea whom to turn to. His few friends from Greece wouldn't have the slightest idea of what to do in this situation, and his parents were very conservative in their views.

"I probably should go over and see Molly and try to talk this out with her. Maybe I can convince her that she should give up Linda and stop this way of life, but what if I say the wrong thing again and hurt her even more?" Alex wondered.

He dreamed about Molly all night, and in the morning, he was exhausted and full of tension. Although he knew he was being narrow-minded and old fashioned, he just couldn't accept the fact that Molly preferred Linda to him.

Discussion

1. What kind of person is Alex Mitopolous?
2. What kind of person is Molly Donnelly?
3. What different types of feelings has Alex experienced in regard to Molly?
4. What are Molly's feelings for Alex?
5. Why did Alex misunderstand the type of relationship he and Molly could have?
6. What is Alex's attitude toward homosexuality?
7. Should Alex try to convince Molly to change her sexual orientation? Why or why not?
8. How can Molly try to change Alex's attitude toward her sexual orientation?

Case Study Report

Working with a partner or in a small group, write a case study report analyzing the problem Alex is facing concerning his relationship with Molly.

    I. Statement of the Problem
   II. Suggestion of Possible Solutions
  III. Evaluation of Possible Solutions
  IV. Selection of a Solution

Vocabulary

Fill in the blanks with the most appropriate words. Use each word only once.

homosexuals	lifestyles	orientation	lesbians	abnormal	gender
conservative	sexuality	factors	genetic	valid	environmental

In the United States since the 1960s, _____ issues, those issues focused on the roles and rights of men and women, have been receiving a lot of attention because of major changes within society. As large numbers of women have entered the workforce, some men have chosen to stay home with the children. Furthermore, the traditional family (mom, dad, two children) has been transformed, and alternative _____ have become more prevalent. In 1994, one in three families with children was headed by a single parent (86.8 percent by the mother).[1] Other families are composed of two men or two women who have made a commitment to each other. Thus, it is no longer easy to define a normal or a(n) _____ living arrangement.

    Because of these social changes, homosexuality is not the secret subject it was in past generations and to some extent has become accepted as just another sexual _____.[2] Today, gay men and _____ do not have to hide their sexual preference. Many choose to live openly with their partners and have attempted to make same-sex marriages legal. This has raised the question of what marriage is. The traditional definition of marriage is the union of two people of the opposite sex. However, there are many who believe that marriages between people of the same sex are just as _____ as marriages between a man and a woman. In fact, in December 1996, Hawaii became the first state not

---

1. John W. Wright, ed., *The Universal Almanac 1997* (Kansas City, MO: Andrews and McMeel, 1996): 310–11.
2. "It's Normal to Be Queer," *Economist* 338 (January 6, 1996): 68–70.

to prohibit same-sex marriages in the United States when its First Circuit Court ruled that denying licenses to same-sex couples violated the state constitution's equal-protection clause. This decision is being appealed to the Hawaii Supreme Court.[3]

In addition to the question of marriage, _____ have fought successfully for their equal rights and against discrimination in the workplace and in the military. One major issue that President Bill Clinton faced when he began his presidency in 1992 was the question of whether gays should be allowed to serve in the military. The fact is that many gay men and women have served with honor and distinction in the military throughout the years. However, a number of _____ lawmakers hold the opinion that a person who is gay should not be allowed to remain on military duty. The issue is still unsettled, but the temporary resolution has been to evade the problem by instituting a "Don't Ask, Don't Tell" policy.

Scientific researchers are studying the possibility that _____ structure influences sexual behavior. Although _____ _____ may also be important, several recent studies have shown a biological basis for sexual orientation.[4] If that is true, the widely held idea that homosexuality is a matter of choice may be challenged. Nevertheless, some people tend to be skeptical about the search for a biological explanation for homosexuality, believing that it is sufficient to explain homosexuality in terms of the rightful pursuit of liberty and happiness. In any case, it is likely that future research will be able to answer the question of whether genes or the environment has a stronger effect on human _____.

What is your opinion?

Write one or two paragraphs expressing your point of view on the issues discussed above.

3. James Kunen, "Hawaiian Courtship," *Time* 148 (December 16, 1996): 44.
4. Eliot Marshall, "NIH's 'Gay Gene' Study Questioned," *Science* 268 (June 30, 1995): 1841.

Before Stonewall; dir. Greta Schiller, Robert Rosenberg, 1986, U.S.

Activities

1. Write a letter from Alex to Molly in which he apologizes for his reactions but tries to convince her to change her sexual orientation.
2. Do library research on the subject of the gay rights movement (also known as the gay liberation movement) in the United States. When was it founded, what are its goals, and what has it achieved? Write a short report presenting this information.
3. Gender stereotyping assigns certain roles, characteristics, and behaviors to people according to whether they are male or female. Make a list of qualities and behaviors that are generally considered to be characteristic of males and a list of qualities and behaviors that are generally considered to be characteristic of females. Then underline those qualities on both lists that apply to you. Compare your lists with your classmates' lists by writing them on the chalkboard.
4. Conduct a survey of at least ten people. Ask them the questions listed here and report your results to the class.
    1. Do you believe that homosexuality is just another sexual orientation?
    2. Do you believe homosexuality is mainly a result of genetic structure?
    3. Do you believe homosexuality is mainly a result of environmental factors?

4. Do you believe that homosexuals should have the same civil rights as other Americans?

5. Do you support making same-sex marriage legal?

5. After the class is divided into two teams, have a debate on the following topic: Genetic factors are more important than environmental factors in influencing sexual behavior.

6. Choose one of the following role plays for presentation in class. Plan and practice your dialogue before presenting it.

(A) Act out the scene between Alex and Molly in Alex's apartment when Molly tells Alex she is a lesbian.

(B) Act out a future scene between Alex and Molly in which they have a rational and friendly discussion about Molly's sexual orientation.

Oral Presentation

Prepare and give an oral presentation on one of the topics listed. Use the suggested methods of development to organize your presentation and do library research to gather information.

- Why Gender Stereotyping Is Invalid (analysis, examples)
- Same-Sex Marriages: Should They Be Legal? (argument, analysis)

Chapter Readings

Search for a Gay Gene

A DNA transplant made these male fruit flies turn away from females. What does that say about the origins of homosexuality?

Larry Thompson

Fruit flies are among the most sexually proficient creatures on earth. Their ability to produce a new generation in two weeks has made them the darlings of genetics research-ers for nearly a century. Put a male fruit fly into a bottle with a female, and he doesn't waste any time before getting down to business.

So it's a bit bewildering to watch the behavior of certain fruit flies at the National Institutes of Health in Bethesda, Maryland. There, in the laboratories of biologists Ward Odenwald and Shang-Ding Zhang, strange things are happening inside the gallon-size culture jars. In some experiments, the female flies are cowering in groups at the top and bottom of the jars. The males, meanwhile, are having a party—no, an orgy—among them-selves. With a frenzy usually reserved for chasing females, the males link up end-to-end in big circles or in long, winding rows that look like winged conga lines. As the buzz of

Larry Thompson, "Search for a Gay Gene," *Time* 145 (June 12, 1995): 60–61.

the characteristic fruit fly "love song" fills the air, the males repeatedly lurch forward and rub genitals with the next ones in line.

What's going on? Without a wink or a chuckle, Odenwald claims that these male fruit flies are gay—and that he and Zhang made them that way. The scientists say they transplanted a single gene into the flies that caused them to display homosexual behavior. And that's very interesting, they assert, because a related gene exists in human beings, although there is no evidence yet that the human gene has an effect on sexual preference.

A report of Odenwald and Zhang's findings, to be published this week in Proceedings of the National Academy of Sciences, adds to the mounting evidence that homosexuality has genetic origins, and is sure to produce new fireworks in the contentious debate over what it means to be gay. The two scientists are not foolhardy enough to claim that a single gene can make a person homosexual. But they think their studies may yield important new insights into how genetic makeup, through a complex series of biochemical reactions, influences sexual orientation.

Such work stirs mixed emotions in the gay community. To some extent, gays and lesbians welcome the research because it supports what most of them have long felt: that homosexuality is an innate characteristic, like skin color, rather than a perverse life-style choice, as conservative moralists contend. And if that is true, then gays deserve legal protection similar to the laws that prohibit racial discrimination. "On a political level, genetic research does seem to move the debate along a certain path," says Denny Lee of the Lambda Legal Defense and Education Fund, a gay advocacy group in New York City. "When people understand that being gay or lesbian is an integral characteristic, they are more open-minded about equality for gay Americans."

On the other hand, many gays are wary of the genetic hypothesis. It could, they fear, help promote the notion that gayness is a "defect" in need of "fixing." "Any finding will be used and twisted for homophobic purposes," says Martin Duberman, head of the Center for Lesbian and Gay Studies at the City University of New York. "If it does turn out that for some people, there is a genetic or hormonal component, the cry will then arise to take care of that." Indeed, the cry is already rising. The Rev. Louis P. Sheldon, president of the Traditional Values Coalition in Anaheim, California, says that if a biological cause of homosexuality is found, then "we would have to come up with some reparative therapy to correct that genetic defect."

No matter how people feel about the issue, it is increasingly hard to argue that genes play no role in homosexuality. The evidence began to pile up in 1991, when studies showed that identical twins were more likely to have the same sexual orientation than other pairs of siblings. That same year, a California scientist reported slight brain differences between gay and straight men, although the conclusion is disputed. And in 1993, an NIH researcher found a stretch of DNA on the X chromosome that seemed to harbor one or more genes affecting sexual orientation. But no one has proved that a particular gene promotes gayness or has offered any convincing theory of how genes could influence a person's choice of sleeping partners.

Odenwald and Zhang do not pretend to have any easy answers. In fact the type of gene they've been studying in fruit flies could not begin to account for the complex variations in human homosexual behavior. For one thing, the gene does not cause flies to renounce heterosexuality altogether. If a "gay" fly is surrounded by females instead of males, he'll fertilize the lady flies. So strictly speaking, the NIH flies are not homosexual but bisexual. And the gene produces no unusual behavior when transplanted into females: the scientists have produced no lesbian fruit flies.

Yet the way the gene works is intriguing, and may offer some clues to the biochemical roots of gayness. Surprisingly, the swatch of DNA in question was discovered long ago, and is one of the most thoroughly studied of all fruit-fly genes. It is called the "white" gene because, among many effects, it influences eye color, and a particular mutation in the gene causes a fly's normally red eyes to be white. The gene's specific job is to produce a protein that enables cells to utilize an essential amino acid called tryptophan. If fruit flies are unable to process tryptophan properly, then they cannot manufacture red eye pigment.

Under normal circumstances, the white gene is active only in certain cells, including brain cells, and does nothing to disrupt standard sexual behavior. In the NIH experiments, Odenwald and Zhang inserted a normal version of the gene into embryonic flies, but transplanted the gene in such a way that it was activated in every cell. That's what apparently played havoc with the flies' sex lives. With every cell sucking in tryptophan from the blood, a shortage of tryptophan developed in the brain, where it has important uses. Since tryptophan levels were altered, the researchers hypothesize, the brain was unable to make enough serotonin, one of the neurotransmitters that carry messages between nerve cells. Serotonin is a multipurpose chemical, and abnormal levels of it in humans have been linked to everything from depression to violent behavior. In the case of the gay fruit flies, the scientists speculate, a shortfall of serotonin produced those all-male conga lines.

Though the idea seems far-fetched, it jibes with two decades of research suggesting that serotonin plays a role in regulating sexual behavior. One piece of evidence is the action of the drug Prozac, which relieves depression by lifting serotonin levels in the brain. At the same time, though, the serotonin boost tends to dampen sexual desire. In contrast low serotonin levels can produce heightened sexual activity, at least in lab animals. In experiments done in the U.S. and Italy, scientists used drugs and special diets to suppress serotonin in rats, mice, cats and rabbits. The result was increased sex drive and, sometimes, homosexual couplings.

As intriguing as it sounds, the serotonin theory is still full of holes. Even if shortages of the chemical increase sexual activity, why would it often be homosexual rather than heterosexual? And if sexual orientation is genetically determined, then why do some identical twins differ in sexual preferences?

Getting the answers, if possible at all, will require much more research. Even harder will be knowing how to use any knowledge that emerges. Will children be given genetic tests to determine the odds of their becoming homosexual? Will prenatal tests lead to abortions of fetuses that might grow up to be gay?

Scientists caution against jumping to conclusions about the meaning of the NIH studies. To complicate the picture, some of the work shows that environment, along with genetics, influences sexual behavior. In one experiment, a small group of "straight" flies was mixed with a larger group of genetically altered "gay" flies. While the gays formed their conga lines, the straights stayed to the side—but only temporarily. After a few hours, the straights joined in and, for the time being, acted gay.

In fruit flies, and certainly in humans, sexual orientation is just not a simple matter. And no amount of scientific research is going to change that fact of life.

No One Has to Send a Gift

I have a right to marry—even if others disapprove.

David Mixner

My partner, Patrick Marston, was asked recently why he wanted to marry me. Patrick looked surprised at the question and replied simply, "Because I love David very much and want to spend the rest of my life with him." It is hard to imagine that such an honest and loving statement could be the subject of a bitter national debate. Last week's Hawaii court ruling has increased the tempo of the morals police, who are determined to impose their values on our lives. Unfortunately, there is no shortage of political demagogues willing to build their careers on the fear of change.

The court ruling has been a cause for jubilation for those who believe in justice. The issue of marriage goes far beyond the commitment of two people of the same sex. It goes to the civil rights of gay and lesbian Americans. The effort to ban same-sex marriage would deny us the basic rights accorded to our neighbors and friends. The issue involves immigration, taxation, family leave, health care, adoption, Medicare and numerous other benefits and rights. I don't know one American who would willingly surrender any of these rights.

Repeatedly I have been told by politicians frantically seeking to avoid leadership that a majority of Americans do not approve of same-sex unions. Although I am sad that people are so frightened of Patrick's and my love, I refuse to allow anyone's discomfort to be the reason why we should be less free than other Americans. I sincerely hope that eventually most of our fellow citizens will be able to understand our love for each other. But nowhere in the Constitution of the United States does the word comfortable appear as a criterion for the full enjoyment of the rights accorded to every American citizen. In fact, this nation's founders went to great pains to protect an unpopular minority from the tyranny of a majority.

Let us be clear what this issue does not do. It does not force any religious institution to perform a same-sex marriage. Such institutions are now free to refuse to marry even heterosexual couples based on certain religious beliefs. Members of those institutions will continue to have the ability to choose whom they want to marry. No citizen will be tied to a chair and forced to watch the happy couple dance at a reception. No one is required to send a gift.

David Mixner, "No One Has to Send a Gift," *Time* 149 (December 16, 1996): 45.

In fact, if our fellow citizens choose, they can do what they did when many of them disapproved of interracial and interfaith marriages. They can sit at home, loudly condemn us, pray for us and express their disgust. But let us be very clear, their beliefs and disapproval are not grounds to commit a grave injustice to millions of their fellow citizens. Gay and lesbian Americans should be accorded the same rights as other Americans . . . no more, but certainly no less.

As for Patrick and me, we are going to get married. We both are blessed because our families and many of our straight friends plan to participate in the ceremony and celebrate with us. I guess we could wait until everyone approves and the laws of the land say we can legally get married, but then I guess Rosa Parks could have waited until the laws of Alabama said she could ride in the front of the bus. She refused to give up her dignity in the face of unjust laws—and so do Patrick and I.

David Mixner is a writer and gay activist whose most recent book is *Stranger Among Friends* (Bantam Books).

Comprehension

"Search for a Gay Gene"
1. Describe the experiment conducted by Ward Odenwald and Shang-Ding Zhang at the National Institutes of Health.
2. What do the findings of this study suggest about human sexual orientation?
3. Why are some gays cautious about the genetic hypothesis?
4. What other evidence suggests that genes influence homosexuality?
5. What is serotonin, and what effect does it have?
6. According to experiments, what other factor influences sexual behavior?
7. What is the main idea of this article?
8. Would Alex, the young man in the case study, agree with the genetic or the environmental theory of homosexuality? Explain your answer.

"No One Has to Send a Gift"
1. What is the main issue involved in the Hawaii court ruling that same-sex marriages are legal?
2. What would be denied to homosexuals if same-sex marriages are banned?
3. What is the author's main argument for making same-sex marriages legal?
4. How convincing is the author's argument?

Strategy Session

Imagine that you are a college professor who teaches a course in human sexuality. You have been asked to add a component to the course on the topic of homosexuality.

Which approach to the subject would you use and why? Provide a written justification for your decision. If none of the listed strategies would be your choice, you may develop your own strategy.

1. Homosexuality is just another sexual orientation, like heterosexuality.

2. Homosexuality is a disease that can sometimes be cured.

3. Homosexuality is mainly a result of genetic factors.

4. Homosexuality is mainly a result of environmental factors.

5. The causes of homosexuality have not been determined.

6. Other: _____

Suggested Films

Before Stonewall (MPI Home Video: 1989)
The Birdcage (1996)
The Boys in the Band (1970)
La Cage aux Folles (1978 France-Italy)
Chasing Amy (1997)
Entre Nous (1983 France)
Everything Relative (1997)
Fried Green Tomatoes (1991)
In & Out (1997)
The Incredibly True Adventure of Two Girls in Love (1995)
Lianna (1983)
Maedchen in Uniform (1931 Germany)
My Beautiful Laundrette (1985 Britain)
Persona (1966 Sweden)
Personal Best (1982)
Philadelphia (1993)
The Question of Equality (KQED Video: 1995)
Sacred Lies, Civil Truths (Gay and Lesbian Emergency Media Campaign: 1993)
The Servant (1963 Britain)
Sotto, Sotto (1984 Italy)
Three of Hearts (1993)
Threesome (1994)
Victim (1961 Britain)
The Wedding Banquet (1993 U.S.-Taiwan)

Additional Readings

Gose, Ben. "The Politics and Images of Gay Students." *Chronicle of Higher Education* 42 (February 9, 1996): A33–34.
Handy, Bruce. "He Called Me Ellen Degenerate?" *Time* 148 (April 14, 1997): 86.
Howe, Rob. "A Fatal Friendship." *People* 46 (July 1, 1996): 65–71.

"It's Normal to Be Queer." *Economist* 338 (January 6, 1996): 68–70.

Krauthammer, Charles. "When John and Jim Say, 'I Do.'" *Time* 148 (July 22, 1996): 102.

Kunen, James. "Hawaiian Courtship." *Time* 148 (December 16, 1996): 44–45.

"Lack of Marriage License Doesn't Stop Gay Men in New York from Exchanging Vows." *Jet* 88 (August 28, 1995): 37.

"Let Them Wed." *Economist* 338 (January 6, 1996): 13–14.

Marshall, Eliot. "NIH's 'Gay Gene' Study Questioned." *Science* 268 (June 30, 1995): 1841.

Rhoads, Robert A. "The College Campus Climate for Gay Students." *Education Digest* 61 (September 1995): 57–60.

"Same-Sex Marriage: A Fair Ruling." *Ms.* 7 (March-April 1997): 17.

Chapter 8
Illegal Activities: Drug Abuse

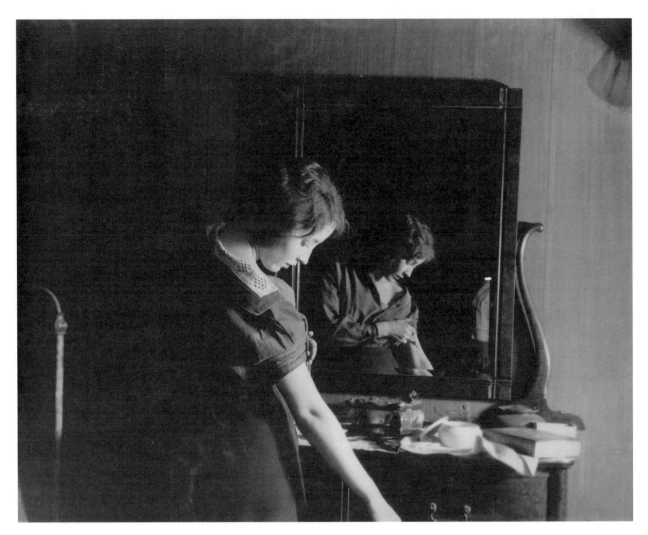

Human Wreckage; 1923, U.S.

What would you do if you realized you had become addicted to marijuana?

Exploration

After reading the following statements, respond to each one by writing *yes* or *no.*

1. The use of illegal drugs on college campuses in the United States is widespread. _____

2. I have never experimented with illegal drugs (marijuana, cocaine, heroin, LSD).

_____

3. The use of marijuana should be legalized. _____

4. Cocaine and heroin are not dangerous drugs if they are used in moderation. _____

5. Drug use by college students is not a problem in my country. _____

6. Smoking marijuana is less harmful than drinking alcohol. _____

7. Drinking alcohol and taking illegal drugs are prohibited by my religion. _____

8. I am addicted to legal drugs such as nicotine in cigarettes, caffeine in coffee, cola drinks, and chocolate, or alcohol in wine, beer, and liquor. _____

9. My parents have educated me on the dangers of using illegal drugs. _____

10. I know people who use illegal drugs. _____

11. Routine drug testing should be implemented in schools to help prevent drug abuse. _____

12. Because drug testing is an invasion of an individual's privacy, it cannot be justified. _____

Glossary

abuse	improper or excessive use; misuse
addicted	physiologically dependent upon a drug
addiction	compulsive physiological need for a habit-forming drug
bury	to submerge
cautious	prudent and careful in the face of danger or risk
close	good friends
cocaine	substance produced from coca leaves that produces intoxication
cool	very good, excellent (slang)
cut	to not attend
dope	marijuana
down	depressed and sad
experimented	tried to discover something not yet known
hangover	headache, nausea as aftereffects of drinking much alcohol
heroin	strongly physiologically addictive narcotic
high	intoxicated by marijuana
hooked on	addicted to
implemented	carried into effect; accomplished
interfere	to meddle; to enter into the concerns of others
introvert	a person who is more interested in himself or herself than in the environment or other people
invasion	intrusion or infringement

ironically	directly opposite to what is or might be expected
justified	shown to have had a sufficient legal reason; shown to be right
marijuana	the dried leaves and flowering tops of the hemp plant that are smoked in cigarettes for their intoxicating effect
moderation	avoidance of excesses or extremes
perplexed	full of doubt and uncertainty; puzzled, confused
pot	marijuana
privacy	one's private life or personal affairs
prohibited	forbidden by law or by an order
reluctantly	feeling unwilling to do something
routine	being in accordance with established procedure; regular and habitual
sobered	made serious and sensible
spaced out	feeling out of touch with reality
spare	free, extra
suspicion	the act of suspecting something wrong without proof or on slight evidence
unsure	not sure
widespread	distributed or occurring over a wide area

Reefer Madness; dir. Louis Gasnier, 1936, U.S.

Case Study: Hooked on Pot

After you read the case study, discuss the major problem the case presents and answer the discussion questions with the members of the class. Then write a case study report following the format that is provided.

Akiko Nakamura, from Kyoto, Japan, is a first-year student at Field College in New York City. She has been having a hard time adjusting to college life despite the fact that she spent her junior year in high school living with an American family in Philadelphia and attending an American high school. Although her English is excellent, she feels a bit unsure of herself and, being an introvert by nature, hasn't made too many friends yet. She tends to bury herself in her studies and to write lots of letters to her friends in Japan and her family. She also often calls her older American host "brother," Kevin, who is studying law in Philadelphia, to get his opinion on different things. She and Kevin have been close ever since she lived with his family, and she chose Field College because it was near Philadelphia.

It was the evening of October 31, and Akiko was sitting at her desk in her dorm room when her friend Barbara Coleman knocked at the open door and came in.

"Hi, Akiko. How about going with me to the Halloween party at Dan and Carl's house? I bet it will be quite a scene," said Barbara with a big smile.

"Oh, thanks, but I have to study for my microeconomics test on Monday," replied Akiko. "I heard it would be tough."

"Hey, come on. You can't study all the time. Let's go on over about ten o'clock. You need to get out and relax a little bit," Barb said.

"Well, okay. I guess I could go. I've never been to a Halloween party," Akiko reluctantly agreed. She had been feeling kind of down lately, so maybe going to a party would cheer her up. Barbara was one of her few friends, and she was such fun to be with.

When she got to the party, Akiko was sorry that she had let Barbara convince her to come because she hardly knew anyone, which made her feel out of place, as usual. But then Jerry Hill, who was in her business law class, came over and started talking to her. He was smoking and offered Akiko a cigarette. Akiko accepted, but after taking her first puff, she realized it tasted funny.

"What kind of cigarette is this?" she asked Jerry.

"Come on, Akiko. You know it's pot," replied Jerry, laughing.

"Oh, well, I guess I never tried pot before. Hey, this is so cool. I like how it's making me feel," Akiko said softly, after several minutes had gone by. Everyone began to seem very friendly, and the music sounded more beautiful, and the colors looked so bright.

From then on, whenever Akiko went out to a party, she smoked marijuana, and she decided that since it didn't hurt her, she wouldn't worry about it. She noticed that now she liked to smoke three or four cigarettes in an evening, which was more than she had smoked in the beginning, but she loved the way pot made her feel—so calm and happy and like she belonged in the group. And she didn't even have a hangover the next morning, which was what often happened when she drank too much beer or wine.

In fact, Akiko had also started smoking dope in her dorm room during the day when she had some spare time. It usually didn't interfere with her studying, and she rarely cut classes unless she was just too spaced out or sleepy, maybe about one day a week. And although her grades had gone down in all of her classes, she didn't really care anymore. School was boring compared to smoking dope and getting high.

The weekend after Thanksgiving vacation, Kevin came to visit from Philadelphia. He immediately noticed that Akiko seemed rather different. She wasn't too open about how her classes were going, and she didn't want to talk about what she was planning to major in or anything else connected to her academic work. Every time Kevin brought up the topic of school, she changed the subject.

In the evening, Akiko took Kevin to a party, and he was startled to see that Akiko and almost all the other students were smoking a lot of marijuana. Finally Kevin decided he'd better find out what was going on, so he sat down next to Akiko on the sofa.

"Akiko, you know smoking dope is illegal, plus it's bad for you. Why are you into this?" asked Kevin.

"What's your problem? There's nothing wrong with dope. This is just part of being a college student, and everyone does it, illegal or not," Akiko said cheerfully.

"Well, your mother and father sure wouldn't like it if they knew you were hooked on pot," answered Kevin quietly. "And I think they have the right to know."

"Why should they have to know about this? Please don't tell them!" begged Akiko, suddenly sobered by the thought of her conservative family back in Kyoto.

"I might have to. Anyway, I'm getting out of here. I can hardly breathe with all this smoke," Kevin said, as he stood up and walked out the door, leaving Akiko at the party.

After Kevin returned to Philadelphia, he thought about Akiko and how dependent she had become on smoking marijuana. He was worried and wondered if he should call his parents to discuss Akiko's situation. Or perhaps he should write to Akiko's parents, but he was afraid of their reaction. If they had even the slightest suspicion that their daughter was using drugs, they might decide to come to New York. Kevin knew that Akiko's father was a strict and traditional businessman who would probably make Akiko drop out of school and return to Kyoto, where he could keep an eye on her every move.

Maybe it would be better to try other ways of convincing Akiko about the danger of drugs. But how? And what if Akiko decided to experiment with more dangerous drugs like cocaine or heroin? Kevin was perplexed. This problem would never have arisen if Akiko had stayed in Japan, and ironically, it was Kevin who had persuaded her parents that sending Akiko to college in the States would be a good idea. How wrong he had been. Of course, he could not have predicted that Akiko would get hooked on drugs. In high school she had been very cautious and almost too well behaved. Living in New York had really changed Akiko, but not for the better.

Discussion

1. Why did Akiko begin smoking marijuana?
2. Is smoking marijuana harming her in any way?
3. What effect is smoking marijuana having on Akiko's academic performance?
4. How dependent is Akiko on marijuana?
5. Should Akiko stop using marijuana? Why or why not?

  6. Should Kevin try to convince Akiko to stop using marijuana?
  7. Should Kevin inform his parents about Akiko's drug use?
  8. If you were Kevin, would you tell Akiko's parents about Akiko's drug use?
  9. What methods could Kevin use to make Akiko stop smoking marijuana?
10. Which of the following sayings best expresses your attitude toward solving this case?
- Live and let live.
- Experience is the best teacher.
- It is better to prevent than to lament.

Case Study Report

Working with a partner or in a small group, write a case study report analyzing the problem of Akiko's use of marijuana.

   I. Statement of the Problem
  II. Suggestion of Possible Solutions
III. Evaluation of Possible Solutions
IV. Selection of a Solution

Vocabulary

Fill in the blanks with the most appropriate words. Use each word only once.

implement	interfering	addictive	marijuana	moderation	suspicion
justified	routinely	privacy	invasion	experimenting	widespread

United States government officials and school administrators have been working to establish guidelines and procedures to prevent drug use among students, but until now, they have not succeeded in winning the war against drugs. The problems of drug use and drug abuse among students of all ages have been getting worse in the past several years. There has been a dramatic growth in drug use in both secondary schools and colleges.[1]

According to *Rolling Stone* magazine, college campuses on the United States are facing a "drug comeback." Nearly fifty percent of college students have tried some form of drugs, and college drug arrests increased by thirty-four percent between 1992 and 1993.[2] Use of _____, commonly referred to as pot or dope, has shown an increase recently, and unfortunately, more young people are using hard drugs like cocaine and heroin.

---

1. David Lipsky, "The Hard-Core Curriculum," *Rolling Stone* (October 19, 1995): 100.
2. Lipsky, 100.

In fact, eighth graders have been _____ with illegal drugs in some of the major cities in the United States.[3]

The greatest danger to a person who uses drugs is that he or she will become physiologically dependent on the drugs. Heroin and cocaine are highly _____, even when used in _____, and anyone who begins taking those substances quickly learns how difficult it is to stop. Although researchers have discovered new methods that help people quit abusing drugs, most people who have a drug habit relapse after a period of being drug free, whether it happens in a month or in a year. Alan Leshner, of the National Institute on Drug Abuse, says: "Addiction is not a failure of the will or morality but a chronic brain disease."[4] If that is true, then there is no real cure for addiction.

One way to help prevent drug abuse is to _____ drug testing in schools on a regular basis for all students. However, this is controversial because of the Fourth Amendment to the U.S. Constitution. This amendment protects citizens from _____ of their privacy by prohibiting government searches without a warrant. There are more than eighteen million children in grades seven through twelve in the public schools in the United States.[5] Is it appropriate to test all these boys and girls even though most of them are not guilty of using illegal drugs? Many proponents of the Fourth Amendment right to _____ would answer no. They argue that drug tests and searches should be limited to those students who appear to be using drugs.

In June of 1995, the U.S. Supreme Court ruled that schoolchildren in public schools may be _____ tested for drug use even if there is no _____ of use because they have fewer Fourth Amendment rights than adults do. The decision was based on a case involving a seventh-grade student in Oregon who refused to comply with his school policy on drug testing. The minority opinion of the Court was that drug testing and searches are not reasonable unless suspicious behavior or signs of drug use exist.[6] But many people agree with the majority decision. They believe that _____ with a person's privacy is _____ when that person may be involved with using illegal drugs.

3. Abigail Trafford, "The Snare of Illegal Drugs," *Washington Post Health,* December 12, 1995, 6.
4. Rosie Mestel and David Concar, "New Treatments for Addiction," *World Press Review* 42 (March 1995): 38–39.
5. "Seventh-Grade Drug Tests," *Washington Post,* June 27, 1995, A16.
6. "Seventh-Grade Drug Tests," A16.

Furthermore, they are willing to weaken their constitutional rights in order to stop the

_____ use of drugs.

What is your opinion?

Write one or two paragraphs expressing your point of view on the issues discussed above.

Activities

1. Write a letter from Kevin to Akiko's parents, telling them about Akiko's drug use but asking them not to let Akiko know that he wrote to them.
2. Make one list of the legal drugs that are available and one list of the illegal drugs that are available in the United States. Circle the drugs that you use in both categories. Then write an essay in which you discuss your use of drugs.
3. Conduct a survey of at least ten people. Ask them the questions listed here and report your results to the class.
   1. Do you believe that drug abuse is a serious problem in the United States?
   2. Do you support the legalization of marijuana?
   3. Do you support the legalization of all illegal drugs (cocaine, heroin, LSD, etc.)?
   4. Do you believe it is acceptable to use illegal drugs on a recreational basis?
   5. Have you ever smoked marijuana?
4. After the class is divided into two teams, have a debate on the following topic: The use of marijuana should be legalized in the United States.
5. Find out if your school offers drug counseling services. If so, conduct an interview with a doctor, nurse, or counselor from the counseling service on the harmful effects of using marijuana, heroin, or cocaine on a prolonged basis. Then write a report on your interview.
6. Choose one of the following role plays for presentation in class. Plan and practice your dialogue before presenting it.
   (A) Act out the scene at the party when Akiko and Kevin talk about Akiko's use of marijuana.
   (B) Act out a future scene between Akiko and a drug counselor in which Akiko explains why she uses marijuana and the counselor explains the dangers of drugs.

Oral Presentation

Prepare and give an oral presentation on one of the topics listed. Use the suggested methods of development to organize your presentation and do library research to gather information.

- Methods of Treatment for Drug Addiction (enumeration, process)
- Should Drug Testing Be Legal? (argument, analysis)

Chapter Readings

The Snare of Illegal Drugs

Abigail Trafford

It seems Santa has put a piece of coal in the nation's health stocking this year—an ominous rise in illegal drug use and addiction.

Heroin that can be smoked is on the upswing in Chicago, New York, Detroit and Miami —increasingly fashionable among some affluent professionals.

Methamphetamine—"speed" and "chalk"—and smokable methamphetamine hydro-chloride—"ice," "crystal" and "glass"—are hot in Los Angeles, San Diego, San Francisco, Denver, Phoenix and Seattle.

Illegal use of the drug Ritalin—grinding it up, injecting it, snorting it, taking it orally— is big in Cleveland. Bingeing with the illegal drug Rohypnol—a benzodiazepine available in Mexico that is more potent than Valium—is a growing favorite in Florida and Texas.

Meanwhile, marijuana use is up everywhere, including rural areas, and is becoming popular among the 13- and 14-year-old set. So are inhalants—breathing in solvents, gases and nitrites. In fact, more eighth-graders are into inhalants than 12th-graders. In this younger age group nationwide, use of marijuana, LSD, cocaine and crack has about doubled since 1991.

In Washington, while crack cocaine appears to be on the decline, marijuana is up. Since 1993, the trend has been to mix marijuana with the hallucinogen PCP or with cocaine or with heroin. "A lot of users are playing around with multiple drugs. Kids are creating their own high," says Calvin C. Johnson, a consultant with the Urban Institute who works on National Institute on Drug Abuse's epidemiology study group. "It's scary and alarming."

The country, according to the latest government surveys, is in the midst of a surge in illegal drug abuse. If current trends continue, we'll be right where we were at the height of the drug crisis of the 1980s.

To be sure, a relatively small proportion of the population uses illegal drugs. Ninety-seven percent of high school seniors, for example, have never tried crack cocaine, according to 1994 surveys. But drug experts are alarmed by the increase and wonder what happened to the vaunted War on Drugs—which seemed to be winning the battle only a few years ago?

Abigail Trafford, "The Snare of Illegal Drugs," *Washington Post Health,* December 12, 1995, 6.

"We became a little complacent," says researcher Jeffrey C. Merrill at the Center on Addiction and Substance Abuse (CASA) in New York. "Now there's a perception that these drugs aren't as scary as people thought and you can use them and lead normal lives."

That's not true, of course. People who become drug addicts do not lead normal lives. Yet more people seem to be trying drugs. Health officials point out that there's no simple explanation for the current resurgence. Drug abuse goes in cycles, they say, and they note the following factors:

• Perception of harm. The current surge follows a major change in how people view the dangers of drugs. As Alan I. Leshner, director of the National Institute on Drug Abuse, explains: "Among high school students there has been a significant decline in the perception of risk that any drug use is harmful."

In 1979, for example, just before the rise in illegal drug use in the early 1980s, 42 percent of high school seniors thought regular use of marijuana was harmful. But by 1991, the proportion had risen to a high of 79 percent. Three years later, however, the figure had dropped back down to 65 percent. "In 1992 we started to see a sudden shift in attitude that would predict an increase in drug use," says CASA's Merrill. "That's exactly what has happened."

• Drug war backlash. While the War on Drugs in the 1980s focused attention on the problem, its scare tactics to keep young people away from drugs may have backfired, drug experts note. Anti-drug messages were delivered in such absolutist terms that the drumbeat of warnings could be dismissed as hyperbole—leaving health officials with a lingering credibility problem. As Leshner says, "We have got to get people to understand credible scientific data."

• Market forces. The quality of some drugs is better. The illegal drug industry follows basic economic laws, explains CASA psychiatrist Herbert Kleber. Almost like the computer industry, the quality of illegal drug products is up and the prices are down. Heroin, for example, can be of such high quality that it doesn't have to be injected. It can be smoked and inhaled. "People think it's not addictive that way—but that's not true," says Leshner.

• Generational link. High school students today are the children of parents who came of age in the 1970s, when use of illegal drugs was embraced in the popular culture. How, ask drug experts, can a generation of former users tell their children to stay away from drugs? Yet parents play a crucial role in educating their children about drugs. "The single biggest factor is parental involvement," says Leshner.

The irony here is that much more is known today about the health consequences of using illegal drugs. Researchers have a much clearer understanding of the biomechanics of addiction. Crack cocaine, for example, is the most addictive substance ever tested.

While starting to experiment with illegal drugs may be a voluntary choice, once the use becomes an addiction, the person is trapped in illness. For many users, the concept of recreational drug use is a cruel mirage. Several months ago, the veneer of chic surrounding upscale heroin use was shattered by the publicized death of a New York stockbroker from an overdose.

"Recreational drug use is not like playing tennis," says Leshner. "We need to change the national attitude so that even recreational use is not acceptable."

These Dorm Rooms a Study in Sobriety

Fern Shen

College dormitories have been hotbeds of many wild trends over the years, from goldfish-gulping to acid-tripping, but one recent campus phenomenon is strikingly un-wild—the rising popularity of drug-, alcohol- and tobacco-free dormitories.

At the University of Maryland and other colleges across the country, growing numbers of students are choosing to reside in "substance-free" living areas, even as the use of those substances has risen among American teenagers. Some students request these sobriety suites simply because they hate cigarette smoke or want a quiet place to study, while others say they developed a deep aversion to drugs, alcohol and tobacco after encountering substance abuse for years in their high schools or homes.

"One friend of mine hung himself under the influence of painkillers. A couple of my other friends were in accidents after drinking," said freshman Sean Bull, 18, of Harrisburg, Pa., as he moved into his room last week in a substance-free dormitory on Maryland's College Park campus.

"A lot of kids, from smoking dope so much, have just gotten stupid," he said, with obvious distaste.

Whatever the reason, the number of students seeking substance-free rooms, and the number of schools rushing to accommodate them, has been skyrocketing.

About 120 University of Maryland freshmen moved into the special substance-free buildings or floors in 1993, when the program, offered to first-year students, began. To satisfy the demand, the school is now offering the option to upper-class students as well. This year, the number of participants has risen to about 1,000 of a total of 8,000 on-campus residents.

The University of Michigan, which started the substance-free dorm room phenomenon in 1989, has seen the same tremendous increase. About 500 students went substance-free when that program began, a number that has risen to 2,600 this year. Vassar College in Poughkeepsie, N.Y.; Washington University in St. Louis; and the Rochester (N.Y.) Institute of Technology are among the dozens of schools that now offer substance-free or "wellness" housing.

"Students want a clean environment around them, not just a clean lifestyle for themselves," said Karla Shepherd, coordinator of programs and orientation for the University of Maryland. "In the morning, they don't want to look in the sink and find the results of someone's drinking too much the night before."

Shepherd said the sobriety rooms have become a selling point for the university at recruitment time, appealing to students and parents alike: "You've got to give people what they ask for, and this is what they want."

Like other forms of specialized housing (African American dorms, vegetarian dorms), substance-free housing has raised fears among administrators that too much self-segregation could deprive students of the diversity that has been considered a valued part of the college experience.

Fern Shen, "These Dorm Rooms a Study in Sobriety," *Washington Post*, September 3, 1996, A1.

"That's why we made a philosophical decision not to have entire substance-free buildings—we just designate certain floors," said Alan Levy, director of campus affairs for housing at Michigan.

In Maryland's program, modeled after Michigan's, students sign a contract agreeing not to have alcohol, cigarettes or tobacco products in their rooms. Those who violate their pledge may be counseled, warned, placed on probation or asked to leave the dorm. Officials said few violations have been reported so far.

Students can use the proscribed substances outside their dorms, but if they come back obviously drunk or disorderly, fellow residents will call them on it or turn them in.

It may sound harsh, but students who have lived in the substance-free dorms say their occupants often look out for each other.

"It's kind of like a fraternity, but one based on something besides booze," said Dan Bukowski, 19, as he guided a visitor through a hall where the doors had name tags in the shape of cigarette butts and booze bottles with X's over them.

To understand what's so special about the substance-free living areas, Bukowski said, try visiting those that aren't.

"You go into regular dorms and the guys' side reeks of alcohol and the girls' side reeks of smoke," said Bukowski, a sophomore from Baltimore. He said his decision to live in the special housing last year was prompted by the experience of two family members. "One died of smoking-related cancer and the other is an alcoholic," he said.

Illegal drugs are, of course, prohibited, and university policy also prohibits students under the legal drinking age of 21 from drinking alcohol in the dormitories. Students who are 21 or older are permitted to drink in their rooms. But students of all ages at Maryland have been known to drink openly in the dorms, smoke and use drugs as well, all mirroring national trends.

Last fall, the university released the results of a survey that showed that drug use among students had increased sharply. From 1991 to 1994, the number of students surveyed who said they had been using marijuana increased from 16 percent to 35 percent, according to the school. In a 1994 survey of Maryland high school students, about 25 percent reported having smoked marijuana in the previous months, bolstering the university's contention that rising marijuana use is a trend that begins in high school.

As for alcohol use, about 28 percent of the University of Maryland students surveyed reported drinking on six or more occasions in the last month, a number that has held steady in recent years.

One recent national study estimated that as many as 40 percent of college students are binge drinkers. Another study describes the "second-hand" effects of this bingeing on other students, who complained that the heavy drinkers interrupted their sleep or study, insulted or humiliated them, damaged their property and physically or sexually assaulted them. Much of that behavior, students said, can be found at Maryland on any given Saturday night, in fraternity and non-fraternity housing, on campus and off.

"Maryland has had a reputation as the place to party. We've been working to change that," Shepherd said. "We don't like to offer this as 'alternative' housing. We're hoping it's becoming the norm."

Maryland students offer a variety of explanations for the popularity of the abstinence housing, many saying it has more to do with an aversion to tobacco smoke than anything else.

"I just can't stand the smell of smoke. It gets in my eyes, my eyes water—I really hate it," said Greg Herbert, 19, of West Chester, Pa. Herbert said he's happy not to be around drugs and alcohol ("I'm hoping it'll be quieter, less distracting"), but he's no teetotaler.

"I was in Germany this summer, in places where there's no drinking age. People drink beer with a meal and it's no big deal. I think that's fine," he said, adding that he hopes his dorm mates won't mind if he hangs up the decorative "Pete's Wicked Ale" and "Red Stripe" beer signs his brother gave him. ("I've kind of got them hidden behind this dresser right now.")

But other students, like Bull, have more ideology behind their decision. Bull, who is majoring in biology, said he refrains from drinking, smoking and taking drugs as part of the "straight-edge" scene, a no-substance-abuse lifestyle that has its own music and symbols. (Bull points to the necklace he's wearing that's made with small X-marked cubes.)

Bull seemed almost jaded about drug and alcohol abuse. "There were kids back in the fifth grade dealing drugs," he said. "It's just getting to be too much." Other students say that they literally have "been there, done that."

"I was drinking and doing all that stuff, and I stopped. I realized it would hurt my studies, hurt my spiritual growth," said Matt Geris, a junior from Oxon Hill, as he carried clothes and stereo equipment into his room in preparation for the start of classes today.

Geris, a criminal justice major who transferred to the university from Prince George's Community College, said he heard about the substance-free dorm from members of his Bible study group who live there.

It's hard to pinpoint a single explanation for the popularity of the substance-free dorms. One statistical oddity of the Maryland program is that a disproportionate number of the participants are men.

Many seemed to view the substance-free dorms as a way to protect themselves from temptation, to keep them from slacking off their studies.

"I went to a big high school and I saw kids party and get wasted every weekend," said Josh Elithorpe, 18, of Albany, N.Y. "I don't want to wind up accidentally getting into it."

"Exactly," said his roommate, Dave Johnson, of Newport News, Va., boiling their decision down to simple economics: "We're not spending $13,000 a year to get plastered."

Comprehension

"The Snare of Illegal Drugs"
1. What drugs are being used in the United States?
2. What has been the trend in drug abuse in the 1990s?
3. According to a 1994 survey, what percentage of high school students have never tried crack cocaine?
4. How do many high school students view the dangers of drugs?
5. Why was there a backlash against the War on Drugs?

6. How do market forces affect drug use?
7. How important is parental involvement in educating children about drugs?
8. What misconception do many people have about recreational drug use?
9. What is the main idea of this article?
10. How would Akiko, the young woman in the case study, feel about the health consequences of using drugs?

"These Dorm Rooms a Study in Sobriety"
1. Why are growing numbers of students at the University of Maryland and other colleges across the country choosing to reside in "substance-free" living areas?
2. Which universities offer "substance-free" dorm rooms?
3. Describe the contract students at Maryland sign if they live in a "substance-free" dorm room and the punishments for violations of the contract.
4. What is the University of Maryland policy on using illegal drugs in dormitories and on drinking alcohol?
5. What did a university survey on drug use show?
6. List some of the reasons that the students give to explain the popularity of abstinence ("substance-free") housing.
7. Would you prefer to live in a "substance-free" dorm room if you had a choice?

Strategy Session

Imagine that you are a person who has been using marijuana and crack cocaine on a recreational basis for a year, and you have gradually become addicted to these drugs.

Which of the following courses of action would you take in this situation and why? Provide a written justification for your decision. If none of the listed strategies would be your choice, you may develop your own strategy.

1. Go to a doctor and ask to be admitted to a drug treatment program in a hospital in order to quit using these drugs.

2. Try to quit using marijuana and crack cocaine on your own, little by little.

3. Continue to use these drugs since you are able to function almost normally and have experienced only a few problems from using drugs.

4. Join a support group for addictive personalities in order to find support if you decide to stop using drugs.

5. Begin therapy with a therapist who specializes in drug addiction.

6. Other: _____

Suggested Films

Annie Hall (1977)
Basketball Diaries (1995)
Clean and Sober (1988)
Dazed and Confused (1993)
Drugstore Cowboy (1989)
Growing up Stoned (Films, Inc.: 1984)
Hair (1979)
I'm Dancing as Fast as I Can (1982)
Jungle Fever (1991)
The Man with the Golden Arm (1955)
The Panic in Needle Park (1971)
Reefer Madness (1936)
Rush (1991)
Trainspotting (1996)

Additional Readings

"Alcohol, Drug Use Increase among U.S. Youth." *Nation's Health* 26 (January 1996): 9.

Drozdiak, William. "Dutch Drugs Irk Neighbors." *Washington Post,* November 4, 1995, A1, A20.

Gest, Ted. "They're Toking up for Algebra Class. Teenagers Need Incentives to Keep It Clean." *U.S. News & World Report* 121 (December 30, 1996): 62.

Gose, Ben. "The Drug Problem." *Chronicle of Higher Education* 41 (July 21, 1995): A29–30.

Gose, Ben. "Dorm Searches Stir Student Complaints at Appalachian State." *Chronicle of Higher Education* 42 (March 22, 1996): A36.

Guernsey, Lisa. "Undercover Operations Yield Drug Arrests at 2 Colleges." *Chronicle of Higher Education* 42 (May 17, 1996): A40.

Kowalski, Kathiann M. "Proving You're Clean." *Current Health* 23 (November 2, 1996): 19–21.

Lipsky, David. "The Hard-Core Curriculum." *Rolling Stone* (October 19, 1995): 99+.

McCaffrey, Barry R. "The Next Front in the Drug War: The Media." *Christian Science Monitor,* May 30, 1997, 19.

Mestel, Rosie, and David Concar. "New Treatments for Addiction." *World Press Review* 42 (March 1995): 38–39.

O'Harrow, Robert, Jr., and Eric L.Wee. "Marijuana Users' Air of Defiance." *Washington Post,* August 3, 1996, A1, A12, A13.

Rist, Curtis, and Laird Harrison. "Weed the People." *People* 46 (October 21, 1996): 75–76.

Scalia, Antonin, and Dave Kindred. "At Issue: Should Schools Have the Right to Randomly Test Athletes for Drug Use?" *CQ Researcher* (September 22, 1995): 841.

"Seventh-Grade Drug Tests." *Washington Post,* June 27, 1995, A16.

Streisand, Betsy. "Thank You for Not Toking." *U.S. News & World Report* 121 (May 19, 1997): 28–29.

Chapter 9
Religious Beliefs: Discrimination

Gandhi; dir. Richard Attenborough; Ben Kingsley, 1982, Britain-India

How would you react if you felt you were being treated unfairly in school because of your religious beliefs?

Cultural Exploration

After reading the following statements, respond to each one by writing *yes* or *no*.

1. I consider myself a religious person. _____

2. I follow the teachings and live according to the rules of my religion. _____

3. A country's government should determine the religion of its citizens. _____

4. People should live according to the moral code taught by their religion. _____

5. I have experienced discrimination or persecution because of my religious beliefs.

   _____

6. The United States gives all people the right to religious liberty. _____

7. There is less religious freedom in my country than in the United States. _____

8. Many people in the United States do not understand my religious beliefs. _____

9. I would prefer to live in a country where everyone is a member of the same religion.

   _____

10. I would not marry a person whose religion is different from mine. _____

11. Learning about other religions is important. _____

12. My country's constitution contains the principle of the separation of church and

    state. _____

Glossary

compel	to force to do something
constitution	the system of fundamental laws and principles of a government, state, country, or society (written or unwritten)
curriculum	all of the courses offered in a school or in a particular subject
dean	the head of a division, faculty, college, or school of a university
discrimination	showing partiality or prejudice in treatment, specifically action directed against the welfare of minority groups
exception	treating someone differently from others of the same class
experiment	to make a test or trial of something to discover something not yet known
fasting	abstaining from all food, as in observing a holy day
Islam	the Muslim religion, a monotheistic religion in which the Supreme Deity is Allah and the chief prophet is Muhammad
liberty	freedom
minority	the smaller in number of two groups; a part of the population differing from others in some characteristics and often subjected to different treatment
Muslim	an adherent of Islam
observant	adhering to a law, rule, custom, or duty
observe	to adhere to a law, rule, custom, or duty
orientation	introduction to and explanation of an academic program
persecution	cruel oppression, especially for reasons of religion, race, or politics

perspective	point of view that shows events in their true relation to one another
pillars	main supporting principles
practice	to observe or adhere to beliefs
precepts	laws, commands, or principles intended as general rules of action
prerequisite	course that must be taken before enrolling in the next course
principle	fundamental truth, law, or doctrine upon which others are based; rule of right conduct
protest	objection
Ramadan	ninth month of the Muslim year, a period of daily fasting from sunrise to sunset
secular	not sacred or religious
separation	division, break; noninterference
separation of church and state	the principle by which religion and government are free of each other's control, as in the United States, France, and other countries
spiritual	showing much refinement of thought and feeling; of the spirit or soul as distinguished from the body
sympathize	to share the feelings or interests of another; to be in accord
worship	religious devotion or reverence; attendance at religious services
unfair	unjust, inequitable; showing prejudice and bias

Case Study: Free to Be Me

After you read the case study, discuss the major problem the case presents and answer the discussion questions with the members of the class. Then write a case study report following the format that is provided.

Ibrahim Khan Abbasi arrived from Pakistan at the beginning of January to attend a state university in the Midwest. He is planning to get a master of science degree and perhaps a Ph.D. in civil engineering with a structural major and then return to Karachi, where his family lives. Ibrahim is a deeply spiritual young man who takes his religion very seriously. He is an observant Muslim, following the five pillars of Islam and praying five times a day. When Ibrahim told his parents that he wanted to study in the United States, they asked him if he thought he would have any problems carrying out his religious practices in a secular country where Muslims were a minority, but Ibrahim was confident that he would have no troubles in that regard. "People have complete religious freedom in the States," he reassured his parents.

Before the semester began, the College of Engineering held an orientation for all incoming students. The first day included sessions on registration, tuition, health insurance, and housing. At the end of the day a buffet dinner was scheduled for the students and faculty so they could meet and get acquainted. Ibrahim had looked forward to the party, but when he arrived at the student center where the event was being held, he was surprised and disappointed to see that the menu was hot dogs and potato chips. Ibrahim didn't eat pork products, and he knew the hot dogs were probably made of pork, so he

Joan of Arc; dir. Victor Fleming;
Ingrid Bergman, 1948, U.S.

was not sure what he would eat. Just as he was looking at the tables with the food, Eric Parker, another new grad student whom Ibrahim had met earlier that day, came up to him and shook his hand.

"Hi, Ibrahim. How're you doing? This looks pretty good, don't you think? I'm starving," said Eric.

"Well, to tell the truth, I can't eat the hot dogs—they're pork, aren't they?" asked Ibrahim.

"Yeah, I guess so. But they're not bad, especially when you're hungry. Why don't you try one?" suggested Eric, grabbing a can of cola and a paper plate.

"I'm Muslim, so I don't eat pork," Ibrahim answered casually.

"Oh, I didn't know that. So what else don't you do?" asked Eric, laughing. "How about having some beer over at Charley's Bar, or is that not allowed either?"

"That's right. Actually, I don't drink alcohol," Ibrahim told Eric with a smile.

"What? Really? That seems kind of strange. Anyway, who would know what you do here in the States? It's a free country. Why not try something new? You're going to be living here for awhile, aren't you? When in Rome, do as the Romans," Eric said as he picked up two hot dogs and buns.

"Maybe you don't understand what I mean; I want to follow the rules of Islam," Ibrahim tried to explain to Eric, putting a handful of potato chips on his otherwise empty plate. "It's a way of life that is important to me."

"Oh, I get it. But if I were you, living far from home, I'd probably experiment a little. You know, just to find out what it's like," Eric replied. "So what do you say? Shall we go drink a few beers?"

Ibrahim thought about what Eric was saying for a few moments. "No, thanks," he replied. "I'd better get back to my place. I have some work to do before tomorrow."

That night, in his apartment, Ibrahim had second thoughts about whether he was going to have problems because of his religious beliefs. Being a hopeful person, he dismissed such negative thoughts and turned his attention to his course selection.

The first week of classes went well for Ibrahim. But on Friday, as he was going to his Advanced Structural Analysis course, which met on Tuesday and Friday from 11:30 A.M. to 1:30 P.M., Ibrahim realized that he would have to leave the class at 12:30 in order to get to the Friday prayer service on time. He decided to talk to his professor, Dr. Miller, before class and ask his permission to leave early every Friday. Ibrahim caught the professor just as he was entering the classroom.

"Dr. Miller, I will have to leave class at 12:30 today because I want to attend Friday prayers," Ibrahim said politely. "And I'll have to do that every Friday."

"Well, I guess that's OK for today since it is the first week, but you must attend class for the entire period during the rest of the semester," Dr. Miller replied as he sorted through the papers he intended to hand out to the students.

Ibrahim stared at his professor. "I'm afraid I can't stay past 12:30 on any Friday. You see, I need to get to the prayers on time."

"I sympathize with you, but rules are rules, and no student can be excused from an hour of class for a whole semester. Why don't you drop the course if you can't be here for the full two hours?" Dr. Miller suggested firmly.

"Well, I really have to take the course this semester since it's a prerequisite for the courses I want to take next, so I can't do that," replied Ibrahim, beginning to get nervous.

"That means that you'll just have to stay in class till 1:30. There's nothing else I can do, unless you wait for next semester. The course meets on Monday and Thursday next semester," Dr. Miller said, turning away to start his lecture.

Ibrahim went to see the dean of the College of Engineering to tell him about the problem. The dean, who was somewhat understanding and sympathetic, told Ibrahim to be patient.

"Maybe Professor Miller will change his mind," said the dean, "but for now, you have to attend class till 1:30 on Fridays, even if that means being late to prayers. Naturally, the university supports freedom of worship. However, the curriculum in the master's program is demanding, and graduate students can't be missing classes, even for good reasons. After all, Ibrahim, you know how challenging the course work is."

Although Ibrahim was angry and confused after his meeting with the dean, he tried to put the issue in perspective, and he concentrated even more on his studies. Still, the fact that he would probably be missing the Friday prayers bothered him a great deal.

Ramadan was beginning soon, and Ibrahim knew from his past experience that fasting was difficult for him, especially during the first few days. He felt more tired and weaker than usual on Monday, the first day of Ramadan. On Tuesday, Professor Miller announced a test for the following Friday. When Ibrahim heard that, he became anxious, and finally he decided to talk to Dr. Miller after class to see if he could reschedule the test.

"Dr. Miller, I was wondering if I could be allowed to take the test next Tuesday, a week from today, instead of this Friday. You see, it's Ramadan, and I'm not feeling my best right now," Ibrahim said. "By next week, I'll be used to the fasting."

Dr. Miller frowned. "Well, if I make an exception for you, I will have to make an exception for any student who asks me to postpone the test. That wouldn't be a good idea. I'm sure you would agree. Of course, I can't compel you to come to class and take the test, but my advice is just come, do your best, and don't worry about it."

"Oh, I see," Ibrahim replied in a discouraged voice, and without saying more, he picked up his books and left the room.

When Ibrahim thought about the way he was being treated because of his religious beliefs, he became convinced that the university was discriminating against Muslims.

"This seems unfair. I thought religious freedom was a major principle in the States. But I am not being given the freedom to practice my religion, or to be what I am," he said to himself as he wondered what to do.

Should he go to the dean again? Or should he talk to the other Muslim students and try to organize them to make a formal protest? Or maybe he should return to Karachi and try to get his master's degree there. Living by the precepts of his religion was just as important to Ibrahim as getting his graduate degree.

Discussion

Answer the following questions before writing the case study report.

1. What kind of person is Ibrahim Khan Abbasi?
2. What is causing Ibrahim's problem at the university?
3. Is Dr. Miller treating Ibrahim fairly? Explain your answer.
4. Are Ibrahim's requests reasonable or unreasonable? Explain your answer.
5. Why does Dr. Miller refuse Ibrahim's requests?
6. Should the dean take an active role in resolving the conflict? Why or why not?
7. What options does Ibrahim have in resolving this problem?
8. Should Ibrahim return to Pakistan, where he can easily practice his religious beliefs?

Case Study Report

Working with a partner or in a small group, write a case study report analyzing the problem Ibrahim is facing in regard to his religous beliefs.

I. Statement of the Problem
II. Suggestion of Possible Solutions

III. Evaluation of Possible Solutions
IV. Selection of a Solution

Vocabulary

Fill in the blanks with the most appropriate words. Use each word only once.

secular	separation	worship	practice	liberty
constitutions	principles	spiritual	persecution	compelled

Religious freedom is one of the basic _____ of the U.S. Constitution, which has been the supreme law of the nation since its adoption in 1789. The religious liberty clauses of the First Amendment ensure the equality of all people and religions before the law and ended the connection between church and state: "Congress shall make no law respecting the establishment of religion, or prohibiting the free exercise thereof."[1] Because of the First Amendment, debate and dissent are accepted in the United States, where religious beliefs are a matter of personal choice.

Although the original English colonists who left England for the New World between 1607 and 1628 were seeking freedom of religion, they did not interpret religious freedom as broadly as we understand it today. The earliest English colonies, Jamestown (1607), Plymouth (1620), and Massachusetts Bay (1628), were based on English law and liberty. They served as a refuge for Protestant Christians and a way to prevent the Catholic Church from taking over the native population of America.[2] In these settlements, Pilgrims and Separatists (Puritans who had left the Church of England) were able to _____ their form of the Protestant religion without fear, but these settlers were not tolerant of other religions, so true religious freedom did not exist.

During the Puritan migration of the 1630s, New England was settled by deeply religious and _____ people who wanted to do the will of God in all aspects of their lives. However, these early colonists did not establish religious freedom. In 1644, the colony of Rhode Island became the first settlement to attempt to separate church and state and to offer freedom of _____ to all settlers. The Reverend Roger Williams, the

---

1. U.S. Constitution. Amendment 1.
2. Samuel Eliot Morison, *The Oxford History of the American People,* vol. 1, *Prehistory to 1789* (New York: Meridian, 1994), 85–86.

founder of Rhode Island, was one of the first advocates of religious _____.

Indeed, Williams believed that the Native Americans' religion was as acceptable to God as

was Christianity.[3]

Another step toward freedom of religion was the Toleration Act of Maryland, which

was passed in 1649. The act, whose purpose was to protect Catholics from religious

_____, stated that no Christian should "be any ways troubled molested or

discountenanced for . . . his or her religion, nor in the free exercise thereof . . . nor any way

compelled to the belief or exercise of any other Religion against his or her consent."[4] The

Toleration Act led to a legalized system of religious tolerance that eventually became full

religious freedom as stated in the U.S. Constitution.

By 1700 religious freedom, already established by Roger Williams in Rhode Island and

William Penn in Pennsylvania, was becoming accepted throughout the other English colo-

nies. After the American Revolution of 1776, in which America won its independence from

England, the leaders of the Revolution wanted to "maintain, develop, and correct the state

of things political and religious, which already existed."[5] Thus, state and federal

_____, each including a bill of rights, were drawn up. The first was the

Virginia Declaration of Rights (June 12, 1776), a historical document asserting the rights to

"the enjoyment of life and liberty, with the means of acquiring and possessing property, and

obtaining happiness and safety." It also contained the right to religious liberty. Pennsylvania's

constitution was even stronger on the right to freedom of religion.[6]

The principle of religious freedom became a part of the state constitutions, but the final

_____ of church and state was not completed until 1785 in Virginia, 1818

in Connecticut, and 1833 in Massachusetts.[7] The Virginia Statute of Religious Liberty (1786),

written by Thomas Jefferson, states: "No man shall be _____ to frequent

or support any religious worship, place, or ministry whatsoever."[8] Today the United States is

a country that accepts all religions. It is a _____ society as a result of the

separation of church and state, which keeps religion and government free of each other's

control, and all people have the right to worship as they please or not to worship if they

choose not to.

3. Morison, 109–10.   5. Morison, 355.   7. Morison, 361.
4. Morison, 129.   6. Morison, 356–57.   8. Morison, 382.

What is your opinion?

Write one or two paragraphs expressing your point of view on the issues discussed above.

Activities

1. Write a letter from Ibrahim to the dean, justifying his request to leave class early on Fridays in order to attend prayers and asking to be treated fairly.
2. Do library research on the subject of the major religions of the world. Take notes about five of these religions in regard to number of members, date of origin, founder, principal beliefs, most important figures, and major holidays. Write a short report presenting this information.
3. Make a list of the religions (or philosophical systems of belief) that are found in your country. Compare your list with your classmates' lists by writing them on the chalk-board. What is the predominant religion in your country? Are there many different religions or just one?
4. Conduct a survey of at least ten people. Ask them the questions listed here and report your results to the class.
    1. Have you experienced any form of religious discrimination?
    2. Do you think that religious belief is getting stronger in the United States?
    3. Do you attend religious services on a regular basis?
    4. Do you pray on a regular basis?
    5. Is there a need for more constitutional protection of religious liberties in the United States? Please explain your answer.
5. After the class is divided into two teams, have a debate on the following topic: The separation of church and state is the appropriate way to organize a government.

Intolerance (St. Bartholomew's Day Massacre); dir. D. W. Griffith; Lillian Gish, 1916, U.S.

6. Choose one of the following role plays for presentation in class. Plan and practice your dialogue before presenting it.

   (A) Act out the scene where Ibrahim asks Dr. Miller to excuse him early from class on Fridays.

   (B) Act out a scene in the future where Ibrahim talks to the dean after the dean has received a letter from Ibrahim justifying his request to leave class early on Fridays in order to attend prayers.

Oral Presentation

Prepare and give an oral presentation on one of the topics listed. Use the suggested methods of development to organize your presentation and do library research to gather information.

- An Introduction to Islam (or another religion) (definition, enumeration)
- An Analysis of the Principle of Separation of Church and State (definition, analysis)

Chapter Readings

Proclamation 6862
Religious Freedom Day, 1996

January 12, 1996

By the President of the United States of America

A Proclamation

On this day over 200 years ago, Virginia's General Assembly passed a law that created the first legal protection for religious freedom in this country. Introducing his bill to the Virginia Assembly, Thomas Jefferson stated that he was not creating a new right confined simply to the State of Virginia or to the United States, but rather declared religious liberty to be one of the "natural rights of mankind" that should be shared by all people. Jefferson's language was shepherded through the legislature by James Madison, who later used it as a model for the First Amendment to the United States Constitution.

Americans have long benefited from our founders' wisdom, and the Constitution's twin pillars of religious liberty—its protection of the free exercise of religion and its ban on the establishment of religion by the Government—have allowed an enormous diversity of spiritual beliefs to thrive throughout our country. Today, more than 250,000 churches, synagogues, mosques, meeting houses, and other places of worship serve to bring citizens together, strengthening families and helping communities to keep their faith traditions alive. We must continue to ensure full protection for religious liberty and help people of different faiths to find common ground.

Our Nation's profound commitment to religious freedom reminds us that many people around the world lack the safeguard of law to protect them from prejudice and persecution. We deplore the religious intolerance that too often tears neighbor from neighbor, and we must remain an international advocate for the ideal of human brotherhood and sisterhood and for the basic rights that sustain human dignity and personal freedom. Let us pledge our support to all who struggle against religious oppression and rededicate ourselves to fostering peace among people with divergent beliefs so that what Americans experience as a "natural right" may be enjoyed by individuals and societies everywhere.

Now, Therefore, I, William J. Clinton, President of the United States of America, by virtue of the authority vested in me by the Constitution and laws of the United States, do hereby proclaim January 16, 1996, as Religious Freedom Day. I call upon the people of the United States to observe this day with appropriate ceremonies, activities, and programs, and I urge all Americans to reaffirm their devotion to the fundamental principles of religious freedom and religious tolerance.

In Witness Whereof, I have hereunto set my hand this twelfth day of January, in the year of our Lord nineteen hundred and ninety-six, and of the Independence of the United States of America the two hundred and twentieth.

William J. Clinton

"Proclamation 6862—Religious Freedom Day, 1996," *Weekly Compilation of Presidential Documents* (January 15, 1996): 54.

Proclamation 6908
A National Month of Unity, 1996

July 1, 1996

By the President of the United States of America

A Proclamation

Our Nation was founded by people who sought the right to worship freely, and religious liberty is enshrined in our Constitution as the "first freedom" granted by our Bill of Rights. The United States is now the most multi-ethnic, multi-religious democracy in history, and we must preserve this precious freedom while making the most of our diversity. Ours is a great and noble struggle to make our national voice a chorus of unity—varied by differing intonations, but carried and lifted by a rich harmony.

The recent rash of arson attacks against black churches and other houses of worship is a stark reminder that our work to build common ground is far from over and that our progress can be threatened by forces that tear at the very fabric of our society. It is hard to think of a more heinous act than the destruction of a sacred structure. The violence that charred and defaced these buildings challenges our fundamental right to worship in safety, and has left us grim emblems of the hatred and alienation that too often darken our daily experience.

And so we must look into our hearts as America approaches the new century, pledging to devote our energies to reinvigorating the shared values that will enable us to embrace the future together. We must never go back to the terrible days of racial and ethnic division, nor can we afford to dismiss our problems by ascribing them to isolated groups or areas of the country. Instead, let us join hands to lighten our burdens and build bridges among people and communities so that we can be one America—a Nation of extraordinary possibility with opportunity, freedom, and respect for all.

Now, Therefore, I, William J. Clinton, President of the United States of America, by virtue of the authority vested in me by the Constitution and laws of the United States, do hereby proclaim July 1996, as A National Month of Unity. I call upon religious leaders of all faiths to emphasize the need for healing and tolerance. I ask all Americans to join these efforts by working together to mend divisions and promote understanding; by reaching out to friends and neighbors of all races and faiths in a spirit of fellowship; and by seeking to strengthen, through words and actions, the ideals of equality and community cherished by generations of Americans. In this birth month of our Nation, let us set an example for the world we welcome to Atlanta for the Centennial Olympic Games by rededicating ourselves to America's fundamental truth: E pluribus unum—from many, one.

In Witness Whereof, I have hereunto set my hand this first day of July, in the year of our Lord nineteen hundred and ninety-six, and of the Independence of the United States of America the two hundred and twentieth.

William J. Clinton

"Proclamation 6908—A National Month of Unity, 1996," *Weekly Compilation of Presidential Documents* (July 8, 1996): 1164–65.

Myths Propel the Push for Prayer in School

Our View: New statement from coalition of religious groups spells out better ways to teach religion in schools.

USA Today editorial staff

"Beware of practicing your piety before men in order to be seen by them," cautioned Jesus, "for then you will have no reward from your father who is in heaven."

Too often, those eager to make a political issue of school prayer seem to forget that part of the Gospel. The most outrageous keep peddling the falsehood that religion has somehow been barred from the nation's public schools.

Fortunately, religious groups from across the theological spectrum have joined in an effort to clear up such misinformation. The drafters of *Religion in the Public Schools: a Joint Statement of Current Law* include the National Association of Evangelicals and the Baptist Joint Committee, as well as the National Council of Churches and the American Jewish Congress, among others.

They meet a lot of myths head-on:

• Courts have declared the schools religion-free zones.

"Simply wrong."

• The law is so murky that school officials can't know what's permitted.

Also wrong: Much of the law is settled, though some difficult issues remain.

• Students can't pray in school.

Again wrong: Students have the right to pray individually and to discuss their religious views. Expressing religious beliefs in reports, art, homework and classroom discussion, even giving religious literature to schoolmates, is constitutionally protected.

• Schools can't teach about religion.

Teaching about the history of religion, comparative religion, the Bible as literature and the religious background of the abolition, women's rights and civil rights movements is "both permissible and desirable."

This common-sense document ought to be required reading for school administrators confused about how to handle religious issues. It is an answer simultaneously to those who say religion has no place in school and those who call for legislation to "permit voluntary prayer."

Religion has a role. And prayer legislation doesn't.

Voluntary prayer never has been curbed. Only the use of coercion, applying the authority of the school to impose religious observances in a form of state-enforced proselytizing— and ostracizing those who object—is barred.

Some of our ancestors came to this continent to escape precisely that kind of tyranny. And because even in the 18th century this was a pluralistic nation, they wrote a ban on official religion into the Constitution. This is no time to start tearing down that bar in a zeal for public displays that marginalize the beliefs of others.

"When you pray, you must not be like the hypocrites; for they love to stand and pray . . . that they may be seen by men," Jesus continued. "But when you pray, go into your room

"Myths Propel the Push for Prayer in School," *USA Today,* April 27, 1995, A12.

and shut the door and pray to your father who is in secret; and your father who sees in secret will reward you."

Stop the Discrimination

Opposing View: We need to protect the rights of religious people. Pass school prayer.

Jay Sekulow

Education Secretary Richard Riley's support of the statement of principles designed to protect the religious liberties of public school students is a good beginning.

But this statement of current law does not go far enough. No matter how many government officials and organizations sign on to this statement of principles, it is ultimately the courts which decide the scope of religious liberties in America.

When you consider that religious discrimination today is a fact of life, the need for affirmative constitutional protection is clear.

In Washington State, a kindergarten child—who was asked to sing her favorite song—was chastised by the teacher after she sang *Jesus Loves Me.* The teacher told her songs like that aren't allowed in school.

A woman in Oregon filed suit after the state rejected her request to use "PRAY" on her license plates.

And in California, a pastor was told that he could not pray at a birthday party for his wife at a rented hall in a city park.

Real stories. They happen every day.

The call for a religious liberties amendment reflects the frustration experienced by people of faith.

This amendment would safeguard religious liberties by providing equal access to the marketplace for all people of faith.

Don't be misled, though. No one is suggesting that one religion be given preference over another. No one is suggesting that a school or state endorse any kind of religious belief.

The religious liberties amendment will complement our Constitution, not create a crisis.

It will serve the First Amendment well by prohibiting discrimination toward religious speech and religious expression.

It will not eliminate the separation of church and state, which we support.

But it will protect the freedoms of students in the public schools, citizens in the public square, and all Americans who support freedom and liberty.

As Supreme Court Justice William O. Douglas argued in *Zorach vs. Clausen* in 1952: "We are a religious people whose institutions presuppose a Supreme Being."

As the debate continues, that's a truth worth remembering.

Jay Sekulow is chief counsel of the American Center for Law and Justice, a public interest law firm and educational organization based in Virginia Beach, Va.

Jay Sekulow, "Stop the Discrimination," *USA Today,* April 27, 1995, A12.

Comprehension

"Proclamation 6862—Religious Freedom Day, 1996"
1. What did Thomas Jefferson state to the Virginia Assembly in 1796?
2. What are the two pillars of religious liberty in the Constitution?
3. How many religious places of worship are there in the United States?
4. For what must the United States remain an international advocate?
5. Clinton urges all Americans to reaffirm their devotion to the fundamental principles of religious freedom and religious tolerance. What is the difference between religious freedom and religious tolerance?

"Proclamation 6908—A National Month of Unity, 1996"
1. What is the "first freedom" granted by the Bill of Rights?
2. How does Clinton describe the United States, and what does this description mean?
3. What do the arson attacks against black churches and other houses of worship show us?
4. What does Clinton ask religious leaders and all Americans to do?

"Myths Propel the Push for Prayer in School"[9]
1. What false claim do supporters of school prayer make?
2. What religious rights do students have in school?
3. What can schools teach about religion?
4. What is barred by the Constitution?
5. What argument does the author make against the prayer amendment?
6. Explain the quote the authors use to support their argument.

"Stop the Discrimination"
1. Who decides the scope of religious liberties in America?
2. Why does the author believe that there is a need for affirmative constitutional protection of religious liberties?
3. How would this amendment safeguard religious liberties?
4. How will the religious liberties amendment complement the Constitution?
5. What will the amendment not eliminate?
6. Explain the quote the author uses to support his argument.

Strategy Session

Imagine that you are a student at a public school that closes on major Christian holidays but not on the major holidays of other religions, including yours. This seems unfair to you because you believe that your school should not support one religion over others.

Which strategy would you use in this situation and why? Provide a written justification for your decision. If none of the listed strategies would be your choice, you may develop your own strategy.

---

9. The religious liberties amendment to the U.S. Constitution was defeated in the U.S. Congress.

Biruma no Tategoto (Burmese Harp); dir. Kon Ichikawa, 1956, Japan

1. Write a letter to the local newspaper asserting that the school is not treating all religious beliefs equally and thus is violating your First Amendment rights.

2. Hire an attorney whose specialty is First Amendment religious liberty clauses to represent you in your dealings with the school.

3. Make an appointment with the president of the school to discuss the manner in which the school is discriminating against students who are not Christians.

4. Don't attend school on the days that are holidays in your religion.

5. Organize all the students who share your point of view in order to have a demonstration on campus, with speakers from different religions.

6. Other: _____

Suggested Films

Au Revoir, Les Enfants (1987 France)
The Crucible (1997)
The Dark at the Top of the Stairs (1960)
Europa Europa (1991 France-Germany)
Gandhi (1982 Britain-India)
Gentleman's Agreement (1947)
Intolerance (1916 silent film)
Joan of Arc (1948)
Michael Collins (1997)
The Night of the Shooting Stars (1982 Italy)
Queen Margot (1994 France-Germany-Italy)
The Scarlet Letter (1926 silent film)
Schindler's List (1993)
School Ties (1992)
Some Mother's Son (1997)
The Witches of Salem (1956 France–East Germany)

Additional Readings

Al-Marayati, Salam. "A Spiritual Course in the Meaning of Life." *Washington Post,* January 11, 1997, C6.

Aziz, Barbara Nimri. "U.S. Muslims Live in Isolation as Public Intolerance Grows." *National Catholic Reporter* 29 (September 10, 1993): 16.

Broadway, Bill. "Dual Devotion." *Washington Post,* January 11, 1997, C1, C6, C7.

"Court Authorities Pray at Graduation." *ABA Journal* 83 (April 1997): 37.

Mack, Tara. "Together as Muslims, Students Learn, Grow." *Washington Post,* January 19, 1997, B1, B3.

McFarland, Steven T. "Students Need Constitution." *USA Today,* September 6, 1995, A12.

Pouliot, Janine S. "Rising Complaints of Religious Bias." *Nation's Business* 84 (February 1, 1996): 36–37.

Wallace, Wendy. "Holding Fast to Faith." *Times Educational Supplement,* January 19, 1996, Second Supplement 1–2.

Wrynn, John F. "Ramadan Is Generous." *America* 172 (May 13, 1995): 21–22.

Chapter 10
Student-Teacher Interactions: Sexual Harassment

Way Down East; dir. D. W. Griffith;
Lillian Gish, 1920, U.S.

What would you do if your teacher sexually harassed you?

Exploration

After reading the following statements, respond to each one by writing *yes* or *no*.

1. Teachers and students should have formal relationships both in and outside of class.

   _____

2. Teachers and students should not become close friends. _____

3. Teachers have a responsibility to be role models for their students. _____

4. Students who want to improve their grades should get to know their teachers better outside of class. _____

5. Teachers can harm students if teachers abuse their power over their students. _____

6. Many college students will do almost anything to get higher grades. _____

7. Students in my country are often afraid of their teachers. _____

8. It is unethical for students and teachers to get romantically involved with each other. _____

9. Universities should make rules that prohibit relationships between students and teachers. _____

10. A teacher who tries to pressure a student into a sexual relationship should be dismissed from the school. _____

11. Sexual harassment is a common problem in the United States. _____

12. Sexual harassment is not considered a problem in my country. _____

Glossary

abuse	to put to a wrong or improper use
accusation	the crime or wrong of which a person is accused
appropriately	proper, suitable; right for the situation or purpose
back up	to support or help
charming	attractive, fascinating, delightful
come forward	to offer one's testimony
come on to	to show sexual interest in someone
dirty old man	immoral older man (slang)
dismissed	discharged or removed from employment
distant	cool in manner; reserved
embarrassment	feeling ill at ease, confused, and self-conscious
file	to initiate a legal action
fired	terminated or dismissed from a job
get away with	to succeed in doing without being discovered or punished
grade on a curve	to evaluate according to performance rather than an absolute scale
handle	to deal with or manage with skill
harm	to injure or hurt
innuendos	indirect remarks usually implying something derogatory
naive	deficient in worldly wisdom or informed judgment

pressure	to exert force or compelling influence
propositions	unethical or immoral proposals of sexual relations in return for some gain
role model	a person who is unusually effective or inspiring in some social role or position and serves as a model for others
sexual harassment	forcing unwanted sexual attention on someone, verbally and/or physically
straighten out	to make less confused and easier to deal with
stroke	to caress; to rub gently in one direction
unethical	not conforming to accepted standards of conduct
upheaval	sudden violent change or disturbance
verify	to confirm or substantiate
victim	a person injured, harmed, or destroyed by some act
warm	friendly, genial, sincere

Queen Kelly; dir. Erich Von Stroheim; Gloria Swanson, 1928, U.S.

Case Study: Grading on a Curve

After you read the case study, discuss the major problem the case presents and answer the discussion questions with the members of the class. Then write a case study report following the format that is provided.

Florence Bokunda comes from Abidjan, a city in the Ivory Coast in Africa. She is in her second semester at Clearhaven College in Florida and is doing pretty well, considering that her English skills are not all that great, especially her writing. However, one course that has been giving her trouble is Third-World Politics. Her professor, Dr. Duke, is an older man with a warm and kind personality, and Florence has been considering whether to go to see him and get some suggestions on how to improve her academic performance.

Although Florence is a little nervous around her professors, Dr. Duke has told all his students that they should come to his office during his office hours if they ever have any problems or questions about the course. And in class, he looks directly at her and smiles quite often, so Florence thinks that he must like her for some reason in spite of her average grades.

After Florence received a C on her paper on Nigerian political upheaval, she decided that she had better make an appointment with Dr. Duke and find out how to meet his requirements in regard to written work. She talked to him after class and asked if she could see him during his office hours that afternoon to discuss her paper.

"Yes, of course. I'll be expecting you at 1:30," Dr. Duke replied with his usual charm. "My door will be open."

Dr. Duke was grading papers when Florence arrived at his office at exactly 1:30.

"Oh, Dr. Duke, I'm sorry to interrupt you," said Florence shyly.

"Never mind. I'm always glad to see a beautiful young lady in my office," laughed Dr. Duke. "Please sit down and make yourself comfortable. How about a cup of coffee? And do call me Charles," he continued as he closed his door and sat down next to her.

Florence got out her paper on Nigerian political instability and asked Dr. Duke if he would mind going over some of his comments in greater detail.

"Sure, but first, why don't you tell me a little about yourself, Florence? What made you decide to come to Clearhaven and how do you like it here?" Dr. Duke asked.

Florence explained to Dr. Duke that she had come to Clearhaven because her cousin had graduated from the school. She told him how much she liked the college but that she was having some difficulty with her course work.

"Well, I would be more than happy to give you extra tutoring. Why not come to my office this evening at 7:30, and we will have plenty of time to concentrate on your problems," said Dr. Duke in a sympathetic voice. Then he reached over and stroked Florence's hand. "I think I understand how hard it is to adjust to a strange culture. Maybe I can be your friend, not just your professor. How do you feel about that?"

Florence remained silent and stared at her paper.

"I'm sure if we work closely together on your papers for my class, you will be able to get A's on all of them. After all, I usually grade on a curve," said Dr. Duke, with a smile.

Florence was not sure how to respond to Dr. Duke. She had never had a teacher as a friend. Her teachers had been polite but distant in her country. She also didn't like Dr. Duke's holding her hand. Suddenly, as Florence was thinking about what to say, Dr. Duke moved closer to Florence and put his arms around her.

"You really are a lovely young woman," he said softly. "Let's see if we can raise your grades by spending some time together, okay?"

Florence stared at Dr. Duke's face, so close to her own. Then she jumped up and, without replying, quickly left the office.

After Florence got back to her dorm room, she sat on her bed and tried not to think about what had just happened. Her whole body was trembling, and she felt cold, so she took a hot shower and changed clothes. Realizing that staying in her room alone wouldn't make her feel better, she decided to go to the library to study. As Florence was entering the periodicals reading room, she ran into her friend Michael, who lived in her dorm.

"Hey, what's happening, Flo?" asked Michael.

"Not too much. Well, actually I do want to ask you about something weird that happened to me this afternoon. But you have to promise to keep quiet about it if I tell you," replied Florence cautiously.

"Sure, I'll never tell," said Michael.

Then Florence explained how Dr. Duke had come on to her in his office and had suggested that her grades would improve if she spent time alone with him.

"What do you make of that?" she asked Michael.

"I think Dr. Duke is a dirty old man, and you should report him to the dean of student affairs. What he did is called sexual harassment. I should know because I just finished writing a paper on that subject. If anyone makes sexually suggestive comments, innuendos, or propositions or engages in inappropriate physical contact of a sexual nature, like touching, patting, or pinching, that's harassment. Isn't that what happened to you?" asked Michael.

"Yes, I guess so." Florence looked embarrassed.

"Well, Duke is just using his power over you to force you to do something you would never do. He shouldn't be allowed to get away with it. If you don't report him, he will continue to do this stuff, and sooner or later someone will get really hurt."

"I can't report him, Michael. He is a professor! What if he tries to prove that it was all my fault, and the dean believes him? Dr. Duke is powerful and smart. I'm just a first-year student with no one to back up my story. I could end up failing his course and even having to leave the college. There's no way I can go to the dean!" answered Florence. "Give me another suggestion, but don't tell me to report Dr. Duke."

"You are making a big mistake, Flo," Michael responded. "Dr. Duke can't harm you if you tell the truth about what happened. I'll go with you to the dean if you want me to and verify your story."

"Thanks, Michael, but no. Let me handle this my way. I'll just try to avoid Duke, and somehow I'll get through the rest of the semester. Maybe it was my fault—I guess I must have been too friendly with him and he misunderstood me. I might even go talk to him about this and see if I can straighten things out," Florence said hopefully.

"Florence, Duke's behavior was highly unethical. If you go alone to his office again, who knows what he might do? That is definitely a bad idea and so naive. Why are you protecting him? I'll bet you are not his first victim, and someone has to be the first to come forward and make an accusation," pleaded Michael.

"I'll think about it, but don't give me a hard time, OK?" Florence replied impatiently as she sat down at the library desk and opened her book. Now she was sorry she had involved Michael in this mess. All she wanted to do was forget that it had ever happened.

Discussion

1. What kind of person is Florence?
2. What kind of person is Dr. Duke?
3. Why did Florence go to Dr. Duke's office?
4. Did Dr. Duke behave appropriately with Florence? Why or why not?
5. Did Florence behave appropriately with Dr. Duke? Why or why not?
6. Why does Michael want Florence to report Dr. Duke to the dean of student affairs?
7. How does Florence feel about making a complaint?
8. What could happen if Florence reports Dr. Duke to the dean of student affairs?
9. Should Florence file a formal complaint with the university against Dr. Duke?
10. What options does Florence have in regard to this problem with her professor?

Case Study Report

Working with a partner or in a small group, write a case study report analyzing the problem Florence is facing in regard to her professor Dr. Duke.

I. Statement of the Problem
II. Suggestion of Possible Solutions
III. Evaluation of Possible Solutions
IV. Selection of a Solution

Vocabulary

Fill in the blanks with the appropriate words. Use each word only once.

come forward	harassment	handle	appropriate	file	accusations
get away with	role models	unethical	victims	back up	dismissal

Sexual _____ has become a major issue in the United States, whether it occurs on military bases, on college campuses, or in private corporations. The definition of sexual harassment is the forcing of unwanted sexual attention on a person, including verbal or physical conduct of a sexual nature and requests for sexual favors. This is a complicated area of the law because of the difficulties involved in determining when such objectionable behavior has taken place. It is generally agreed that sexual harassment exists when there is a pervasive pattern of behavior that results in a hostile environment and makes the other person feel uncomfortable. However, individual reactions differ greatly, and words and actions that are acceptable to one person may be unacceptable to another. Furthermore, some people still do not realize that making jokes or remarks of a sexual nature is not considered _____ in today's environment of gender equity and political correctness.

_____ of sexual harassment have often been reluctant to _____ to press charges against the person who has harassed them. First, they worry that they may not have the evidence to _____ their claims, especially if there are no witnesses. It is one person's word against another's. Second, they may fear that they will be seen as having encouraged the person to harass them, so they may prefer to _____ the situation on their own privately, without making the problem public. Thus, until recently, many people managed to _____ sexual harassment despite the U.S. Supreme Court ruling in 1986 that employers can be sued for sexual harassment by those who faced a hostile work environment or received "quid pro quo" offers of benefits in return for sexual activity.[1]

In 1991, the nomination of Clarence Thomas to the U.S. Supreme Court brought the issue of sexual harassment into the spotlight. During the hearings on his nomination, Anita Hill, a law professor at the University of Oklahoma, testified before the Senate committee that Thomas had sexually harassed her when she worked for him at the Equal Employment Opportunity Commission in the 1980s. Although Hill's testimony was convincing to many, Thomas strongly denied her _____ and was ultimately confirmed as a Supreme Court Justice. Nevertheless, after these hearings, more women began to _____ lawsuits claiming they had been sexually harassed, and most private companies and government agencies now offer training courses to their employees on the subject of sexual harassment.

---

1. Meritor Savings Bank, *FSB v. Vinson*, 477 U.S. 57 (1986).

A nationwide survey in 1994 revealed that twenty-two percent of women in the United States have been sexually harassed.[2] Studies show that sexual harassment frequently occurs in schools, beginning in the sixth grade and continuing through graduate school. According to research, thirty to seventy percent of women experience sexual harassment during their four years of college.[3] In the past few years, a growing number of teachers and professors have been accused of sexual harassment, making this a major issue within academic institutions. In fact, in February of 1992, the U.S. Supreme Court ruled that students could collect money in sexual harassment cases from educational institutions that receive federal funds.[4]

For those found guilty of sexual harassment of students, the punishment usually is _____ from the university or school. Even if a person is acquitted of the charges, his or her reputation is often ruined. Teachers are expected to serve as _____ for their students; thus, it is particularly _____ for them to abuse their power through the forcing of sexual attention on their students. In some universities, policies have been developed to strictly define the relationship between student and teacher in an attempt to prevent such immoral actions. However, these policies may conflict with the right of free speech, a basic value in American higher education, because "First Amendment rights apply to the speech of students and teachers."[5]

What is your opinion?

Write one or two paragraphs expressing your opinion on the issues discussed above.

2. Joannie M. Schrof, "Sex in America," *U.S. News & World Report* 117 (October 17, 1994): 80.
3. Michele A. Paludi, *Sexual Harassment on College Campuses: Abusing the Ivory Power* (Albany: State University of New York Press, 1996), 5.
4. *Franklin v. Gwinnett County Public Schools,* 503 U.S. 60 (1992).
5. U.S. Department of Education, "Office of Civil Rights: Sexual Harassment Guidance: Harassment of Students by School Employees, Other Students, or Third Parties," *Federal Register* 62 (March 13, 1997): 12045.

The Wedding March; dir. Erich Von Stroheim; Fay Wray, 1928, U.S.

Activities

1. Write a letter from Florence to the dean of student affairs, describing the episode in Dr. Duke's office and accusing Dr. Duke of sexual harassment.

2. Does your educational institution have a sexual harassment policy? If so, get a copy of the policy, read it, and discuss it in class. (It is probably in the student handbook.)

3. Make a list of activities that could be considered sexual harassment in the university or in the workplace. Include both speech and conduct. Compare your list with your classmates' lists by putting them on the chalkboard.

4. Conduct a survey of at least ten people. Ask them the questions listed here and report your results to the class.

    1. Do you believe that sexual harassment is a serious problem in the United States?
    2. Have you ever experienced sexual harassment of any kind? If so, please answer questions 3–5.
    3. Where and when did the harassment take place?
    4. What type of action did you take in response to the harassment?
    5. What was the result of your action?

5. It is difficult to balance the prevention of sexual harassment with the right to free speech. Read one of the articles listed here that discuss this issue. Then, after the class is divided into two teams, have a debate on the following topic:

It is more important to prevent sexual harassment than to protect freedom of speech.

Nicks, Sandra D. "Fear in Academia: Concern over Unmerited Accusations of Sexual Harassment." *Journal of Psychology* 130 (January 1996): 79–82.

"Professors Once Shielded by Academic Freedom Now Risk Charges of Sexual Harassment." *CQ Researcher* 6 (February 16, 1996): 162–63.

Small, Mary Jo. "The Guardians of Heloise? Sexual Harassment in Higher Education." *Educational Record* 70 (Spring 1989): 42–45.

Veraldi, Lorna. "Academic Freedom and Sexual Harassment." *Education Digest* 61 (September 1995): 36–39.

6. Choose one of the following role plays for presentation in class. Plan and practice your dialogue before presenting it.

(A) Act out the scene between Florence and Dr. Duke in his office.

(B) Act out a future scene between Florence and Dr. Duke in which she tells him that she is thinking of filing a sexual harassment complaint against him.

Oral Presentation

Prepare and give an oral presentation on one of the topics listed. Use the suggested methods of development to organize your presentation and do library research to gather information.

- What Is Sexual Harassment? (definition, examples)
- Student-Teacher Relationships in the United States and in My Country (contrast)

Chapter Readings

Romancing the Student

Rattled by lawsuits, colleges are cracking down on faculty-student love affairs.

Nancy Gibbs

During the three months in 1993 when she was sleeping with her English professor, Lisa Topol lost 18 pounds. She lost interest in her classes at the University of Pennsylvania, lost her reputation as an honor student and wondered if she was losing her mind. If she tried to break up, she thought, he could ruin her academic career. Then she made some phone calls and learned a bit more about the professor she had come to view as a predator. In June she will tell her story in federal court, but even before a verdict is rendered, the case has prompted Penn to consider more stringent rules on student-teacher sex. Depending on the outcome of her trial, love life on campus may never be the same.

Nancy Gibbs, "Romancing the Student," *Time* 145 (April 3, 1995): 58–59.

Lisa was a senior at the University of Pennsylvania when she found herself embroiled in an affair with a young English professor named Malcolm Woodfield. His tastes ran to whips and riding crops, she told *Philadelphia* magazine, and when she tried to get out of the relationship, the professor bullied her into continuing. She need not worry about flunking his course, she recalls his saying, because "your grade is not based on your work anyway."

In March 1993 Lisa finally told another English professor about the affair; encouraged by assistant ombudsman Gulbun O'Connor, Topol charged Woodfield with sexual harassment. A university ethics committee supported her allegation that Woodfield had abused his academic power. The embattled professor resigned last April, after admitting that he once slept with Topol and engaged in "unethical conduct," though he has denied the other details of their affair.

But Topol has since taken her case even further, in a gesture that is rattling the teeth of campus administrators everywhere. Topol had heard rumors that Woodfield had been in trouble before, and she began asking questions. Before coming to Penn, she learned, he had taught at Bates College in Maine, where some students had also accused him of harassment, but he was allowed to leave quietly in 1991, with the recommendations that helped him land the Penn job.

Topol has since filed civil suits not only against Woodfield and Penn but against Bates as well for failing to warn Penn of Woodfield's record. Having supported her before, Penn has reversed course: in a pretrial memorandum filed in February, Penn charges that the affair "grew out of her strong sexual attraction to and romantic feelings for Woodfield." Penn has asked for her diary to prove her consent; meanwhile, says Topol's lawyer, Alice Ballard, Bates is trying to get records from her psychotherapist.

In the midst of this furor, the Penn faculty executive committee has called for tougher rules against faculty-student romances; it wants to amend the policy that calls such relationships "unethical" so that it would prohibit professors from dating students under their supervision. For her part, Topol doubts this will do any good. "I can't imagine how any student would come forward after seeing what Penn has done to me," she says. "Penn's response has done nothing but make the wounds deeper and more painful."

Penn thus becomes the latest school to turn itself inside out over an issue that dates back to Abelard and Héloise. Through the years so many professors have romanced and often married their students that it seems a quaint, even hypocritical exercise to suddenly try to stop them. "If this policy were applied retroactively," remarks Penn history professor Alan Kors, who married one of his students 20 years ago, "I think a third of the faculty would have resigned."

It has been easy for some critics to cast efforts to legislate sexual mores on campus as the latest prudish gambit of a feminist police state. But the universities that tackled this issue are actually engaged in a practical—rather than an ideological—enterprise: they are trying to prevent lawsuits. In fact, in this era of heightened sensitivity, the legal pressures are coming from all sides. Even as Penn wrestles with the Topol case, another Penn professor, economist David Cass, is charging that the university has sexually harassed *him* by asking about his relationship with a former student and then denying him a post to head the department's graduate program. Last week Cass was busy circulating a petition to try to block the new rules. "I resent the fact that because I'm standing up for my privacy people are drawing an inference that I'm some kind of lecher who has had numerous affairs," he says.

Administrators respond that they are merely extending to the university the same strictures that apply in the workplace: when there is power involved, whether between boss and employee or teacher and student, a sexual relationship opens the door to extortion, exploitation and favoritism. Drawing the lines more boldly, they argue, will protect friendly faculty from oversensitive students, as well as vulnerable students from lascivious professors.

The potential for misunderstandings was amply illustrated this winter at Cornell, where the faculty ethics committee charged that Professor James Maas, a star of the psychology department, harassed four of his former students by hugging and kissing them, buying them expensive presents and making suggestive remarks. Maas calls his behavior affectionate and innocent, an effort to make Cornell a more "warm and caring place"; the angry students call it unwelcome and intimidating. Cornell, with no written policy on student-faculty romance, had a typically equivocal response: the popular professor was stripped of a $25,000 teaching award that he had received in 1993—honoring him for, among other things, creating an "atmosphere of intimacy" in his enormous lecture courses—and told to go and sin no more. Any more complaints, the committee said, and Maas would lose his job.

Harvard claims to have instituted the first restrictions on faculty-student relations in 1984, followed by the University of Iowa in 1986. But the most draconian proposal was debated at the University of Virginia two years ago, where the faculty considered a total ban on student-teacher liaisons, even if the individuals were from different departments. "The majority of the faculty agreed, but they weren't happy about more rules," says Richard Rorty, a Virginia philosophy professor. In the end Virginia fell into the mainstream and approved rules that simply "discourage" relationships in situations where there could be favoritism or the appearance of abuse.

According to a survey by Cynara Stites, a clinical social worker at the University of Connecticut, professors themselves admit the potential for exploitation in such romances: 9 out of 10 agreed that a student who breaks up with a professor risks "unfair reprisals." More than half the male faculty members agreed that a professor who sleeps with a student he supervises is taking advantage of her. "There's a real risk of her losing her entire academic career," explains Stites. "It undermines her self-confidence. She doesn't know whether [her success is] based on her lover or based on merit."

Moreover, the damage of such an affair can extend far beyond the people directly involved. Undoing it is "like unscrambling eggs," says Susan Mask, assistant to the president of the University of Iowa. "It creates serious problems for the faculty. It can fracture a department. The damage has to be weighed against the fun."

Yet many professors insist that even a limited ban can't work; others think it shouldn't be tried. Most college students, after all, are legal adults, capable of consent, and a university of all places should respect personal liberty. Professor bell hooks at City College in New York, who had affairs with professors while a student and once became the lover of a younger man after she had taught him, says, "No feminist thinks that banning abortions would keep women from having them. So why do we think that banning relationships between faculty and students will keep them from having them?"

Barry Dank, a sociologist at California State University at Long Beach who argues that such prohibitions "infantilize" students, has formed a loosely knit group of about 100 professors and students called Consenting Academics for Sexual Equity. He believes the spread of campus rules on romance will leave professors less accessible to students. "It's creating a paranoia that is really affecting whatever is left of an academic community," he says.

But Stites, for one, is confident that "once faculty members know where the line is, people can relax about normal mentoring, normal faculty-student relationships. If they do not know where the line is, they will not feel safe to do anything that might be misconstrued."

Students, Soldiers, Justice

One of the worst crimes is likely to be concealed by its victim.

Tom Gerety

To a college president, the United States Army looks like an awfully big campus, with dorms and dining halls, playing fields, and an astonishing number of vehicles. But what does not look so different is the number of people not much past their 18th or 19th birthdays and a long way from home. Coeducation has given campuses decades of experience with the sexual assault and harassment problems that the military now confronts. Campus experience suggests a number of insights that the military should take to heart:

• Underreporting is not going to go away soon. Female soldiers and college students feel the same burden of shame and guilt on and off their bases and campuses. Our culture, along with most others, imposes this additional victimization on women subjected to sexual assault. Education is the only way out of the cruel irony—that one of the worst crimes one human being can perpetrate on another is the crime most likely to be concealed by its victim.

Again and again on our campuses, we teach that students must not hesitate to report what has happened to them. Deans, peer counselors, professors, doctors and nurses, and police reinforce the same message: "We will support you if you complain and we will help you to prosecute the charges of sexual assault and harassment." But fear remains a powerful deterrent: the fear, in the first place, of stepping forward to accuse someone who is either in a position of authority or else a member of a relatively close-knit peer group. It is not an unreasonable fear, because the accusation of sexual assault is almost always met with a counteraccusation: "You consented; you asked for it; you lied." Most perniciously, there is the fear that the institution will side with the person you accuse, out of resistance to the "bad news" or because of due process.

Tom Gerety, "Students, Soldiers, Justice," *Christian Science Monitor,* January 2, 1997, 19.

So the education that is called for is both broad and deep. Ultimately, it must engage the entire legacy of shame that our culture attaches to sexuality.

• Procedures should be simple, straightforward—and fair. But no procedure yet devised makes this easy or risk-free for the victim who comes forward. Typically, physical evidence is in short supply in date-rape and harassment cases. Complaints are often made days or weeks after the event. The better the victim and the perpetrator knew one another, the more likely the perpetrator did what he did without witnesses, in a private setting. Often the perpetrator used force without leaving bruises or cuts. The result is that the prosecutor has a case that depends on circumstances observed by few, on conflicting testimony, and on inferences about the character and motivation of the perpetrator.

Standards of proof

On campuses, the standard of proof is lower than in a criminal trial, and lawyers are often barred. The military may not have the luxury of trying such cases under procedures less stringent than criminal law. The upshot in these cases is that any system of due process—and certainly one that presumes the innocence of the accused—will lead to a high number of acquittals. And acquittals after bitter trials discourage victims from pressing charges. Thus the road is long and difficult, requiring tenacity, with cynicism a constant temptation.

• Any institution that wants to reduce the incidence of sexual assault will need to accept the limits of its own rules and procedures. In many, perhaps most, cases, prosecution will not be successful—not because no crime occurred but because none can be proven. This means that prevention efforts cannot rely very much on deterrence. The likelihood of escaping conviction, or of not even being accused in the first place, remains high for many perpetrators. Procedures that make the victims feel that they should come forward will gradually change the culture of shame and intimidation that surrounds rape and harassment. But the most important lesson for those of us who supervise young men and women in residential settings is that prevention is not only the most humane but also the more practical strategy.

The starting point

This raises the question of the best preventive strategies: Peer counseling; women's support groups; explicit discussion of techniques for resisting male imposition whether forceful or seductive; clear and repeated condemnation of abusive and insulting sexism. These and other promising efforts all have a common starting point. Without exception they involve an insistence on the equality of women in general and on the power of individual women to tell men—including men in authority—that insult and assault will not be tolerated.

On campuses we have abolished most arrangements or traditions that put upper-class males in positions of authority over underclass females. We are committed to making men and women equal participants in our work, with no jobs or assignments off-limits to women. So far, the military continues to insist on unequal numbers of men and women and to limit the kinds of jobs to which women can aspire. Moreover, the military's drilling and training seem at present to require some senior-level men—the drill sergeants—to exercise authority over the daily lives of the most vulnerable women in the services. The advice from colleges and universities would be to find another way to train young female recruits for a coeducational Army.

Equality is the hardest lesson of all in the military as it is on campus. On campuses like mine, where coeducation is two decades old, women continue to feel that many of our practices and expectations reflect the males-only campus we once were. The military wants equality for women, but it also wants to limit their numbers and close off many assignments to them. It is hard to believe sexism will go away until full equality is the goal.

Tom Gerety is president of Amherst College in Amherst, Massachusetts.

Comprehension

"Romancing the Student"
1. Explain the case of Lisa Topol and Professor Malcolm Woodfield of the University of Pennsylvania.
2. Why do university administrators want to impose tougher rules against faculty-student romances?
3. Describe the case of Professor James Maas at Cornell.
4. What risks do students face if they have sexual relationships with their professors?
5. Why do some professors think a ban on student-faculty relationships won't work or shouldn't even be tried?
6. What is the main idea of this article?
7. Do you believe that all student-faculty relationships should be banned?

"Students, Soldiers, Justice"
1. Why are cases of sexual harassment and sexual assault underreported and concealed?
2. What kind of education does the author believe is called for to end this underreporting?
3. Even if the procedure for filing complaints is simple, why is it difficult and risky for victims to come forward?
4. What does *due process* mean?
5. Why is prosecution not successful in most cases of sexual assault or harassment?
6. What is the most important lesson for those who supervise young men and women in residential settings?
7. What are the best prevention strategies?
8. What advice does the author give the military?
9. What is the hardest lesson of all in the military and on college campuses?
10. Why does the author, who is president of Amherst College, believe he can make suggestions to the military about how to handle sexual assault and sexual harassment?

Zorba the Greek; dir. Michael Cacoyannis, 1964, U.S.-Greece

Strategy Session

Imagine that you are a college student who has been sexually harassed by your professor on many occasions throughout the semester. You have experienced both unwanted behavior and verbal harassment of a sexual nature.

Which strategy would you use in this situation and why? Provide a written justification for your decision. If none of the listed strategies would be your choice, you may develop your own strategy.

1. Continue to act unresponsive and to ignore the inappropriate behavior, hoping that the professor will lose interest in you and leave you alone.

2. Write a letter to the professor stating that you will take legal action if the inappropriate and unacceptable behavior does not stop.

3. Make an appointment to meet with the dean of student affairs, the professor's

supervisor, to inform the dean of the professor's inappropriate and unacceptable behavior.

4. File a formal complaint with the university, charging the professor with sexual harassment.

5. Hire a lawyer to file a lawsuit against the university alleging sexual harassment, under the federal education statute (Title IX of the Education Amendments of 1972).

6. Other: _____

Suggested Films

Disclosure (1994)
Don't Do It, Don't Allow It (Intermedia: 1994)
Educating Rita (1983 Britain)
Queen Kelly (1928 silent film)
Sexual Harassment in the Academic Workplace (Intermedia: 1993)
Sexual Harassment in the Workplace (American Media, Inc.: 1990)
Sexual Harassment in the Workplace and Classroom: What You Should Know (Cambridge Research Group: 1994)
Thelma & Louise (1991)

Additional Readings

Adato, Allison. "Campus Report: Student-Faculty Sex." *Seventeen* 52 (December 1993): 50.

Bryant, Anne. "Sexual Harassment in School Takes Its Toll." *USA Today: The Magazine of the American Scene* 123 (March 1995): 40–41.

Kent, Debra. "Sexual Harassment." *Seventeen* 50 (November 1991): 46, 48.

Patai, Daphne. "Never Offending Anyone: What Price Utopia?" *Education Digest* 61 (January 1996): 48–51.

Pichaske, David R. "When Students Make Sexual Advances." *Chronicle of Higher Education* 41 (February 24, 1995): B1–2.

Pollan, Stephen M., and Mark Levine. "Confronting an Alleged Harasser." *Working Woman* 21 (January 1996): 59.

Roth, Elizabeth. "The Civil Rights History of 'Sex': A Sexist, Racist Congressional Joke." *Ms.* 3 (March–April 1993): 84–85.

Saltzman, Amy. "Life after the Lawsuit." *U.S. News & World Report* 121 (August 19, 1996): 57–61.

Sanchez, Rene. "In School, Early Lessons on Sexual Harassment." *Washington Post,* October 4, 1996, A1, A4.

Woodhull, Angela Victoria. "Coping with Sexual Harassment." In *Coping with Difficult Teachers*. Rochester, VT: Schenkman Books, 1996.

Chapter 11
Academic Integrity: Plagiarism

Horse Feathers; dir. Norman Z. McLeod; the Marx Brothers, 1932, U.S.

What would you say if a friend offered to pay you to write the research paper that was required in his or her course?

Exploration

After reading the following statements, respond to each one by writing *yes* or *no*.

1. I have a clear understanding of what plagiarism is and know how to avoid it. _____

2. I am familiar with the correct format for footnotes and a bibliography or reference list. _____

3. Plagiarism is not a common academic offense in my country. _____

4. I would not turn in a paper that someone else had written for me. _____

5. I know students who have plagiarized their papers and other written work. _____

6. Handing in a paper as your own when someone else has written it is unethical. _____

7. Students who intentionally plagiarize or commit other serious academic violations should be expelled from their university or college. _____

8. Many students try to find ways to beat the system and get better grades. _____

9. Professors should not accuse students of plagiarism unless they have definite proof. _____

10. Plagiarism by students is a natural result of the excessive pressure put on college students today. _____

11. It is not necessary to cite the source when you copy several sentences from a book or an article if you change a few words. _____

12. Nearly all students have plagiarized at one time or another. _____

Glossary

abstract	a short summary of a longer written document
accuse	to bring charges against someone for doing wrong, breaking the law
ache	to have dull, steady pain
allegations	statements of accusation that must be proven
bibliography	a list of the books and articles used or referred to by an author
brain trust	a group of experts acting as advisers, specifically during the Franklin Delano Roosevelt New Deal (1933–45)
bucks	money (slang)
citations	references to author, title, source, date, and page of quotations; passages cited or quoted by an author
contemplated	considered; thought about intently
credits	units that certify a student's successful completion of courses
defiantly	with open and bold resistance
excessive	being too much or too great
expelled	forced to leave by official action
first rate	excellent; very good; of the highest rank or quality
footnotes	notes giving author, title, source, date, and page number for a citation in a paper, usually at the bottom of a page (called *endnotes* if at the end of the paper)

format	the general plan of organization or arrangement of materials
grinned	smiled broadly as in amusement
intentionally	done for a purpose and by design
irritation	annoyance, impatience
offense	the act of breaking a law; crime
panic stricken	badly frightened; hysterical and out of control from fear
plagiarism	passing off the words or ideas of another person as one's own
plagiarize	to present as one's own an idea or a product derived from another
prestigious	having an honored position in people's minds
principle	a fundamental truth or law upon which others are based
probation	the status of a person being tested or on trial because of misconduct
proof	conclusive evidence; anything serving to establish the truth
proposing	putting forth for consideration; making a proposal
references	sources of information in a paper, such as books and articles, to which a reader is referred
severe	serious or grave; harsh or strict
stammered	said with rapid repetitions of syllables because of embarrassment
strict	exact, precise; inflexibly maintained
sweat it	worry about something (slang)
tempted	inclined strongly to do something immoral
throbbing	beating strongly or fast
treated	dealt with
unethical	not ethical; not conforming to standards of conduct
violations	infringements or breaches of a law or rule

Case Study: What Money Can Buy

After you read the case study, discuss the major problem the case presents and answer the discussion questions with the members of the class. Then write a case study report following the format that is provided.

Igor Zakarov, a Russian student from Moscow, has a 3.8 GPA and is in the honors program at a prestigious university in Virginia. He has taken 16 credits each semester and is now in his third year, with plans to go to summer school in order to graduate a semester early. Igor already is looking into which graduate schools to apply to for his MA in political science. But right now, April 24, Igor is totally exhausted and feeling somewhat annoyed that although the semester is almost over, he still has to turn in a twenty-five-page research paper in his American Presidency course by May 1.

Igor wants badly to get an excellent grade on that paper, but he is so worn out that he feels unable to even walk over to the library and begin his research, which he should have completed by now. In addition, writing has always been extremely difficult for Igor: his papers take him a long time to complete, and they usually have minor errors in grammar, particularly the use of articles and sometimes verb tenses and prepositions.

The Paper Chase; dir. James Bridges, 1973, U.S.

After drinking a few cups of coffee and eating a sandwich, Igor had finally gotten himself into the mood for the library. But just then his best friend, George, arrived at his door. Igor and George decided to go out for a beer at Houlihan's, and two hours later, Igor was starting to tell George about his research paper that was due in a week.

"George, I just can't get going on this damn paper," said Igor with irritation in his voice. "And to make matters worse, if I don't get an A on the paper, my final grade for the course could be a B since the paper counts for 60 percent of the course, and I didn't do too well on the midterm."

"Hey, don't sweat it, Igor. I can solve your paper problem in no time. What topic are you writing on?" asked George.

"Oh, anything about Franklin Delano Roosevelt. I was going to concentrate on his brain trust mostly, but it could have another focus if I want. Why? Do you have material on this subject?" Igor looked at George with curiosity.

"Not really, but I can get you a paper—did you say about twenty-five pages long—on Franklin Roosevelt if you want me to," said George.

"What do you mean by 'get me a paper'? Are you joking? Don't tell me you are in the business of buying term papers for lazy students," laughed Igor.

"No, actually, I'm not in the business, but I can get my hands on papers on just about any topic you need, so how about if I help you out, and you'll owe me something when you get your A," replied George. "It won't be the first time this has happened on this campus."

Igor considered what George was proposing for a few minutes. It wasn't that Igor had not heard of students buying ready-made term papers, but until now he hadn't seriously contemplated doing such a thing. He knew several students back in Russia who had done it. Of course, plagiarism was not treated in the same way in Russia as it was in the United States because in Russia, published ideas were seen as belonging to everyone. So the rules about borrowing other people's ideas were less strict, which made a lot of sense, especially for university students, and it really cut down on the footnotes.

The more he thought about it, the more he could see the practical value in George's suggestion, and he felt tempted but worried.

"George, what if Professor Graham finds out I didn't write the paper?" Igor said fearfully. "Maybe I could be expelled from the university."

"That won't happen," promised George. "Your writing is good, and this paper will be similar to your other papers, except you won't be spending your valuable time writing it. Oh, sure, it will cost you a few bucks—maybe $50, but look what money can buy," said George, laughing.

"I guess that's not too much, considering how busy I am and how I hate to do research. When can you get the paper?" Igor asked.

"I'll have it in a couple of days," promised George.

Igor grinned and drank some more beer. He had to admit that George really knew how to play the academic game. What a relief not to have to read all those books and articles and write all those pages. As Igor continued to turn the idea over in his mind, it began to make total sense.

"Well, give me a call as soon as you have the paper so I can read it to make sure it is good. I can't turn in something unless it is first rate, you know," he warned George.

"Relax, Igor," George replied. "It'll be great."

Igor was pleased with the twenty-five-page paper on Franklin Roosevelt that George brought him two days later. It was clearly and logically written, with excellent use of supporting sources, plenty of footnotes, and a long bibliography. After he turned it in, he relaxed and began planning his summer school schedule. When the phone rang the following day, Igor was surprised to hear the voice of Professor Graham.

"Igor, could you drop by my office this afternoon? I would like to talk with you about your paper," said the professor.

"Oh, sure," stammered Igor. "What time?"

"How about three o'clock?" suggested Professor Graham.

"That's fine," said Igor, whose head was beginning to ache at the thought of what his professor might ask him.

Professor Graham was not looking cheerful when Igor entered his office.

"Igor, I am surprised that you would hand in this paper on Franklin Roosevelt. It is very different from your usual writing style, and I regret that I must ask you if it is your own work or if you have plagiarized it," said Graham.

"Uh, yes, sure, it is my own work. I did all the research and spent a long time writing it, and there were so many revisions and rewrites over the past month," answered Igor defiantly.

"Well, I have some serious doubts and will have to ask you to bring me all your notes and also to write an abstract of the paper at this time," said Graham.

"Now? I have another appointment—couldn't I just take the paper home and write the abstract there tonight?" asked Igor.

"No, I'm sorry, but you have to write it here. Let's get going on it, Igor. Since you have been reading about this topic for so long and rewriting and revising, you should have no trouble doing a 200-word abstract," said Graham with a severe expression on his face.

Igor began his abstract, but it wasn't easy for him, and when he finished one hour later, his headache had become an intense throbbing pain. He handed the abstract to Professor Graham, who handed him a piece of paper in return.

"This is a section of the University Academic Integrity Policy that you might want to read," said Graham. "I'll be in touch."

As Igor left Professor Graham's office, he quickly read the following statement: "In accordance with the University's Academic Regulations, cheating in any form will not be tolerated. This includes plagiarism and receiving inappropriate assistance on examinations and assignments. Cheating is an extremely serious academic offense. Allegations of cheating will be referred to the dean for action."

Igor felt sick. How would he ever be able to explain this if Professor Graham decided to formally charge him with plagiarism? He was ashamed and panic stricken. If only he had written the paper himself. Why had he listened to that dumb George? What a major mistake!

Discussion

1. Have you ever been tempted to plagiarize anything?
2. Why do students intentionally plagiarize?
3. How does Igor feel about writing papers in general?
4. What is George's attitude toward academic regulations?
5. Why did Igor agree to buy the paper from George?
6. Should Igor blame George for his situation? Why or why not?
7. What made Professor Graham suspicious that Igor had not written the paper?
8. Why did Professor Graham ask Igor to write an abstract of the paper?
9. What should Professor Graham do about this situation?
10. What options does Igor have in this situation?

Case Study Report

Working with a partner or in a small group, write a case study report analyzing the problem that Igor is facing in regard to the paper he turned in to Professor Graham.

I. Statement of the Problem
II. Suggestion of Possible Solutions

III. Evaluation of Possible Solutions
IV. Selection of a Solution

Vocabulary

Fill in the blanks with the most appropriate words. Use each word only once.

plagiarizing	expelled	principle	tempting	bibliography
severe	citation	probation	treated	violations

The number of cases of plagiarism on college campuses as well as in the world of publishing in general is increasing. Recently, several well-known American authors and journalists have been accused of _____ material in order to use it in their books, and lawsuits have been filed against them. Other authors have filed lawsuits against those who have accused them of plagiarism and have won their cases. Obviously the issue is quite complex. Many people throughout history, including Shakespeare, have copied from other sources. The real question is: What is plagiarism?

It is often _____ to use the words and sentences of those whose ideas are expressed with beauty and originality. Moreover, some students, when writing papers, unintentionally borrow the language and thoughts of other writers because they are unfamiliar with the strict rules on plagiarism in the United States. But the knowledgeable writer understands that whenever he or she uses material written and developed by someone else, citations in the form of footnotes and a(n) _____ listing all sources must be part of the document. Otherwise, the writer, in failing to cite his or her sources, is taking credit for other persons' ideas. These rules apply not only to direct quotations from an author's text but also to paraphrases of an author's language.

At academic institutions in the United States, _____ of the academic integrity code result in a wide range of punishments. For example, for opening a book during a closed-book exam, a student could receive a letter of warning or a failing grade in the course or be placed on one semester of _____. However, while other types of violations may result in less _____ punishment, plagiarism is considered an extremely serious offense that reveals a total disregard for honesty, so students who intentionally plagiarize are usually _____ from their schools.

Cheating of any kind is unethical, but plagiarism goes against the basic _____ of a person's right to ownership of his or her intellectual property when it is in written or recorded form. As a result, in the United States, it is _____ as a major offense. The U.S. Constitution and the Copyright Act of 1976 both protect the author's exclusive right to his or her writing. Nevertheless, today the Internet and the World Wide Web are making the detection of plagiarism even more difficult and complicated. Currently, copyright law does not apply to the Internet, and writers can publish whatever they want.[1] As James R. Kincaid says: "Who will police property in cyberspace, with words going who knows where and coming from who knows where, folding in on themselves, lawless and rootless?"[2]

Not all cultures view plagiarism in the same light. In some parts of the world, people do not subscribe to the idea that authors own their words; rather, language is considered to belong to everyone. Thus, copying or imitating another writer's language is acceptable. However, in other cultures, such as the North American culture, where it is illegal to borrow or share another's words, a writer must follow the rules of copyright and _____ of sources. According to Darsie Bowden in "Coming to Terms," these clashing value systems can lead to confusion and emotional conflict for teachers and students: "Especially in a culture where classrooms are increasingly diverse, both teachers and scholars need to address more fully the value systems that make plagiarism a crime."[3]

What is your opinion?

Write one or two paragraphs expressing your point of view on the issues discussed above.

1. Kavita Varma, "Footnotes in Electronic Age," *USA Today*, February 7, 1996, D7.
2. James R. Kincaid, "Purloined Letters," *New Yorker* 72 (January 20, 1997): 97.
3. Darsie Bowden, "Coming to Terms," *English Journal* 85 (April 1, 1996): 82.

Askndrie . . . Lie? (Alexandria . . . Why?); dir. Youssef Chahine, 1978, Egypt/Algeria

Activities

1. Give a solution to the case study from the points of view of
   - Igor;
   - George; and
   - Professor Graham.

2. Find out if your educational institution has a statement on plagiarism. If so, get a copy of the document, read it, and discuss it in class. (It is usually part of the school's academic integrity code, which is probably in the student handbook.)

3. Write a letter from Igor to Professor Graham in which he admits that he plagiarized the paper, explains why, and suggests a method of punishment for his unethical behavior.

4. The definition of plagiarism varies from country to country. For example, in some societies, copying the words of an author without citing the source may be considered acceptable rather than unethical behavior. Describe your country's rules about a writer's citation of sources by answering the following questions.
   - Are words considered the property of the writer?
   - When are footnotes required?
   - When are quotation marks used?

- When is a bibliography or list of references necessary?
- In what ways, if any, do these rules differ from the rules in the United States?

5. After the class is divided into two teams, have a debate on the following topic: The rules on plagiarism in the United States are too strict and should be revised.

6. Choose one of the following role plays for presentation in class. Plan and practice your dialogue before presenting it.

   (A) Act out the scene between Igor and Professor Graham in Graham's office.

   (B) Act out a future meeting between Igor and Professor Graham in which Igor admits that he plagiarized, explains his behavior, and asks for a second chance.

Oral Presentation

Prepare and give an oral presentation on one of the topics listed. Use the suggested methods of development to organize your presentation and do library research to gather information.

- Forms of Academic Violations and Types of Punishments (classification)
- How to Write a Research Paper (process)

Chapter Readings

Telling Students about Copyright

Paulette Bochnig Sharkey

What can you do to stop students from copying a literary gem and calling it their own? You can appeal to their conscience *and* you can tell them about copyright, *if* you understand the basics yourself. This explanation is in the form of answers to questions students will probably ask:

What is copyright? Copyright is the legal right of authors to prohibit others from copying their work. The official notice of copyright is the letter "C" within a circle, followed by the year of the copyright and the name of the copyright owner.

You'll often see two copyright notices in a book, one for the author, another for the illustrator. In fact, once you're aware of copyright, you'll be amazed at where that little C turns up—on posters, comic strips, even record albums. That's because copyright law covers not only poems, magazine articles, stories, and books, but also computer programs, songs (both music and words), choreography, photography, drawings, movies, and sound recordings.

Can I ever quote from someone else's work? Those who wrote the copyright law realized that writers often want to quote from copyrighted materials. They provided a legal way to do this in certain cases, within certain limits. It's called *fair use,* and it means you may quote short excerpts from copyrighted materials for educational and critical purposes. Despite years of debate, there are no definitions of exactly how brief those quotations must be to qualify as fair use. But as a general guideline, the courts have ruled that you can quote up to 300 words from a book for discussion in your writing. You may also quote a

Paulette Bochnig Sharkey, "Telling Students about Copyright," *Education Digest* 58 (September 1992): 66–68.

line or two from a poem. Use quotation marks or block indentations to set off the words, and be sure to identify who said the words and where you found them.

To quote copyrighted material beyond fair use, you need written permission from the copyright owner to avoid infringement (violation of the copyright owner's rights). Write to the magazine or book publisher stating what you want to use and how you will use it. Send an envelope for the reply, stamped and addressed to yourself.

How long does copyright last? Copyright protection for literary works published since 1978 lasts the life of the author plus 50 years. Works published before 1950 are protected for a maximum of 75 years—those published between 1950 and 1977, for a maximum of 56 years. After that, the copyright expires, and the work becomes part of the public domain. Public domain material may be freely quoted by anyone. No permission is necessary, even if you exceed fair use, because there is no copyright left to infringe upon. Of course, this doesn't mean you can copy material written by someone else and pretend it's your own. That's plagiarism. If you quote from someone else's writing in your own work—whether the quoted material is copyrighted or in the public domain—give credit where it's due by identifying your source.

Is everything covered by copyright? No. Copyright law protects works that are "fixed in a tangible form of expression." That means a speech never written down or recorded doesn't count. And neither do the good ideas residing in a writer's head! Ideas cannot be copyrighted; only the words put together to express the ideas can be. You can get ideas for your writing from many places. You might read a magazine article about wind surfing and decide to write about it yourself. That's fine—you haven't infringed on the magazine writer's copyright because you plan to write your own piece, not copy his. The other writer served as your inspiration.

There are a few more categories of material that cannot be protected by copyright. Names, titles, and other short phrases are not eligible (although these are often protected by trademarks). Neither are lists of information considered common property (for example, height and weight charts) or encyclopedia-type facts such as dates and places. These are not original works as required by copyright law. And imagine how hard research would be if facts were copyrighted! Names, titles, and facts are in the public domain, and you may use them freely without quotation marks and without paying homage to anyone else. (Of course, if you start "borrowing" whole sentences from an encyclopedia to insert into your own writing, it's a different story!)

How can I avoid infringing on copyright? All writers build on the ideas of others who wrote before them. Information in books, newspapers, and magazines is there for you to use, but keep in mind these basics:

1. Give credit to other writers when you use information prepared by them. This is citing or acknowledging your sources, done through footnotes and bibliography you include in your writing. If you use part of another writer's work without citing your source, you are presenting it as your own. That's plagiarism, plain and simple. Your footnotes and bibliography allow your readers to judge how reliable and up-to-date your sources are, and tell them where to find more about the subject.

2. Follow fair-use guidelines when you use quotations in your writing. This is easier if you choose your quotations carefully. Don't quote straightforward statements you could

write yourself. Quote what adds authority and color to your writing. Show clearly those words that are not your own by putting quotation marks around them and giving your source. Be absolutely accurate in your quotations. Authors are usually pleased to be quoted but not to be misquoted.

3. Whenever possible, put things into your own words. If you're tempted to copy word-for-word when you do research, try this: Read part of the material, and then write down the same ideas you have read without looking at the original. This is paraphrasing—expressing someone else's ideas in your own words.

What happens if I violate copyright law? Sirens will not sound; police officers won't appear at your door. Copyright law is enforced by copyright owners. Authors must discover you have "stolen" their work and file a lawsuit against you to prove copyright infringement. But it does happen. And consider, too, that respect for the property of others—in this case, their writing—is simply a matter of honesty.

Is my writing covered by copyright? Yes. Copyright law recognizes you as the owner of your writing. You don't need to register your work with the U.S. Copyright Office or publish it to claim copyright. Even the official copyright notice isn't necessary. The moment your poem or story is in "fixed form," whether written on paper, typed into a computer, or read into a tape recorder, it is protected by copyright law.

Where can I get more information about copyright? Write to the Register of Copyrights (Copyright Office, Library of Congress, Washington, DC 20559) for a free booklet called "Copyright Basics." Give your name, address, and zip code.

Paulette Bochnig Sharkey, formerly a university reference librarian, is a freelance indexer and writer.

Note Book

Students at Middlebury College who plagiarize may soon face a new punishment: having the offense recorded on their transcript.

Until now, the college punished plagiarizers by denying them credit for the work that was copied. In some cases, students were suspended, but their academic records did not indicate that they had plagiarized.

A committee of faculty members and students is now considering a proposal to specify on the transcripts of some students that they were found guilty of plagiarism.

"The threat of having it on their transcript has a cautionary effect," says Don J. Wyatt, vice-president for undergraduate affairs, who originated the proposal. "It will make students be more thoughtful before they cheat."

Some faculty members object to the change. "After students have carried out their punishment, they ought to be given a second chance," says John Emerson, a professor of mathematics and computer science. "Their mistake shouldn't have to hang over them for the rest of their lives."

But Mr. Wyatt points out that the new penalty would apply only to repeat offenders and to students who directly lied to the college about plagiarizing.

The committee studying the proposal is to issue a report in March.

"Note Book," *Chronicle of Higher Education* 43 (November 22, 1996): A35.

Comprehension

"Telling Students about Copyright"
1. Define copyright and explain its purpose.
2. What is *fair use* and how can you apply it?
3. What is public domain material?
4. How can a writer avoid plagiarism?
5. What things are not protected by copyright?
6. How can you obey the copyright laws?
7. When does your writing become protected by copyright law?

"Note Book"
1. What may be the new punishment for Middlebury College students who plagiarize?
2. How does this policy differ from the previous policy?
3. What effects does the vice president think the policy will have on students?
4. Why do some faculty members object to the change in policy?
5. To whom will the new penalty apply?

Strategy Session

Imagine that you are a professor who is teaching a course in which every student has to write a ten-page research paper. One of your students who has very weak writing skills has turned in a perfectly written paper that is obviously plagiarized.

Which strategy would you use in this situation and why? Provide a written justification for your decision. If none of the listed strategies would be your choice, you may develop your own strategy.

1. Before you grade the paper, ask the student to bring you all his or her notes, outlines, and sources and warn the student that plagiarism is a serious offense.

2. Return the paper to the student without a grade and ask him or her to write another paper because you do not accept plagiarized work.

3. Give the student an F on the paper and an F in the course.

4. File a formal complaint charging the student with violating the university academic integrity code.

5. Meet with the chairperson of your department to tell the chairperson that a student has plagiarized a paper and ask for advice on what to do.

6. Other: _____

Suggested Films

Back to School (1986)
Cyrano de Bergerac (1950 and 1990 France)
Issues Facing the Nation (C-SPAN: 1991)
The Paper Chase (1973)
Roxanne (1987)

Additional Readings

Bowden, Darsie. "Coming to Terms." *English Journal* 85 (April 1, 1996): 82–84.

DeLoughry, Thomas. "Self-Detection Programs Help Students Deal with Plagiarism." *Chronicle of Higher Education* 35 (December 14, 1988): A14.

Freedman, Morris. "Plagiarism among Professors or Students Should Not Be Excused or Treated Gingerly." *Chronicle of Higher Education* 34 (February 10, 1988): A48.

Goldin, Davidson. "A Brisk Market Develops in College Term Papers." *New York Times,* November 22, 1995, B9.

Goode, Stephen. "Trying to Declaw the Campus Copycats." *Insight on the News* 9 (May 3, 1993): 10–13+.

Gorin, Julia. "Copy Comrades." *New York* 28 (December 25, 1995): 26–27.

Hitchens, Christopher. "Steal This Article." *Vanity Fair* no. 429 (May 1996): 58–63.

Kincaid, James R. "Purloined Letters." *New Yorker* 72 (January 20, 1997): 93–97.

McCollum, Kelly. "Web Site Where Students Share Term Papers Has Professors Worried about Plagiarism." *Chronicle of Higher Education* 42 (August 2, 1996): A28.

Meikle, James. "Degree Thesis Proves a Steal." *Guardian,* September 27, 1994, 1, 6.

Newman, Richard. "How to Write A-Grade Papers." In *The Complete Guide to College Success: What Every Student Needs to Know.* New York: New York University Press, 1995.

Sanchez, Rene. "University Tries to Pull Plug on Internet Paper Mills." *Washington Post,* November 5, 1997, A1, A14.

Thompson, Lenora C., and Portia G. Williams. "But I Changed Three Words! Plagiarism in the ESL Classroom." *Clearing House* 69 (September 1995): 27–29.

Varma, Kavita. "Footnotes in Electronic Age." *USA Today,* February 7, 1996, D7.

"What Plagiarism Is—And Isn't." *Washington Post,* January 8, 1994, A12.

White, Edward. "Too Many Campuses Want to Sweep Student Plagiarism under the Rug." *Chronicle of Higher Education* 39 (February 24, 1993): A44.

Witherspoon, Abigail. "This Pen for Hire." *Harper's* 290 (June 1995): 49–57.

Chapter 12
Personal Relationships: Racism and Prejudice

Guess Who's Coming to Dinner; dir. Stanley Kramer; Katherine Hepburn, Sidney Poitier, Spencer Tracy, 1967, U.S.

How would you respond if an attractive and intelligent person who was not a member of your religion or ethnic group asked you out on a date?

Exploration

After reading the following statements, respond to each one by writing *yes* or *no*.

1. I feel comfortable being with people of all religions and ethnic groups. _____

2. I prefer to spend time with people who are like me in terms of religion and culture. _____

3. The kind of social life I have in the United States is different from my social life in

   my country. _____

4. My parents would be displeased if I dated someone whose religion was different

   from mine. _____

5. My parents would be displeased if I married someone whose ethnic background was

   different from mine. _____

6. Racism is a problem in the United States. _____

7. Minority groups in my country face prejudice and discrimination. _____

8. There is very little racism in my country. _____

9. I consider myself an open-minded, tolerant person who treats all people equally.

   _____

10. In the United States, there is a great deal of prejudice against minorities and foreign-

    ers. _____

11. The laws in the United States protect people against racial discrimination. _____

12. I have not been the victim of prejudice or discrimination. _____

Glossary

abolish	to put an end to; to do away with completely
affirmative action	a system encouraging the hiring and admission of minorities
belligerently	with hostility and aggression
boy	demeaning term used by whites for African American males
browse	to glance through books in a casual way
cops	police officers
deal with	to handle; to cope with
dean	the head of a division, faculty, college, or school of a university
desegregating	abolishing the separation of races in public schools
discriminate	to show partiality or prejudice in treatment, specifically action directed against the welfare of minority groups; to make a difference in treatment or favor on a basis other than individual merit
discrimination	showing partiality or prejudice in treatment, specifically action directed against the welfare of minority groups; prejudicial outlook, action, or treatment; denial of equal opportunity
encounter	to face
equal	the same for each member of a group, class, or society

ethnic group	group distinguished by customs, characteristics, language, common history
extrovert	a person whose interest is more in the environment and other people than in himself or herself; a person who is active and expressive rather than introspective
First Amendment	the amendment to the U.S. Constitution that guarantees the right to freedom of speech
hang out	to spend time with
harass	to annoy persistently
ignorant	having little knowledge, education, or experience; uneducated
ignore	to pay no attention to; to disregard deliberately
integrate	to abolish segregation and permit free and equal association among racial groups
intolerant	unwilling to grant or share social, political, or professional rights
judged	formed an idea or opinion about someone or something
minority	a racial, religious, ethnic, or political group smaller than and differing from the controlling group in a community or nation
narrow-minded	lacking in tolerance or breadth of vision
outspoken	frank; spoken boldly or candidly
poor white trash	derogatory term for poor white people
prejudice	an irrational attitude of hostility directed against an individual, a group, or a race or their supposed characteristics
racism	racial prejudice or discrimination; a belief that racial differences produce an inherent superiority of a particular race
racist	having the belief that racial differences produce an inherent superiority of a particular race
segregate	to compel racial groups to live apart from each other, to go to separate schools, and to use separate social facilities
self-confidence	a belief in oneself and one's own abilities; confidence
sexist	believing in the exploitation and social domination of members of one sex by the other, specifically of women by men
shrugged off	dismissed or disregarded in a carefree way
slam	to hang up with force and noise
slashed	cut with a sweeping stroke of a knife
stand	to put up with; to tolerate; to go on enduring
staring	looking steadily and intently at a person
threatening	expressing one's intention of hurting or punishing
tolerant	showing sympathy or indulgence for beliefs or practices differing from or conflicting with one's own
transition	passing from one condition, activity, or place to another

Guess Who's Coming to Dinner; dir. Stanley Kramer; Katherine Hepburn, Sidney Poitier, Spencer Tracy, 1967, U.S.

Case Study: Seeing the World as Black or White

After you read the case study, discuss the major problem the case presents and answer the discussion questions with the members of the class. Then write a case study report following the format that is provided.

> Francine Claudel has only been living in the United States for two months. However, as a sophomore transfer student from a large university in Paris, France, she has been making the transition to life at the large state university in Louisiana rather easily. Francine, who is completely fluent in English, comes from a diplomatic family and has lived all over the world. She is an independent young woman and an extrovert who makes friends quickly and enjoys being with all kinds of people. Her self-confidence is high, and she is rarely influenced by the opinions of others.

When the doorbell rang after dinner on Tuesday night, Francine was surprised to see Tony Gates and Joe Hawkins standing on the doorstep. Although she knew both of them from her African American Literature class, she had not spent any time with them outside of class.

"Hey, Francine, we were in the neighborhood, so we decided to come by. What's happening? Want to go out to Border's Books and browse around and get a cup of espresso?" asked Tony.

"That sounds good. I love the espresso there," said Francine.

Walking into Border's, Francine noticed that some of the students were staring at her and her two friends. She wondered what their problem was but just shrugged it off.

Later, when the three of them were leaving Border's, a student who was standing by the door said in a low voice, "What's wrong, honey, can't you find a white man?"

Francine tried to ignore the remark, but Tony heard it and walked up to the student. "What did you say? Did I hear you correctly?" he asked the student coldly.

"Yeah, man, you did," the student replied belligerently.

Tony began to shake the guy, but Francine pulled him away and told Tony to leave the student alone.

"Let's get out of here," she begged.

Joe agreed, and finally Tony moved away and they all three left the bookstore.

That night Francine and Tony and Joe sat around Francine's kitchen table and discussed what had happened. Francine was shocked and worried, but Tony and Joe tried to explain to her that nothing unusual had taken place. Racism was a fact of life in the university town, and many students were outspoken about their prejudice, especially regarding mixed race relationships.

"I had a white girlfriend last year, but the stress got to her and she broke off our relationship," revealed Tony. "I hope this won't keep you from hanging out with us," he said to Francine.

"No way!" answered Francine. "I don't care what other people think about my actions."

"Great. So how about going to a movie on Friday?" asked Tony.

Friday night Francine and Tony went to see the show at the Multiplex. It was a terrible movie, so they decided to leave in the middle. When they were about to get into Tony's car, a group of students standing across the street from where they were parked began making comments.

"Look at that poor white trash. She's really asking for it," one of them said loudly. "Maybe we should call the cops in case that black guy tries to push her around."

Francine and Tony looked at each other and at the group of students. Then they quickly got into the car and drove away, but their evening was ruined. Francine couldn't believe that so much racial prejudice existed in this town. It made no sense to her. The worst part was that she was beginning to care about Tony, and she knew that she didn't want to stop hanging out with him just because some people were narrow-minded and intolerant in this part of the world.

For the next several weeks, Francine and Tony spent a lot of their free time together. They got along so well that it seemed as if they had known each other for a long time. But Francine didn't tell Tony that she had been getting threatening phone calls. Some man was phoning her and saying horrible things before she could slam down the phone. And one day when she went out to her car, she found the tires had been slashed.

Another day, several students were watching when she and Tony left their classroom together. They yelled to Tony, "Hey, boy. Better watch out!" Tony was furious.

"No one is going to call me 'boy' and get away with it. I think I'll report them to the dean of student affairs. Maybe the university has a policy that prohibits racist or sexist remarks on campus," he told Francine. "If students use that kind of speech, they should be expelled from the university, and I'd sure like to see that happen."

When Tony went to the dean to report the racist remarks and identify the students who made them, the dean asked him to testify about the racist incident before the student judiciary board. But the dean also told Tony that the First Amendment right to freedom of speech might make it difficult to get a guilty verdict.

"This is a complex issue, especially on this campus. Since we're a public, not a private, university, the First Amendment protection of free speech is very strong. Are you sure you want to go ahead with it?" the dean asked.

"Well, I thought the university was committed to nondiscrimination," answered Tony with anger. "I guess I need some time to think it over. I'll call you in a few days."

After Tony reported what the dean had said, Francine was so annoyed that she finally decided to go to the campus police about the tire slashing. She hoped that they could find out who was harassing her and Tony and make them quit. Unfortunately, the campus police said there was nothing they could do for Francine. She had to handle her situation on her own. Too many students had too many problems for the campus police to solve. They were sympathetic but not interested. Incidents like the ones she experienced happened all the time, the police told her.

Francine and Tony continued to see each other, and their relationship was getting more serious. But since they never knew what kind of attitudes they might encounter, they spent much of their time together at Francine's place. It just seemed like the safest thing to do. One night, while they were watching TV in the living room, a rock came flying through the window and almost hit Tony. Francine began to scream, and Tony ran outside to try to catch the person who threw it, but he was too late.

"Now, I am really scared," cried Francine, as Tony held her in his arms and comforted her. "What can we do? If this is what life in America is like, I want to go back to France. We have our problems with prejudice there too, but the people in this town are so ignorant and inhumane. I've never judged people by the color of their skin or even thought about whether they were black or white. How can you stand it?"

"I have to stand it, Francine. There's no choice," said Tony. "Besides, if you think it's bad now, you should have seen it forty years ago. You wouldn't believe what my mom and dad went through. Blacks couldn't even attend this university until the Supreme Court decision in 1954 desegregating all schools. Today at least I can get an excellent education and a good job after that, so I just look to the future and concentrate on my opportunities. No use worrying about the past. But maybe this is too much for you to deal with."

"Well, I'm trying to deal with it, but this sure doesn't seem like what America, the land of the free, is supposed to be," answered Francine sadly as she began to sweep up the glass from the broken window.

Discussion

1. What causes people to be prejudiced against other people?
2. What kind of person is Francine Claudel?
3. How do some of the students at the university feel about interracial dating?
4. What should Francine and Tony do about the harassment from the students?
5. Should Francine continue her relationship with Tony? Why or why not?
6. Should Francine take legal action against the students who are harassing her? Why or why not?
7. Should Tony take legal action against the students who made racist remarks on campus? Explain your answer.
8. Do racist and sexist remarks fall in the category of speech protected by the First Amendment to the U.S. Constitution? Explain your opinion.
9. What could the dean do to improve the situation?
10. How can racism be decreased at this university?

Case Study Report

Working with a partner or in a small group, write a case study report analyzing the problem Francine and Tony are facing as a result of their relationship.

  I. Statement of the Problem
 II. Suggestion of Possible Solutions
III. Evaluation of Possible Solutions
IV. Selection of a Solution

Vocabulary

Fill in the blanks with the most appropriate words. Use each word only once.

segregated	equality	prohibiting	opportunity	tolerant	discrimination
transition	inhumane	narrow-minded	integrated	racist	abolished

Deeply rooted racial prejudice in the United States had its beginning in the system of slavery that was instituted in the seventeenth century.[1] In 1619 the first twenty African slaves were

1. George M. Fredrickson, *The Black Image in the White Mind* (Hanover, NH: Wesleyan University Press, 1987), 322.

brought to America on a slave ship.[2] During the next two hundred years, thousands of slaves were imported into the United States from Africa. Unfortunately, much of the economy of the South, which was agricultural, depended on this slave labor, so the South fought hard to maintain slavery. Nevertheless, many Americans believed that the institution of slavery was immoral and had to be _____. This struggle culminated in the Civil War (1861–65). The history of the modern day civil rights movement goes back to 1865, when the sixteenth president of the United States, Abraham Lincoln, freed the slaves at the end of the war. African Americans, who are the central minority in the United States, have been fighting for full _____ since that time.

Slavery was _____, and slaves, who were considered the property of the slaveholders, suffered great physical and mental cruelty. It was even against the law to teach a slave to read or write because the slaveholders knew it would be harder to control educated men and women. Throughout the nineteenth century, people who wanted to do away with slavery (abolitionists) were organizing and speaking out against the evils of the slave system. The abolitionists believed that Christianity and the Declaration of Independence supported equality of races. Famous abolitionists included Harriet Beecher Stowe, the author of *Uncle Tom's Cabin,* and Frederick Douglass, who escaped from slavery and wrote three autobiographies about his life as a slave. The writer and philosopher Ralph Waldo Emerson also lectured about the immorality of slavery.

Although all slaves were freed in 1865, they were greatly disadvantaged by their years of mistreatment and lack of education. Furthermore, African Americans continued to be treated unfairly in every area of life. These extreme _____ attitudes led to legalized segregation.[3] The U.S. Supreme Court ruled in 1896 that racial segregation in public schools and other facilities in the South was not a violation of the Constitution. This ruling was based on the "separate but equal doctrine," which the Court used to justify racial segregation.

---

2. Ronald Takaki, *A Different Mirror: A History of Multicultural America* (Boston: Little, Brown, and Company, 1993), 7.
3. Fredrickson, 325.

Uncle Tom's Cabin; 1903, U.S.

Thus, African Americans had to live in their own separate neighborhoods, attending

_____ schools and not eating in restaurants where white people went. In fact,

they could not even drink out of the same water fountain or sit in the same section of the

movie theater as whites, and they had to sit in the back of public buses. It was a courageous

African American woman named Rosa Parks who started the civil rights movement of the

1950s when she refused to give her seat to a white man and move to the back of a bus in

Birmingham, Alabama, in 1955.

Because of racial prejudice, it was hard for African Americans to advance in a competi-

tive society, but attempts were made to eliminate _____ through legislation, beginning with the Civil Rights Act of 1866 and the Fourteenth Amendment.[4] In the 1950s and 1960s, many Americans joined the civil rights movement and helped bring about the changes that led to making America a country of equal _____. In 1954 the U.S. Supreme Court ruled in *Brown v. Board of Education* that segregation was illegal and public schools had to be _____.[5] Finally in 1964, President Lyndon Johnson signed the civil rights legislation that changed American society by _____ the many forms of public discrimination and establishing affirmative action laws to increase the number of African Americans admitted to universities and hired by companies or government agencies.[6]

After 1964, African Americans began to make some gains in their struggle to live according to the words of the United States Constitution: "with equal protection under the law." The Voting Rights Act of 1965 was extremely important legislation that resulted in political equality for all U.S. citizens. However, African Americans have yet to achieve complete equality, and racism remains a problem in the United States. More time is needed before America makes the _____ from being a(n) _____ society to being an open-minded and _____ society.

What is your opinion?

Write one or two paragraphs expressing your point of view on the issues discussed above.

4. Fredrickson, 183.
5. *Brown v. Board of Education,* 347 U.S. 483 (1954).
6. The origin of affirmative action is the Civil Rights Act of 1964. Title 7 of the act prohibited employment discrimination because of a person's race, color, religion, sex, or national origin. On September 24, 1965, President Lyndon Johnson signed Executive Order 11246, the basis of affirmative action. The order prohibited discrimination by companies doing business with the government and created the obligation to take affirmative action in hiring women and minority groups.

Activities

1. According to the historian Ronald Takaki: "America has been racially diverse since our very beginning on the Virginia shore, and this reality is increasingly becoming visible and ubiquitous. Currently, one-third of the American people do not trace their origins to Europe; in California, minorities are fast becoming the majority."[7]

   Consult a current world almanac in the library to find the following information about the U.S. population:
   - (1) racial and ethnic composition of the United States (percentage of population that is white, black, American Indian–Eskimo-Aleut, Asian–Pacific Islanders, Hispanic origin);
   - (2) percentage of U.S. population that is foreign born; and
   - (3) the top ten countries from which immigrants come.

2. Write a three-paragraph essay expressing your opinion on interracial or intercultural dating and marriage.

3. *Political correctness* is a term that applies to using correct language, language that will not offend or demean others. For example, the word *woman* is generally preferred to the word *lady* today because *lady* has negative connotations to many people. To encourage political correctness, some schools have developed speech codes defining acceptable and unacceptable language, but many believe that these speech codes violate the First Amendment right to free speech.

   Working with a partner, make a list of English words that you think are unacceptable and should be avoided because they may be offensive or insulting. Share your list with the other members of the class by writing the words on the chalkboard.

4. Conduct a survey of at least ten people. Ask them the questions listed here and report your results to the class.
   1. Have you ever experienced discrimination of any kind? If so, please explain.
   2. Do you believe the relationship between African Americans and whites in the United State is getting better, getting worse, or remaining the same?
   3. Have African Americans achieved full equality in the United States?
   4. Do you support the continued use of affirmative action?

5. After the class is divided into two teams, have a debate on the following topic: Racist and sexist remarks should be in the category of speech that is protected by the First Amendment to the U.S. Constitution.

6. Choose one of the following role plays for presentation in class. Plan and practice your dialogue before presenting it.
   - (A) Act out the scene between Francine and Tony when he tells her about the problems African Americans have faced in the United States.
   - (B) Act out a future scene in which Tony and Francine return to tell the dean that they have decided to testify before the student judiciary board about the prejudice they have experienced on campus.

7. Takaki, 2.

Oral Presentation

Prepare and give an oral presentation on one of the topics listed. Use the suggested methods of development to organize your presentation and do library research to gather information.

- The History of the Civil Rights Movement in the United States (chronology)
- The Life and Death of Martin Luther King, Jr. (chronology)

Chapter Readings

**Proclamation 6861
Martin Luther King, Jr., Federal Holiday, 1996**

January 12, 1996

By the President of the United States of America

A Proclamation

Our country's motto, "E Pluribus Unum"—out of many we are one—charges us to find common values among our varied experience and to forge a national identity out of our extraordinary diversity. Our great leaders have been defined not only by their actions, but also by their ability to inspire people toward a unity of purpose. Today we honor Dr. Martin Luther King, Jr., who focused attention on the segregation that poisoned our society and whose example moved our Nation to embrace a new standard of openness and inclusion.

From Montgomery to Birmingham, from the Lincoln Memorial to Memphis, Dr. King led us to see the great contradiction between our founders' declaration that "all men are created equal" and the daily reality of oppression endured by African Americans. His words have become such a part of our moral fabric that we may forget that only a generation ago, children of different races were legally forbidden to attend the same schools, that segregated buses and trains traveled our neighborhoods, and that African Americans were often prevented from registering to vote. Echoing Abraham Lincoln's warning that a house divided against itself cannot stand, Dr. King urged, "We must learn to live together as brothers, or we will perish as fools."

Martin Luther King, Jr.'s call for American society to truly reflect the ideals on which it was built succeeded in galvanizing a political and moral consensus that led to legislation guaranteeing all our citizens the right to vote, to obtain housing, to enter places of public accommodation, and to participate in all aspects of American life without regard to race, gender, background, or belief.

But despite the great accomplishments of the Civil Rights Movement, we have not yet torn down every obstacle to equality. Too many of our cities are still racially segregated, and remaining barriers to education and opportunity have caused an array of social problems that disproportionately affect African Americans. As a result, blacks and whites often

"Proclamation 6861–Martin Luther King, Jr., Federal Holiday, 1996," *Weekly Compilation of Presidential Documents* (January 15, 1996): 53–54.

The Birth of a Nation; dir. D. W. Griffith; Lillian Gish, 1915, U.S.

see the world in strikingly different ways and too often view each other through a lens of mistrust or fear.

Today we face a choice between the dream of racial harmony that Martin Luther King, Jr., described and a deepening of the rift that divides the races in America. We must have the faith and wisdom that Dr. King preached and the convictions he lived by if we are to make this a time for healing and progress—and each of us must play a role. For only by sitting down with our neighbors in the workplace and classroom, reaching across racial lines in our places for worship and community centers, and examining our own most deep-seated beliefs, can we have the honest conversations that will enable us to understand the different ways we each experience the challenges of modern life. This is the peaceful process of reconciliation that Dr. King fought and died for, and we must do all we can to live and teach his lesson.

Now, Therefore, I, William J. Clinton, President of the United States of America, by virtue of the authority vested in me by the Constitution and laws of the United States, do hereby proclaim January 15, 1996, as the Martin Luther King, Jr., Federal Holiday. I call upon the people of the United States to observe this occasion with appropriate programs, ceremonies, and activities.

In Witness Whereof, I have hereunto set my hand this twelfth day of January, in the year of our Lord nineteen hundred and ninety-six, and of the Independence of the United States of America the two hundred and twentieth.

William J. Clinton

The Story in Our Genes

A landmark global study flattens *The Bell Curve*, proving that racial differences are only skin deep.

Sribala Subramanian

Mention *The Bell Curve* in polite company these days, and it may not be polite for long. Critics have pummeled the best-selling book by Charles Murray and the late Richard Herrnstein, which blames genetics for the gap between the average I.Q. of whites and blacks. But most of the assailants haven't noticed that perhaps their best weapon lies almost unused right under their noses. At about the same time that Murray threw his *Curve,* Princeton University Press put out *The History and Geography of Human Genes* by population geneticists Luca Cavalli-Sforza, Paolo Menozzi and Alberto Piazza. Not only is the tome physically hefty (1,000 pages, 7 1/2 lbs.), but the evidence it contains may carry enough weight to flatten Murray's thesis once and for all.

While not exactly best-seller material, *The History and Geography of Human Genes* is a remarkable synthesis of more than 50 years of research in population genetics. It stands as the most extensive survey to date on how humans vary at the level of their chromosomes. The book's firm conclusion: once the genes for surface traits such as coloration and stature are discounted, the human "races" are remarkably alike under the skin. The variation among individuals is much greater than the differences among groups. In fact, the diversity among individuals is so enormous that the whole concept of race becomes meaningless at the genetic level. The authors say, there is "no scientific basis" for theories touting the genetic superiority of any one population over another.

The book, however, is much more than a refutation of the latest pseudoscientific pronouncement. The prime mover behind the project, Cavalli-Sforza, 72, a Stanford professor, labored with his colleagues for 16 years to create nothing less than the first genetic atlas of the world. The book features more than 500 maps that show areas of genetic similarity—much as contour maps match up places of equal altitude. By measuring how closely current populations are related, the authors trace the pathways by which early humans migrated around the earth. Result: the closest thing we have to a global family tree.

The information needed to draw that tree is found in human blood: the antigens, antibodies and other proteins that serve as markers to reveal a person's genetic makeup. Using data collected by scientists over decades, the authors compiled profiles of hundreds of thousands of individuals from almost 2,000 communities and tribes. And to ensure a de-

Sribala Subramanian, "The Story in Our Genes," *Time* 145 (January 16, 1995): 54–55.

gree of "purity," the study was confined to groups that were in their present locations as of 1492, before the first major migrations from Europe began—in effect, a genetic snapshot of the world when Columbus sailed for America.

Collecting blood, particularly from ancient tribes in remote areas, was not always easy; potential donors were often afraid to cooperate, or raised religious taboos. On one occasion, when Cavalli-Sforza was taking blood samples from schoolchildren in a rural region of the Central African Republic, he was confronted by an angry farmer brandishing an ax. Recalls the scientist: "I remember him saying, 'If you take the blood of the children, I'll take yours.' He was worried that we might want to do some magic with the blood."

Despite the difficulties, the scientists made some myth-shattering discoveries. One of them jumps right off the book's cover: a color map of world genetic variation has Africa on one end of the spectrum and Australia on the other. Because Australia's aborigines and sub-Saharan Africans share such superficial traits as skin color and body shape, they were widely assumed to be closely related. But their genes tell a different story. Of all humans, Australians are most distant from the Africans and most closely resemble their neighbors, the southeast Asians. What the eye sees as racial differences—between Europeans and Africans, for example—are mainly adaptations to climate as humans moved from one continent to another.

The same map, in combination with the fossil record, confirms that Africa was the birthplace of humanity and thus the starting point of the original human migrations. Those findings, plus the great genetic distance between present-day Africans and non-Africans, indicate that the split from the African branch is the oldest on the human family tree.

The genetic atlas also sheds new light on the origins of populations that have long mystified anthropologists. Example: the Khoisan of southern Africa (Bushmen and Hottentots). Many scientists consider the Khoisan a distinct race of very ancient origin. The uniqueness of the clicking sounds in their language has persuaded some linguists that the Khoisan are direct descendants of the most primitive human ancestors. But their genes beg to differ. They show that the Khoisan may be a very ancient mix of west Asians and black Africans. A genetic trail visible on the maps shows that the ancestral breeding ground for this mixed population probably lies in Ethiopia or the Middle East.

The most distinctive members of the European branch of the human tree are the Basques of France and Spain. They show unusual patterns for several genes, including the highest rate of the Rh-negative blood type. Their language is of unknown origin and cannot be placed within any standard classification. And the fact that they live in the region adjoining the famous Lascaux and Altamira caves, which contain vivid paintings from Europe's early hunter-gatherers, leads Cavalli-Sforza to a tantalizing conclusion: "The Basques are extremely likely to be the most direct descendants of the Cro-Magnon people, among the first modern humans in Europe." All Europeans are thought to be a hybrid population, with 65% Asian and 35% African genes.

In the Americas, a look at native tribes showed that they were not all blood brothers. The three main groups, classified by language, were found to be genetically distinct, suggesting that three separate populations from Asia may have crossed the Bering Strait at different times to settle in America. The Amerind, who predominate in most of North and South America, possess only type O blood; among the Na-Dene, who cluster in Alaska,

Canada and the U.S. Southwest, O prevails but A makes an appearance; in the Alaskan and Canadian Inuit (Eskimo), A, B, AB and O blood groups show the pattern seen in the rest of the world.

Now that Cavalli-Sforza's mammoth study is finally complete, it's time to start a fresh survey. Reason: new analytical techniques that in recent years have revolutionized the field of genetics. Instead of using indirect markers like blood groups, researchers can now determine the exact chemical sequences of long strands of DNA itself. Cavalli-Sforza and his colleagues believe this technology can be used to resolve questions they were ill-equipped to answer, such as the origins of the Negrito tribes in the Indian Ocean, Malayan peninsula and the Philippines. Anthropologists suspect that they are descendants of a wandering people who had once formed an ancient human bridge between Africa and Australia.

The daunting task of making a more refined genetic atlas now lies with the Human Genome Diversity Project (an offshoot of the ambitious Human Genome Project), which was set up by a committee of scientists chaired by Cavalli-Sforza. Its objective is to create a global data base over the next 10 years using the new techniques—and unlock more secrets of the human gene pool.

Before the researchers can even get started, however, they will have to confront some major questions: How will the genetic sequences be used, and who will benefit from them? Genetic information is the raw material of the burgeoning biotechnology industry, which uses human DNA to build specialized proteins that may have some value as disease-fighting drugs. Activists for indigenous populations fear that the scientists could exploit these peoples: genetic material taken from blood samples could be patented for commercial use without adequate compensation to the tribes that provide the DNA.

The researchers believe they can ease such concerns. Already, the Human Genome Diversity Project is working with a U.N. organization to establish some guidelines. Cavalli-Sforza stresses that his mission is not just scientific but humanitarian as well. The study's ultimate aim, he says, is to "undercut conventional notions of race" that cause discrimination. It is a goal that he hopes will resonate among indigenous peoples who have long struggled for the same end.

Comprehension

"Proclamation 6861—Martin Luther King, Jr., Federal Holiday, 1996"
1. What does the motto of the United States ("E Pluribus Unum") mean?
2. Why is this motto appropriate to the United States?
3. On what problem did Dr. Martin Luther King, Jr., focus attention?
4. What forms of discrimination did African Americans experience in the United States one generation ago?
5. What resulted from the political and moral consensus that Martin Luther King, Jr., built?
6. What obstacles to equality still exist in the United States?
7. What choice do Americans face today?
8. How can African Americans and whites understand the different ways they each experience modern life?

"The Story in Our Genes"

1. What are the conclusions of *The History and Geography of Human Genes?*
2. What do the 500 maps in the book show?
3. Where did the researchers find the information needed to draw the global family tree?
4. What caused the surface "racial differences" among people?
5. What was the birthplace of humanity?
6. Who are the most distinctive members of the European branch of the human tree and why?
7. What new analytical techniques have revolutionized the field of genetics?
8. What is the objective of the Human Genome Diversity Project?
9. What do the activists for indigenous populations fear about this research?
10. What is the main idea of this article?

Chronique des Années de Braise (Chronicle of the Burning Years); dir. Mohammed Lakhdar-Hamina, 1975, Algeria

Strategy Session

Imagine that you are a student at a college in which you are a minority. During the past month, several students have been verbally harassing you, using what you believe is discriminatory and racist language.

Which strategy would you use in this situation and why? Provide a written justification for your decision. If none of the listed strategies would be your choice, you may develop your own strategy.

1. Try to avoid the harassing students and hope that they will forget about you.

2. Talk to the students forcefully and insist that they stop using such language.

3. Report the students to the dean of student affairs.

4. File a formal complaint with the student judiciary board, charging the students with racist speech and discriminatory harassment.

5. Complete an application to transfer to a different university where you would no longer be a minority.

6. Other: _____

Suggested Films

Amistad (1997)
The Autobiography of Miss Jean Pittman (1974)
The Birth of a Nation (1915 silent film)
A Class Divided (PBS Video: 1992)
The Color Purple (1985)
Crooklyn (1994)
Do the Right Thing (1989)
Evolution and Human Equality (Insight Video: 1987)
Guess Who's Coming to Dinner (1967)
Hoop Dreams (1994)
In the Heat of the Night (1967)
Jungle Fever (1991)
The Long Walk Home (1990)
Mississippi Burning (1988)
Mississippi Masala (1992)
Racism 101 (PBS Video: 1988)
Rosewood (1997)
Safe Speech, Free Speech, and the University (Columbia University Seminars: 1991)
School Colors (PBS Video: 1994)
Skin Deep: College Students Confront Racism (Iris Films: 1995)
White Men Can't Jump (1992)

Additional Readings

Alter, Jonathan. "The Long Shadow of Slavery." *Newsweek* 130 (December 8, 1997): 58–63.

Gates, Henry Louis, Jr. "Second Thoughts: After the Revolution." *New Yorker* 72 (April 29 and May 6, 1996): 59–61.

Gottleib, Scott. "There's No Such Thing as Justice on Campus." *USA Today. The Magazine of the American Scene* 123 (March 1995): 42–43.

Gwynne, S. C. "Back to the Future." *Time* 149 (June 2, 1997): 48.

Hentoff, Nat. "Against the Odds: A Historic Free Speech Victory." *Village Voice* 40 (May 2, 1995): 20–21.

Kotlowitz, Alex. "Colorblind." *New York Times Magazine,* January 11, 1998, 22–23.

Kreyche, Gerald F. "Political Correctness: Speech Control or Thought Control?" *USA Today. The Magazine of the American Scene* 123 (March 1995): 98.

Morrow, Lance. "The Cure for Racism." *Time* 144 (December 5, 1994): 106.

Rowe, Chip. "The Safe Generation." *Playboy* 42 (June 1995): 74–78.

Sidel, Ruth. "Battling Bias: College Students Speak Out." *Educational Record* 76 (Spring–Summer 1995): 45–51.

Sowell, Thomas. "Drive a Stake Through It." *Forbes* 158 (August 26, 1996): 53.

Wilson, John K. "Many of the More Vocal Critics of Political Correctness Simply Want to Impose Their Own Version." *Chronicle of Higher Education* 41 (July 28, 1995): B3.

Chapter 13
Cultural Traditions: Arranged Marriage

Banshun (Late Spring); dir. Yasujiro Ozu, 1949, Japan

How would you feel if your parents wanted you to have an arranged marriage?

Exploration

After reading the following statements, respond to each one by writing *yes* or *no*.

1. I believe in arranged marriages in most cases. _____

2. My parents' marriage was arranged. _____

3. Arranged marriages were common in my country in the past, but today most people choose their own marriage partners. _____

4. If my parents choose my husband or wife, I will probably agree with their choice.
_____

5. Divorce is more common when people marry for romantic love than when they marry by arrangement. _____

6. Dating before marriage in order to get to know your partner is a good idea. _____

7. Living together before marriage is a good way for two people to decide if they should get married. _____

8. Since parents have more experience, they are better at choosing marriage partners for their children. _____

9. I would consider using a matchmaker to find the right person to marry. _____

10. I intend to choose the person I will marry without any help from my parents or a matchmaker. _____

11. I would not marry a person of whom my parents disapproved. _____

12. Living in the United States has caused me to question some of my traditional beliefs about marriage. _____

Glossary

accomplishments	achievements; things accomplished or done successfully
Allah	the Supreme Being of Islam
annoyance	temporary disturbance of mind caused by something that displeases or irritates
arranged	brought about through an agreement or understanding
assimilated	absorbed into the cultural tradition of a country
assume	to take on the role
call off	to cancel
calm	to become calm, peaceful, quiet
compatible	capable of living together harmoniously or getting along well together
concerns	worries, anxieties
consent	to give approval of what is proposed by another; to agree
devout	devoted to religion or to religious duties
disapproved	considered wrong; had an unfavorable opinion of
drawback	shortcoming; anything that prevents full satisfaction
favorable	expressing approval; disposed to favor
furious	extremely angry
hardly	barely, scarcely; only just

intend   to have in mind as a purpose or plan
lose touch with   to fail to keep involved with
matchmaker   a person who arranges marriages for others
motioning   making a meaningful movement of the hand
Muslim   a member of the Islamic faith
overreact   to react in a highly emotional way, beyond what seems called for
pacing   walking with slow or regular steps
potential   possible
prevalent   widely existing; generally practiced, occurring, or accepted
question   to dispute or challenge; to doubt
reassures   assures again; restores to confidence
reputation   good name; estimation in which a person is held by others
ridiculous   absurd; so unreasonable as to be laughable
romantic   marked by the imaginative or emotional appeal of what is idealized
shocked   greatly surprised and distressed
state   a particular mental or emotional condition
tempted   inclined strongly
tentatively   not definitely or finally; done with hesitancy and uncertainty

Two Daughters (Teen Kanya); dir. Satyajit Ray, 1961, India

Case Study: A Marriage Made in Heaven

After you read the case study, discuss the major problem the case presents and answer the discussion questions with the members of the class. Then write a case study report following the format that is provided.

Maryam Al-Fazawi is from Riyadh, Saudi Arabia. She is in her last semester of studying for her B.S. in management information systems. Although not too many Saudi Arabian women come to the United States for their education, Maryam's family agreed to her request to study at a well-respected university in Michigan because many other members of her family had gotten their degrees from this university, and they knew that Maryam would be near several of her cousins who were also studying there.

Maryam has done unusually well during her four years in college and was recently asked by her department chairperson to consider staying at the school for another two years to get her master's degree in information technology. Maryam is very tempted by this suggestion, as she really would like to continue her studies. However, she knows how much her mother and father want her to return to Saudi Arabia. They often write to her expressing their worries that she will lose touch with her Islamic traditions and religious beliefs. Maryam constantly reassures them that while she has adjusted easily to life in the States and become somewhat assimilated into the culture, she remains a devout Muslim.

Today, when Maryam went to class, she noticed that Mark Sullivan, her classmate, was motioning to her to come sit next to him. Maryam had gotten to know Mark quite well during the semester since they had been assigned to work on several programming projects together.

"Hi, Mark. Have you started studying for the final exam?" Maryam asked.

"Not really, but I'm not too worried. I guess I'm feeling relaxed because it's so close to the end of the semester and to graduation," answered Mark.

"You always get A's, so you don't have to worry," replied Maryam, laughing.

"Well, speaking of relaxing, how about grabbing a sandwich after class and maybe trying out the new software I just got?" suggested Mark.

Maryam paused before she answered. She knew her parents had no idea that she had friends like Mark. They would be disapproving and so would her brothers and cousins if they found out that she had gone out with him. But it certainly wouldn't be the first time. Maryam decided to ignore her thoughts of her family and accept Mark's invitation. What could be wrong with spending a pleasant evening with an interesting person like Mark?

When Maryam got home later that night, she saw a letter from her father waiting for her. She opened it and began to read it quickly. Suddenly she sat down and started to read the letter again more slowly.

Dear Maryam,

We hope everything is fine with you. All of the family members are well, and we are looking forward to your return. You know how proud your mother and I are of your academic accomplishments. But now that you are about to graduate, it is time to think of the next stage in your life: marriage. Mohammed Al-Ahmadi, who, as you know, is from one of the finest and most respected families in Riyadh, has asked for your hand in marriage. His father is an adviser to the King, his mother is my third cousin, and he is a successful businessman with an excellent reputation.

For these reasons, your mother and I have agreed to your engagement to Mohammed. We believe that you will find him a most intelligent and kind husband. Therefore, we would like you to come home immediately after your graduation to become officially engaged, and the wedding, if Allah is willing, will take place in August. Of course, we are hoping that your reaction to this will be favorable and that you will agree with our decision and consent to marry Mohammed. This seems to us to be a marriage made in heaven. We are both convinced that Mohammed will give you a rich and happy life.

With love,
Father

For a long time, Maryam sat in her chair, trying to calm herself and not overreact. But she was shocked and afraid that the plans she had tentatively made for her future were about to be ruined. Naturally, she loved her country, and she had always known that one day she would return to Saudi Arabia, get married, and assume the role of a traditional wife and mother. She would probably even be able to work if she wanted to.

But having lived in the United States for four years, she had changed many of her former ideas about what an educated woman could and should accomplish in her life. Even the Saudi belief that women must cover their hair and wear a veil and robe when outside the home no longer made sense to Maryam. And not being able to drive would take a lot of getting used to after she had been driving everywhere for the past four years. Not that Maryam wanted to stay in the States forever, but she really had some strong concerns about the kind of life she would have to live in Saudi Arabia.

"I have to talk to someone about this," thought Maryam. "Maybe I should go to see the foreign student adviser and she can suggest a counselor or another Muslim woman who has had these kinds of problems."

The longer Maryam thought about her parents' letter, the more furious she became, and many questions kept running through her mind.

"Coming to the States has really changed me," she said to herself, "and I may never again be the person I was before. How can I be expected to marry a man I hardly know? That seems crazy! What if we aren't compatible? The best way I can solve this might be to call Mother and explain my feelings to her. Since she's so understanding, she can tell Father, and perhaps they will call off this engagement," she thought hopefully.

Maryam couldn't sleep that night. She tossed and turned, falling into a light sleep but then waking with her heart beating rapidly. She wished the day would come so she could call her parents and ask them not to agree to her marriage. But in the morning, Maryam was too frightened to make the phone call. Instead of going to her classes, she stayed in her apartment all day, pacing the floor and planning what to tell her parents.

By evening, she was in a terrible state, and when the phone rang, she nearly jumped. It was her friend Mark.

"Hey, Maryam, how about going out for some pizza?" he asked.

Maryam hesitated and then replied, "Sure, that would be great. Come by in thirty minutes."

After she hung up the phone, Maryam looked in the mirror. "Who am I?" she wondered aloud. "And who do I want to be?"

Later her doorbell rang, and she let Mark in.

"Hi, Mark, I'm so glad you're here. I need to talk to you about something important," Maryam said nervously.

"I bet I know what you're thinking about," replied Mark. "You're trying to decide whether to apply to graduate school, aren't you? Well, of course you should. Why not?"

Maryam couldn't help smiling. "I hope I will have that choice, but my life is not that simple," she answered.

Discussion

1. What kind of person is Maryam?
2. What conflict is she facing?
3. Should Maryam continue her friendship with Mark Sullivan?
4. Should Maryam call her parents and tell them how she feels about getting engaged?
5. Do Maryam's parents know what is best for her? Explain your answer.
6. Why do Maryam's parents approve of Mohammed as a potential husband for Maryam?
7. How does Maryam feel about the traditional lifestyle for women in Saudi Arabia?
8. Why is Maryam not ready to return to Saudi Arabia?
9. Should Maryam apply to graduate school in the States? Explain your answer.
10. What options does Maryam have in solving this problem?

Case Study Report

Working with a partner or in a small group, write a case study report analyzing the problem that has arisen between Maryam and her parents.

  I. Statement of the Problem
 II. Suggestion of Possible Solutions
III. Evaluation of Possible Solutions
IV. Selection of a Solution

Vocabulary

Fill in the blanks with the most appropriate words. Use each word only once.

potential	consent	compatible	drawback	arranged
status	favorable	hardly	prevalent	accomplishments

Many people decide to get married on the basis of romantic love, which is "an intense, erotic relationship that involves commitment (resources and time), intimacy, and idealization of the other."[1] However, in earlier ages, parents determined whom their children would marry. Marriage was a contract between two families rather than two individuals, and love was not the major concern. Today, almost everyone hopes to get married and live happily ever after. But are you more likely to succeed in this if you marry for love or marry by arrangement? Statistics show that four out of ten marriages will end in divorce in the United States today,[2] while in countries where arranged marriages are the rule, divorce is far less frequent. That would seem to be an argument in favor of having parents or another person choose the husband or wife instead of allowing young persons to date, fall in love, and marry on their own.

_____ marriages are still _____ in many parts of the world. For example, in India, Pakistan, Japan, China, and some Middle Eastern countries like Egypt, it is common for parents to help their children select their mates. The process differs from country to country. In India, families may place marriage advertisements in the newspapers or ask astrologers to match the horoscopes of their children to find the best marriage partner. But generally the parents make an appointment with a person known as a matchmaker. At this meeting, they describe the type of person they would like their son or daughter to marry. The matchmaker will then set up a time and place for two _____ people to meet. Her arrangements are made by trying to match young men and women from families that are similar in religious beliefs, social and financial _____, and educational _____.[3]

This matchmaker, sometimes called a go-between, acts as the manager of the process. She often knows both families and has a large number of people from whom she can choose in making introductions. After the two individuals have met, they each report to the matchmaker on their reactions to one another. If their reactions are _____, they may

1. Jan Clanton Collins and Thomas Gregor, "Boundaries of Love," in *Romantic Passion: A Universal Experience?* edited by William Jankowiak (New York: Columbia University Press, 1995), 74.
2. Barbara Vobedja, "Children of Divorce Heal Slowly, Study Finds," *Washington Post*, June 3, 1997, E3.
3. Anthony Clare, *Lovelaw: Love, Sex, and Marriage around the World* (London: BBC Publications, 1986), 40.

have a second and a third meeting. Then it is time to make the decision to marry. However, if one of the parties is against the marriage, the matchmaker will introduce that person to someone else. Thus, even in arranged marriages, the parties are free to make up their own minds. In fact, when a marriage has been arranged with the complete _____ of both parties, it is usually successful.[4]

The _____ to arranged marriages, if there is one, is that the two people involved _____ get a chance to know each other or fall in love before they must decide whether or not to marry. Love is expected to come after marriage, not before.[5] This is quite different from the custom of dating, in which two people spend time together and get acquainted gradually. Dating generally begins in the teenage years. Thus, in countries where dating is popular, a man or woman may have the chance to get to know a variety of _____ marriage partners before finally choosing the right one. This process appears to be a better method of finding the one person with whom you would want to spend your whole life. Nevertheless, many of these love marriages end in divorce, while a high percentage of arranged marriages do not. Perhaps there is some truth to the saying "Parents know best."

What is your opinion?

Write one or two paragraphs expressing your point of view on the issues discussed above.

4. Clare, 42.
5. Clare, 20.

The Wedding March; dir. Erich Von Stroheim; Fay Wray, 1928, U.S.

Activities

1. Write a letter from Maryam to her parents, explaining why she does not want to get engaged to Mohammed Al-Ahmadi.
2. In a five-paragraph essay, describe the marriage customs in your country. Compare and contrast the traditional ways in which people get married with the more modern ways. If arranged marriages are common, explain how the process works.
3. Read *Arranged Marriage,* a book of short stories by the Indian writer Chitra Bannerjee Divakaruni (published by Doubleday in 1995). Write a two-page report on one of the short stories. Use the following format: I. Introduction; II. Summary; III. Critique; IV. Conclusion.
4. Conduct a survey of at least ten people. Ask them the questions listed here and report your results to the class.
    1. What is your current status: single, married, divorced, widowed?
    2. If you were unmarried, would you agree to enter into an arranged marriage?
    3. What is the best foundation for a lasting and successful marriage?

    4. Is it too easy to get a divorce in the United States?

    5. Have you or any of your family members ever been divorced? Please explain.

5. After the class is divided into two teams, have a debate on the following topic: Arranged marriages are more likely to be lasting and successful than love marriages.

6. Choose one of the following role plays for presentation in class. Plan and practice your dialogue before presenting it.

   (A) Act out the scene in which Maryam meets Mohammed for the first time, and they have a friendly conversation.

   (B) Act out the scene in which Maryam tells her parents, after meeting Mohammed, that she would like to get to know him better before agreeing to marry him.

Oral Presentation

Prepare and give an oral presentation on one of the topics listed. Use the suggested methods of development to organize your presentation and do library research to gather information.

- How to Find the Right Marriage Partner (process, examples)
- A Comparison of Arranged Marriages and Love Marriages (comparison-contrast)

Chapter Readings

Could I Accept an Arranged Marriage?

I grew up thinking like an American. But in countries like mine, love is considered a transient emotion—and therefore unimportant.

Shandana Durrani

For years my parents pressured me to have an arranged marriage. As kids growing up in America, my sisters and I all understood that we would have to marry men who not only shared our religion, culture and class but had been picked out by our parents. At first we never worried, because adulthood seemed so far away. But as we grew older it became more apparent how important arranged marriages were to my parents.

Adolescence is tough, and it's even tougher when your feelings of not belonging are not paranoid but justified. Almost all of our friends were white, and their parents' rules were drastically different from ours. My friends could date, go to parties and attend that most important of social events: the prom. Too afraid even to talk back to my parents, I had no idea where I would find the nerve to resist an arranged marriage. But at least I was third in line.

My eldest sister was the first to be approached, on behalf of friends of our family in Pakistan. I had never seen my sister so upset until the day my father asked her to marry this man she'd never met. Always in tight control, she snapped when my father began berating her for being selfish and not thinking about her family or her Pakistani community. She was so upset that my father apologized the next day and withdrew his request. My other sister and I were never approached. But none of us is married either.

When I went away to college, seven years ago, it was as if I were reborn. My parents could not know where I was at every moment of the day, and I did a lot of dating and partying that six months earlier would have been unthinkable. I learned a lot that first year. Not from the classroom but from the places I went and the people I encountered. One of those people was my friend Geeta.

Geeta and I met in the dormitory as freshmen. Finally encountering someone who came from a similar background was momentous for me. None of my American friends had ever been able to understand my parents' beliefs and rigid rules; they thought that I should speak my mind to my parents and do what I wanted. But in Eastern countries, respect is more important than love; it is one of the greatest gifts you can bestow upon your parents. Geeta could understand this, and it formed a bond between us that has never been broken.

Geeta always knew that she would have to have an arranged marriage. Our cultures are slightly different (Geeta is an Indian Hindu and I am a Pakistani Muslim), and it is much more difficult for her to resist tradition. On the Indian subcontinent, love is considered a foolish, transient—and therefore unimportant—emotion. It is hard for many Americans to understand that marrying for love is a truly Western practice, that in many countries even today, people marry for every reason but love.

Geeta is now ready to be married and seems resigned to her fate. She believes that this is what she wants, that it is her destiny. Her parents have presented her with a couple of prospective mates, via photographs, but she has rejected both offers. She is free to continue rejecting her suitors but her position in her community as a virtuous and respectful Indian girl is at stake. She hopes to find someone like her, untraditional in a lot of ways, and of course attractive. I can only wish her the best and hope that, by the luck of the draw, she finds true love and happiness.

Watching Geeta come to terms with her fate has helped me understand my parents and the value of our rich heritage. Even so, I will never agree to an arranged marriage for a reason that even my parents don't know: I have never been attracted to Pakistani men. In my experience, the majority of them see women as their property, an opinion that I felt was confirmed when I visited Pakistan as a teenager. They would follow my sisters and me home from the bazaar. They would harass us at the zoo or wherever else we ventured, calling us degrading names if we didn't show interest in them. I knew then that I did not want to marry a Pakistani man, which to me meant someone who would see me as an ornament, or worse, a slave.

I have always been attracted to blond, blue-eyed men. Part of me simply likes their looks; the contrast between our coloring is so stunning. But underneath it all, I like them because they are the opposite of the men my parents expect me to marry. I know my parents want what is best for me, and their intentions come from the heart. I just wish they could look inside my heart for once. If they did, they would know that they set these rebellious wheels in motion when they arranged my marriage to America itself, so many years ago.

When Life's Partner Comes Pre-Chosen

Shoba Narayan

We sat around the dining table, my family and I, replete from yet another home-cooked South Indian dinner. It was my younger brother, Shaam, who asked the question.

"Shoba, why don't you stay back here for a few months? So we can try to get you married."

Three pairs of eyes stared at me across the expanse of the table. I sighed. Here I was, at the tail end of my vacation after graduate school. I had an Air France ticket to New York from Madras in 10 days. I had accepted a job at an artist's colony in Johnson, Vt. My car, and most of my possessions, were with friends in Memphis.

"It's not that simple," I said. "What about my car. . .?"

"We could find you someone in America," my dad replied. "You could go back to the States."

They had thought it all out. This was a plot. I glared at my parents accusingly.

Oh, another part of me rationalized, why not give this arranged-marriage thing a shot? It wasn't as if I had a lot to go back to in the States. Besides, I could always get a divorce.

Stupid and dangerous as it seems in retrospect, I went into my marriage at 25 without being in love. Three years later, I find myself relishing my relationship with this brilliant, prickly man who talks about the yield curve and derivatives, who prays when I drive, and who tries valiantly to remember names like Giacometti, Munch, Georgia O'Keeffe and Kandinsky.

My enthusiasm for arranged marriages is that of a recent convert. True, I grew up in India, where arranged marriages are common. My parents' marriage was arranged, as were those of my aunts, cousins and friends. But I always thought I was different. I blossomed as a foreign fellow in Mount Holyoke, where individualism was expected and feminism encouraged. As I experimented with being an American, I bought into the American value system.

I was determined to fall in love and marry someone who was not Indian. Yet, somehow, I could never manage to. Oh, falling in love was easy. Sustaining it was the hard part.

Arranged marriages in India begin with matching the horoscopes of the man and the woman. Astrologers look for balance and cyclicality, so that the woman's strengths balance the man's weaknesses and vice versa. Once the horoscopes match, the two families meet and decide whether they are compatible. It is assumed that they are of the same religion, caste and social stratum.

While this eliminates risk and promotes homogeneity, the rationale is that the personalities of the couple provide enough differences for a marriage to thrive. Whether or not this is true, the high statistical success rate of arranged marriages in different cultures —90 percent in Iran, 95 percent in India, and a similar high percentage among Hasidic Jews in Brooklyn and among Turkish and Afghan Muslims—gives one pause.

Although our families met through a mutual friend, many Indian families meet through advertisements placed in national newspapers.

Shoba Narayan, "When Life's Partner Comes Pre-Chosen," *New York Times*, May 4, 1995, C1, C8.

My parents made a formal visit to my future husband's house to see whether Ram's family would treat me well. My mother insists that "you can tell a lot about the family just from the way they serve coffee." The house had a lovely flower garden. The family liked gardening. Good.

Ram's mother had worked for the United Nations on women's-rights issues. She also wrote humorous columns for Indian magazines. She would be supportive. She served strong South Indian coffee in the traditional stainless steel tumblers instead of china; she would be a balancing influence on my youthful radicalism.

Ram's father had supported his wife's career even though he belonged to a generation of Indian men who expected their wives to stay home. Ram had a good role model. His sister was a pediatrician in Fort Myers, Fla. Perhaps that meant he was used to strong, achieving women.

Nov. 20, 1992. Someone shouted, "They're here!" My cousin Sheela gently nudged me out of the bedroom into the living room.

"Why don't you sit down?" a voice said.

I looked up and saw a square face and smiling eyes anxious to put me at ease. He pointed me to a chair. Somehow I liked that. The guy was sensitive and self-confident.

He looked all right. Could stand to lose a few pounds. I liked the way his lips curved to meet his eyes. Curly hair, commanding voice, unrestrained laugh. To my surprise, the conversation flowed easily. We had a great deal in common, but his profession was very different from mine. I learned that he had an M.B.A. from the University of Michigan and had worked on Wall Street before joining a financial consulting firm.

Two hours later, Ram said: "I'd like to get to know you better. Unfortunately, I have to be back at my job in Connecticut, but I could call you every other day. No strings attached, and both of us can decide where this goes, if anywhere."

I didn't dislike him.

He called 10 days later. We talked about our goals, dreams and anxieties; we argued over which was the best pizza place in New York, and we teased and joked with each other. He never seemed to be in a rush.

"What do you want out of life?" he asked me one day. "Come up with five words, maybe, of what you want to do with your life." His question intrigued me. "Courage, wisdom, change," I said, flippantly. "What about you?"

"Curiosity, contribution, balance, family and fun," he said. In spite of myself, I was impressed.

One month later, he proposed and I accepted. Our extended honeymoon in Connecticut was wonderful. On weekends, we took trips to Mount Holyoke, where I showed him my old art studio, and to Franconia Notch in New Hampshire, where we hiked and camped. We huddled under the covers on rainy summer days and caught up on each other's lives.

It was in Taos, N.M., that we had our first fight. Ram had arranged for a surprise visit to the children's summer camp where I used to work as a counselor. We visited my old colleagues with their Greenpeace T-shirts and New Age commune mentality. Ram, with his clipped accent, neatly pressed clothes and pleasant manners, was so different. What was I doing with this guy? On the car trip to the airport, I was silent. "I think, perhaps, we might have made a mistake," I said slowly. The air changed.

"Your friends may be idealistic, but they are escaping their lives, as are you," he said. "We are married. Accept it. Grow up!"

He had never spoken to me this harshly before, and it hurt. I didn't talk to him during the entire trip back to New York.

That fight set the pattern of our lives for the next several months. In the evening, when Ram came home, I would ignore him or blame him for bringing me to Connecticut. Half-heartedly, I searched for a job and mutely handed him the rejection letters. He would hold me, whispering soothing words, but I was too depressed to care about it. Or him.

Two years into our marriage, something happened. I was ashamed to realize that while I had treated Ram with veiled dislike, he had always tried to improve our relationship. I was admitted to the journalism program at Columbia, where, at Ram's insistence, I had applied.

Falling in love, for me, began with small changes. I found myself relishing a South Indian dish that I disliked, mostly because I knew how much he loved it. I realized that the first thing I wanted to do when I heard some good news was to share it with him. Somewhere along the way, the "I love you, too" that I had politely parroted in response to his endearments had become sincere.

My friends are appalled that I let my parents decide my life partner; yet, the older they get the more intrigued they are. I am convinced that our successful relationship has to do with two words: tolerance and trust. In a country that emphasizes individual choice, arranged marriages require a familial web for them to work. For many Americans that web doesn't exist. As my friend Karen said, "How can I get my parents to pick out my spouse when they don't even talk to each other?"

Pakistani Court Clears Couple Who Wed for Love

Associated Press

Lahore, Pakistan, March 10—A Pakistani couple who married for love did not violate the teachings of Islam, even though the union was not arranged by their parents, Pakistan's High Court ruled today.

For more than a year, Saima Waheed, who flouted tradition by choosing the man she married, lived in a women's shelter in Lahore while her parents tried to have her marriage declared invalid. They argued that Islam requires parental permission before a woman can marry and asked the court to annul the February 1996 marriage to Arshad Ahmed. In Islamic Pakistan, civil courts rule on some religious issues, including whether a woman can marry without her parent's consent.

Ahmed was jailed for four months before being granted bail and released pending the court's decision.

In today's ruling, the court said Waheed's decision to choose her husband does not violate Islamic teachings, meaning the couple is now free to live together.

"Pakistani Court Clears Couple Who Wed for Love," *Washington Post*, March 11, 1997, A12.

The ruling was considered a milestone for women in Pakistan, where men dominate and tradition and Islam are often cited as reasons to restrict women's rights.

But the three-judge panel's 2 to 1 ruling declaring the marriage legal was confusing on some important issues, said the bride's lawyer, Asma Jehangir. One of the judges who upheld the marriage based his decision on the fact the bride's parents let Ahmed into their home to teach her brothers English, which he interpreted as tacit approval.

Comprehension

"Could I Accept an Arranged Marriage?"
 1. What was the belief of the author's parents about their daughters' marriages?
 2. How did the author feel during her adolescence in the United States?
 3. What change took place when the author went to college?
 4. Why did the author form a close friendship with Geeta?
 5. How do people tend to view love on the Indian subcontinent?
 6. Why will Geeta accept an arranged marriage?
 7. Why won't the author agree to an arranged marriage?
 8. What do the author of this article and Maryam, the young woman in the case study, have in common?
 9. What is the main idea of this article?
10. How convincing do you find the author's point of view?

"When Life's Partner Comes Pre-Chosen"
 1. Why did the author agree to let her family arrange a marriage for her?
 2. What happened to the author when she was attending Mount Holyoke?
 3. What is the statistical success rate of arranged marriages in different cultures?
 4. Describe Ram's family.
 5. How did their first meeting go, and what was the author's initial reaction to Ram?
 6. How well did the author and Ram know each other before Ram proposed?
 7. What caused the author and her husband to fight after they got married?
 8. Explain the process by which the author fell in love with her husband.
 9. What does the author believe forms the basis of her successful relationship with her husband?
10. What is the main idea of this article?
11. What are the similarities and what are the differences between Shandana Durrani, the author of "Could I Accept an Arranged Marriage?" and Shoba Narayan?
12. How convincing do you find the author's point of view?

"Pakistani Court Clears Couple Who Wed for Love"
 1. What was the ruling of Pakistan's High Court on the Pakistani couple who married for love?
 2. What was the argument of Saima Waheed's parents?
 3. What did Saima's parents ask the court to do?

4. What was the court's ruling, and what is the result of the ruling?

5. Why is the ruling considered a milestone for women in Pakistan?

6. If you had been a judge in this case, would you have upheld the marriage or declared it invalid? Explain your answer.

Father of the Bride; dir. Vincente Minnelli; Spencer Tracy, Elizabeth Taylor, 1950, U.S.

Strategy Session

Imagine that you are twenty-five years old, well educated, and single. Your parents are urging you to meet with a matchmaker in order to find the right person to marry.

Which strategy would you use in this situation and why? Provide a written justification for your decision. If none of the listed strategies would be your choice, you may develop your own strategy.

1. Ask the matchmaker to draw up an astrological chart with your horoscope and to introduce you only to a person whose horoscope is compatible with yours.

2. Bring your parents with you to the meeting and let them make suggestions to the matchmaker about potential marriage partners for you.

3. Give the matchmaker a detailed written description, including appearance and personality, of the type of person whom you hope to marry.

4. Show the matchmaker photographs of people whom you consider attractive.

5. Tell the matchmaker that you will be willing to meet only one person, and if that person isn't appealing to you, you will not come back for any other introductions.

6. Other: _____

Suggested Films

Crossing Delancey (1988)
Father of the Bride (1950 and 1991)
Gabbeh (1997 Iran)
Green Card (1990 Australia-France)
Ju Dou (1989 China-Japan)
Kolya (1997 Czechoslovakia)
The Matchmaker (1958 and 1997)
Muriel's Wedding (1994 Australia)
The Piano (1993 Australia-France)
Picture Bride (1994 Japan)
The Scar of Shame (1926 silent film)
Shall We Dance? (1996 Japan)
Two Daughters (1961 India)
The Wedding March (1928 silent film)
Wedding Song: Henna Art among Pakistani Women in New York City (Queens Council on the Arts: 1990)
Women and Islam (Films for the Humanities and Sciences: 1994)

Additional Readings

Applbaum, Kalman. "Marriage with the Proper Stranger: Arranged Marriage in Metropolitan Japan." *Ethnology* 34 (winter 1995): 37–51.
Bhutto, Benazir. "Story of an Arranged Marriage." *New Woman* 19 (August 1989): 78–82.
Dolgoff, Stephanie. "They Said It Would Never Last." *McCall's* 124 (December 1996): 100–104.
Fisher, Ian. "Love for Country, If Not for Each Other." *New York Times*, March 9, 1997, I, 33, 38.
Galston, William A. "Making Divorce Harder Is Better." *Washington Post*, August 10, 1997, C3.

Haberman, Clyde. "In Citizenship, in Sickness and in Health." *New York Times,* February 21, 1997, B1.

Kendall, Laurel. "The Marriage of Yongsu's Mother." *Natural History* 97 (July 1988): 6–10.

Moreno, Manuel. "A Bride for Raman." *Natural History* 97 (March 1998): 6–10.

Peterson, Scott. "Saudis under Cover: Women Live on Own Terms behind the Veil." *Christian Science Monitor,* July 31, 1996, 1, 10.

Yoshida, Ritsuko. "Getting Married the Corporate Way." *Japan Quarterly* 37 (April–June 1990): 171–75.

Wood, Eve. "Arranged Marriage, China, 1921." *Poetry* 164 (June 1994): 138.

WuDunn, Sheryl. "Cupid's a Korean Computer, Making Wise Matches." *New York Times,* April 17, 1997: A4.

Appendixes

She's Working Her Way through College; dir. Bruce Humberstone; Ronald Reagan, 1952, U.S.

Appendix A
Questionnaire on Culture Shock

Please answer the following questions as honestly as possible and explain your answers.

1. Culture shock is the powerful emotional and physical distress that a person experiences when coming to live in a country whose culture differs from his or her own. How much culture shock did you experience in your first weeks or months in the United States?

2. Which of the following did you do to prepare yourself for coming to study in the United States?
   - Talked to others who had been to the United States
   - Read books and magazine articles about the United States
   - Took courses in English
   - Took courses in U.S. history and/or literature
   - Other _____

3. Which of the following is your main reason for coming to the United States?
   - To get an academic degree
   - To acquire professional or academic expertise
   - To master the English language
   - To learn about another culture
   - To achieve personal development
   - Other _____

4. What preconceived ideas and stereotypes did you have about the United States and North Americans before you came here?

5. What has surprised you about life in the United States?

6. Which of the following have been difficult for you to adjust to in the United States?
   • individualism   • women's rights   • racism and prejudice   • food
   • violence and crime   • freedom of speech   • laws and regulations   • climate

7. How would you rate your English language skills?
   • superior   • excellent   • very good   • good   • fair   • poor

8. Do college students in the United States have fewer restrictions than in your country?

9. How easy is it to make friends with North Americans in the United States?

10. Do most North Americans seem to be honest and direct when they talk to you?

11. Have you had any misunderstandings with your teachers? If so, please explain.

12. Do you agree with the North American idea that time is money?

13. How similar are the cultural values in your country to those in the United States?

14. What stereotypes do North Americans have about your culture or country?

15. Would you like to return to your native country soon after you finish your studies, or would you like to remain in the United States?

[This form is reproducible.]

Questionnaire on Culture Fatigue

Please complete the following questionnaire as honestly as possible.

1. Culture fatigue is the exhaustion that results from trying to adjust to the customs, traditions, and values of a culture that is different from your own.[1] Have you experienced culture fatigue since you came to the United States? Explain your answer.

2. List five customs or traditions in the United States that are different from those in your country.
   a.

   b.

   c.

   d.

   e.

3. List five customs or traditions in the United States that you have come to accept and enjoy.
   a.

   b.

   c.

   d.

   e.

---

1. F.T. Murray and Alice Haller Murray, "Global Managers for Global Businesses," *Sloan Management Review* 27 (Winter 1986): 77.

4. Which customs and traditions in the United States are the hardest for you to accept and enjoy? Explain your answer.

5. According to Craig Storti in *The Art of Crossing Cultures:* "We cannot expect that we will like everything about another culture any more than we approve of everything about our own. Nor should we force ourselves to try."[2]
Write one or two paragraphs describing what you do not like about North American culture.

2. Craig Storti, *The Art of Crossing Cultures* (Yarmouth, ME: Intercultural Press, 1990), 67.

[This form is reproducible.]

Appendix B
Case Study Report

    I. Statement of the Problem
       A. Definition
       B. Analysis
   II. Suggestion of Possible Solutions
       A. Solution 1
       B. Solution 2
       C. Solution 3
  III. Evaluation of Possible Solutions
       A. Solution 1
          1. Advantages
          2. Disadvantages
       B. Solution 2
          1. Advantages
          2. Disadvantages
       C. Solution 3
          1. Advantages
          2. Disadvantages
  IV. Selection of a Solution
       A. Choice
       B. Justification

Case Study Report (chap.1)

The following case study report is based on the case study in chapter 1. It should serve as a model for writing case study reports in the remaining chapters of the book.

    I. Statement of the Problem
       A. Definition: Dita Rantung, suffering from culture shock and feelings of alienation, is having a hard time adjusting to her first semester at college in the States. She has no one to turn to, and her adviser is on vacation.
       B. Analysis: Dita Rantung is not doing well in adjusting to her new life in the United States because she has a number of obstacles facing her, but she has no means of emotional support. She needs to improve her English skills, she can't seem to make friends, she dislikes American food, and she is extremely homesick for her family and her country, Indonesia. Thus, she is thinking of dropping out of school and going home to Indonesia.
   II. Suggestion of Possible Solutions
       A. Dita can withdraw from college immediately and return to Indonesia.
       B. Dita can wait for the adviser to return and make an appointment with him or her.
       C. Dita can talk honestly to her roommate and ask for her help in trying to get used to attending college in the United States.

III. Evaluation of Possible Solutions
   A. Dita can withdraw from college immediately and return to Indonesia.
      1. Advantages: She will no longer have to experience culture shock and alienation. She will be reunited with her family and friends.
      2. Disadvantages: She will give up the opportunity to study in the United States, and she will lose her scholarship. She will feel that she has failed to overcome the challenges that she is facing. She may regret her decision at a later date when she is feeling better.
   B. Dita can wait for the adviser to return and make an appointment with him or her.
      1. Advantages: Her adviser may have good advice that will enable Dita to remain at college and overcome her culture shock. Her adviser may send Dita to a counselor or a therapist who can help her and give her moral and emotional support. As time goes by, Dita may begin to feel better.
      2. Disadvantages: Dita may be too unstable to wait for help for a week. Dita's mental state may deteriorate even further while she is waiting for the adviser to return. Dita may not benefit from meeting with her adviser if she and the adviser are not compatible or the adviser is not sympathetic to her problems.
   C. Dita can talk honestly to her roommate and ask for her help in trying to get used to attending college in the United States.
      1. Advantages: Dita's roommate may be willing to help her once she becomes aware of how isolated and insecure Dita has been feeling. Dita may begin to feel better after she talks to her roommate if her roommate is empathetic and kind.
      2. Disadvantages: Dita may become even more depressed if her roommate is not empathetic and kind to her. She may feel embarrassed about revealing her feelings to her roommate.
IV. Selection of a Solution
   A. Choice: (B) Dita can wait for the adviser to return and make an appointment with him or her.
   B. Justification: Dita should not immediately withdraw from college. Although she is experiencing severe symptoms of culture shock, it would be better for her to remain in school and try to meet with her adviser as soon as the adviser returns. Dita may gradually begin to feel better after she talks to the adviser, and if the adviser offers her practical suggestions and emotional support, Dita will probably be able to build a successful life in the United States. At the end of the semester, if Dita has still not adjusted well to her college life and has not made any friends, she could choose to return to Indonesia. However, she would know that she had not given up her scholarship and her dream of studying in the United States without having tried her best.

Glossary for Case Study Report

compatible	getting along well together; in agreement
counselor	a person who gives advice and help
deteriorate	to become worse
embarrassed	self-conscious, confused, and ill at ease
empathetic	understanding and being sensitive to the feelings, thoughts, and experience of another person
insecure	not confident; filled with anxieties
isolated	set apart from others; alone
obstacles	barriers that prevent or delay progress
regret	to feel sorry about or troubled over something that has happened
reveal	to make something known; to disclose
sympathetic	feeling compassion for and sensitivity to another person's emotions
therapist	a person who treats mental and physical disorders
withdraw	to remove oneself from an organization, group, or community

Appendix C
Guidelines for an Oral Presentation

To be successful in giving an oral presentation, speakers should use a direct, natural, and relaxed style. They must know their subject well and present the information in logical order. Planning, preparation, and practice are the keys to making effective oral presentations.

The following are seven suggestions for a successful oral presentation.

(1) Know your subject well by planning, preparing, and practicing in advance.
(2) Organize your material logically so that one idea leads to the next.
(3) State the main idea at the beginning and restate it at the end of your presentation.
(4) Speak in a loud and clear voice and do not speak too quickly.
(5) Maintain eye contact with every member of the audience.
(6) Stand up straight and use natural gestures.
(7) Use concrete language and words that create mental images.

The following are seven suggestions for organizing an oral presentation.

(1) Organize your material into a main idea, major points, and supporting details or examples.
(2) Divide your talk into three parts: introduction, body, and conclusion.
(3) State your purpose and the main idea in the introduction and give necessary background information.
(4) Organize the major points logically and explain them clearly in the body.
(5) Restate your main idea in the conclusion.
(6) Use visual aids (pictures, charts, graphs) to support your major points.
(7) Put your information in outline form on 3"× 5" or 4"× 6" index cards that you can refer to whenever necessary. Do not read your entire oral presentation from the index cards and do not memorize it.

Example of a Purpose Statement: The purpose of this presentation is to explain the major differences in communication styles between the United States and Japan.

Example of a Main Idea Statement: Communication styles in the United States are different from those in Japan in regard to two major characteristics: directness and equality.

Outline for an Oral Presentation

A Comparison of Communication Styles in the United States and Japan

I. Introduction
  A. Definition of Communication
  B. Background and History of Japan
  C. Statement of Main Idea: Communication styles in Japan differ a great deal from communication styles in the United States.

II. Communication Styles in the United States
    A. Direct self-expression in speaking to others
    B. Language showing equality
III. Communication Styles in Japan
    A. Indirect self-expression in speaking to others: *sasshi*[1]
    B. Language showing differences in rank
IV. Conclusion
    A. Summary: Directness and equality in United States. Indirectness and rank in Japan.
    B. Restatement of Main Idea: Communication styles in Japan differ a great deal from communication styles in the United States.

Tokyo Monogatari (Tokyo Story); dir. Yasujiro Ozu, 1953, Japan

1. *An English Dictionary of Japanese Culture* states: "*Sasshi* can loosely be translated as 'conjecture,' 'understanding,' 'sensibility,' 'consideration,' etc. It is an important concept in interpersonal relationships in Japan. According to the concept of modesty and sincerity that Japanese people esteem, direct self-expression is frowned upon. People are expected to guess what others intend to say. If they are not perceptive enough and dare to ask for information left unsaid, they are branded as rude. This communication pattern, often referred to as *ishin-denshin* (tacit understanding), is possible in a closely-knit community where people share a great many cultural assumptions. It also prevails in a tightly-ordered society where people tend to seek harmonious agreement while avoiding ideological confrontation. Since Japan is becoming an individualistic society with a diversity of cultural values, people are now abandoning the traditional communication style and acquiring more self-assertive language" (Bates Hoffer and Noboyuki Honna, *An English Dictionary of Japanese Culture* [Tokyo: Yuhikaku Publishing Co., Ltd.], 1986).

Appendix D
Film Analysis Form

After you have watched the assigned film, fill in as much of this form as possible.

Title of Film: _____ Date: _____

Director of Film: _____

Actors: _____

Type of Film: Comedy   Documentary   Drama   Historical Drama   Mystery   Musical

Romance   Romantic Comedy   Science Fiction   Thriller   Western

Summary and Analysis
Write a summary of the film. Include the important characters, major events, central conflicts, and resolution of these conflicts.

Relation to Case Study
Explain how the film deals with the topics presented in the case study.

Reaction to Film
Explain your reaction to the film. Did you like it or dislike it? Will you remember it? How will it affect your thinking about the topic in the case study?

[This form is reproducible.]

Film Analysis Form

After you have watched the assigned film, fill in as much of this form as possible.

Title of Film: ___"Crocodile" Dundee_____ Date: __1986__

Director of Film: __Peter Faiman_____

Actors: _Paul Hogan ("Crocodile" Dundee) and Linda Kozlowski (Sue Charlton)_____

Type of Film: (Comedy) Documentary Drama Historical Drama Mystery Musical

Romance Romantic Comedy Science Fiction Thriller Western

Summary and Analysis

Write a summary of the film. Include the important characters, major events, central conflicts, and resolution of these conflicts.

Michael J. "Crocodile" Dundee was a man from the far country in Australia. He was well known in his town because he could catch and kill crocodiles with his hands and make giant water buffaloes look away. Sue Charlton, a reporter from a newspaper in New York City, went to this small town in Australia to get to know Crocodile and to write about him for the newspaper.

When she arrived in Australia, Sue experienced culture shock, but she tried to adapt to life in the bush country. Later, the hero in the movie, Mr. "Crocodile" Dundee, had to face a difficult challenge, which was traveling to New York City, an unknown place to him. Thus, in New York, he suffered great cultural shock because the huge and complex city was so different from his simple life in the Australian countryside. Eventually, Sue and "Crocodile" Dundee fell in love and decided to join their lives in marriage.

Relation to Case Study

Explain how the film deals with the topics presented in the case study.

In the case study from chapter 1 and in this movie, we see that culture shocks are experienced by the characters in both of these stories. In case study 1, Dita Rantung suffered from culture shock when she came to the United States to attend college. "Crocodile" Dundee also suffered from culture shock when he came to New York City with his friend Sue. In addition, Sue, the reporter, experienced culture shock when she traveled to the Australian bush country to interview "Crocodile" Dundee.

Reaction to Film

Explain your reaction to the film. Did you like it or dislike it? Will you remember it? How will it affect your thinking about the topic in the case study?

I enjoyed this film very much because it was so funny. At the same time, I could see how culture shocks could be experienced not only by people who go from a small town to a large city like New York but also by people who go to small towns or the countryside after living in a large city. Whenever you move to a place that is much different from the place where you have grown up or have been living for a long time, you will find it hard to adjust to the strange customs and traditions. However, it is possible to get used to these surroundings if you have patience and the willingness to live a new life. I will remember this film for its humor and happy ending to the problems caused by culture shock.

Appendix E:
Reading Report Form

After you have read one of the suggested articles, complete this form.

Author: _____   Title: _____

Source: _____   Date: _____

Main Idea of the Article
Write one or two sentences paraphrasing the main idea of the article.

Summary of Article
Write a summary of the article. Include the main idea of the article and all the major points.

Reaction to Article
Explain your reaction to the article. How will it affect your thinking about the topic in the case study?

[This form is reproducible.]

Reading Report Form

After you have read one of the suggested articles, complete this form.

Author: ___Jill Smolowe___   Title: ___"The Pursuit of Excellence"___

Source: ___*Time* magazine___   Date: ___April 13, 1992___

Main Idea of the Article
Write one or two sentences paraphrasing the main idea of the article.

Universities in the United States are very attractive to foreign students because these students will receive an excellent education that offers more freedom and diversity in courses than they can find in their native countries.

Summary of Article
Write a summary of the article. Include the main idea of the article and all the major points.

U.S. universities are appealing to foreign students for several reasons. First, they offer a diversity of opportunities to these students such as freedom, academic excellence, and the possibility to choose the courses they prefer to take. Second, U.S. schools have a great deal of flexibility. In these schools, students can change their field of study without a problem. Also, they can enroll in school again after a long period of absence, like soldiers do when they return from military duty. Furthermore, U.S. universities offer students direct contact with professors, professional counseling, and personal supervision, which makes these colleges responsive to cultural trends and requirements.

Reaction to Article
Explain your reaction to the article. How will it affect your thinking about the topic in the case study?

American universities are among the best in the world, so enrollments are increasing. Therefore, it is hard to believe that, as the author says, "By the year 2000, American higher education will no longer be dominant in the world." It is incredible that the North American methods of education are not found everywhere throughout the world, knowing how powerful the United States is. Also, if many foreign students come to the United States looking for academic excellence, why don't the universities of other countries use the U.S. universities as a model? The educational system in the United States is the best because students can choose whatever field they want to study and whatever courses they want to take. Also they can obtain a superior education that will prepare them to be competent professionals.

However, as the case study in chapter 1 shows, coming to study in the United States involves adjusting to the academic and social systems as well as learning the English language well enough to be able to study in English. For some students, this adjustment comes easily, but for others, like Dita, the first few months can be extremely difficult and depressing, especially if they do not receive adequate support from the university. I would expect any university that I attend to provide me with support services to help me adjust.

Index